MY AMAZING ADVENTURES WITH THE SEX PISTOLS

© Dave Goodman Estate & Phil Strongman 2006

Editor: Phil Strongman
Co-editor: Kathy Manuell
Special thanks to: Richard Veal, Colin Wilkinson, Ray Stevenson

Published by The Bluecoat Press, Liverpool
Printed and bound by Compass Press Ltd of London
Book design by MARCH Graphic Design Studio, Liverpool

Sex Pistols photographs by kind permission of Ray Stevenson
© Ray Stevenson

ISBN 1 904438 48 2

Dave Goodman

My Amazing Adventures with the Sex Pistols

The Bluecoat Press

FOREWORD BY MALCOLM McLAREN

The last time I heard from Dave Goodman, after an interval of many years, was when he sent me an email saying that he was living in Malta and working in his own studio there. This was at the end of 2004. It all sounded so fascinating as I have simply never heard of anyone ever working in Malta! The mind boggles ... But David had been such a beautiful pirate, blessed with selling Sex Pistols 'bootlegs' – or, rather, live and demo recordings – for God knows how long and getting away with it. I never got to the bottom of all the various legal angles of any of it, and frankly didn't care that much. It just made me smile how such a great character got away with it all! I enjoyed David's success from afar in this regard.

More importantly Dave was always someone that absolutely believed in the Sex Pistols more or less from day one and soon enough became our engineer at every gig. He came along at exactly the right time, appearing in the Nashville's backstage room and raving about how good the band were (back when 'good' was the last word we expected to be hurled at the band). And, though he looked like a hippy – a throwback to early Glastonbury like his PA partner Kim Thraves compete with his blonde ringlets – Dave was a true music biz professional in the best sense of the word (as well as being virtually the first one to see the Sex Pistols' potential). In fact, he did in so many ways contribute to the Seventies scene – not just with our ragtag little outfit but with his own groups before, with his innate generosity, with his Soundforce PA and with things like his record company The Label, one of the very first UK Indies after Stiff and Chiswick (and it was the Label, of course, who brought us such wonders as the 14 year old tearaways who were known as Eater).

Dave later went on tour with the Sex Pistols, up North, to Wales and Scotland and even on the legendary Anarchy Tour, seeing them play far more times than I did. With hindsight it seems obvious to me now that Dave must have been secretly recording at almost every gig, accumulating tape after tape of their various shows as they built their career. And a good thing too! (it would never have occurred to me to do that, never in a million years ... but Dave always did have that bit more 'musical hindsight' than the rest of us – he'd been in the business a fair bit longer and he really could appreciate the Pistols phenomena far more than the rest of us could at the time).

He was also a supreme engineer-mixer-producer back in the day, and all responsibility in that regard fell upon him, particularly as most of us had little idea about studios and recording. He usually worked for nothing, or very very little, and he made the first major stab at recording the Sex Pistols, both live and in the studio. As a matter of fact, the first three records – for EMI, A&M Records and Virgin! – all contained tracks produced by Dave. And, of course, he continued to release such recordings long after he had left the field (contractually speaking).

And Dave did so with some justification – since most of the majors gave him pretty short shrift as did some of the music magazines. It was more than a little irritating to hear that he'd had his production credits removed from album sleeves – *Spunk* was all his while most of the *Great Rock'n'Roll Swindle* soundtrack simply wouldn't have existed without him either – just as it was annoying when he seemed to be written out of the Sex Pistols' history by various magazine and newspaper articles – how amazing it is to understand the culture of deception which some elements of the English press are so good at. Deceptions which leave us all with so many untruths …

Not that Dave seemed too worried by all these obstacles and omissions – and, after all, his notorious 'unlicensed' tapes did end up being extremely popular! I just loved the fact that he was doing something so brilliantly anti-corporate. The record companies always seemed to accuse me of doing such things. I only wish I had!

In some respects David became quite the dark knight and truly subversive with his recording and distributing activities – and in today's world of musical hacking and legit – and illegit – downloading he should really be considered quite a visionary icon …

I am so sad not to have seen him more often. In fact, we hadn't spoken in the flesh since those wonderful roller-coaster days of the late Seventies and I miss him – just as I miss those interesting little chats we used to have … but this book will rectify that, in part – as well as revealing another side to that never ending search for the truth behind the Sex Pistols. Long live Dave Goodman!

Malcolm McLaren September 2006

"The truth is more interesting than lies!"
John Lydon

"The truth is, you can't make this stuff up!"
Dave Goodman

This is the story of the time I spent with the Sex Pistols, on the road, in the studio and behind the scenes as live sound engineer, tour manager, record producer and mate. For the record, I happened to witness them perform more than anyone else in the Galaxy, including Malcolm McLaren. I've really enjoyed writing it and was surprised at how much I could remember. It was like living through it again. I hope you, the reader, experience a similar feeling. I've consciously written it so you can imagine you were there. Enjoy the journey and don't forget – LIVE FOR THE PROCESS, NOT FOR THE PROFIT – and all that bollocks!

Dave Goodman
January 2005

CONTENTS

I noticed something else that was different about this group. Apart from being younger than 'yer average pub band', they had shorter hair, and Rotten's was a mess of orange spikes. They wore tight trousers, ripped t-shirts and teddy boy boots (this was, remember, at a time when virtually everyone from street kids to TV news-readers wore flared denim baggies, patterned shirts and long hair, me included). Joe Strummer and the 101ers looked a bit edgy too but not as wild as the Sex Pistols did.

MY FIRST TASTE OF SEX PISTOLDOM

THE WHOLE SEX PISTOLS THING BEGAN for me on a Tuesday afternoon. It was March 1976, the 23rd to be precise. There I was sitting at home, trying to raise the enthusiasm to take back a van I'd hired for a gig the day before. The big problem was unloading it first! It contained a rather large blue PA – public address system – that I'd been building up and lugging round for the last five years.

Humping gear wasn't my favourite pastime, but as no one else was around the thankless task was mine yet again! Just then the phone rang. I had a feeling it would be the van hire firm wondering where the hell their vehicle was. Some quick talking was needed. Which excuse could I use this time? I'd already used the 'flat battery sketch'. I know ... the key's stuck in the lock, that will stall 'em for a day or two.

Instead of an irate hire company, it was Dai Davies from the Albion talent booking agency. He wanted to know if I would do a cheap gig at the Nashville pub that night. It was for some young band that could only afford £15. Although my price was normally double that, and still a bargain, I accepted. At least I wouldn't have to unload the van and drive 10 miles to return it. I was told that evening's band was called the Sex Pistols. Odd name I thought, I wonder what sort of music they play?

When I arrived at the gig Kim Thraves, my partner in the PA company, was already outside waiting for me. I started giving him the gig details, when suddenly this old van spluttered round the corner. It had slogans painted all over it, the doors were literally tied on with string and the passengers were hanging out of the windows engaging the passers-by. It kangaroo'd to a halt a couple of inches away from me. This must be the Sex Pistols, I thought ...

"Hi, are you the PA?" one of them said.

"Yeah, and you must be the Sex Pistols?" I replied.

"Who? No, we're The 101ers, they must be the support band."

Oh no! We'd been conned again! Here we were, operating at less than half price and now we were gonna be doing two bands instead of one! Kim ran off to phone the Albion agency and complain, but there was no one there except the cleaner – as usual.

At this time pub gigs were in abundance. You could walk into any number, any night of the week and hear a band sounding somewhere between Steely Dan and the Average White Band – for free. The volume levels would be tame and you could sit there comfortably supping your ale whilst making conversation. But the 101ers were different, or so their frontman, Joe Strummer, kept telling me. They were keeping a raw breed of 'rhythm and blues' alive, and they proved it at the sound-check.

With half an hour to go before the bar opened there was still no sign of the support band. We were just about to give up and go for a drink, when four young musicians and their manager ambled in. They announced themselves as the 'Sex Pistols'. Steve Jones and Paul Cook came over and started chatting while John Rotten kept his distance. Malcolm, their manager, stood in the shadows, hands in pockets and collar upturned, viewing proceedings from afar. Glen Matlock was already in the dressing room – washing his feet I believe! They erected their gear, we moved the mikes into position and the stage was set.

"OK, let's get on with the sound-check," I commanded.

"What's a sound-check?" leered John.

"You know, you have to go 'One, Two, Testing' into the mike."

"God, sounds like fun," he winced.

"OK, just turn everything full up, let's make sure they can really hear us tonight!" shouted Malcolm from a far corner. They knocked out a few old covers like the Who's 'Substitute', the Small Faces' 'Whatcha Gonna Do Bout It' and 'Understanding', and an obscure Kinks song called 'I'm Not Like Everybody Else'.

I love the Kinks and have all their early albums, so I was overjoyed to see this raggle taggle bunch of misfits attempt to play a Ray Davies – it was a shame it swiftly got dropped from their set. They also did a few interesting songs I'd not heard before, which turned out to be originals. It was a marvellous noise and reminded me of my old band Frinton Bassett Blues from 1966 (in fact we'd covered 'Substitute', 'Whatcha Gonna Do Bout It?' and 'Understanding' too).

The band were incredibly loud during the sound-check and I was soon wondering how the hell we were going to get away with it. I mean, my own jazzy-funky band, Orange Rainbow, were half their volume and when we'd recently played the Nashville the landlord still asked us to turn down. Anyway, Malcolm insisted and I was game for it – it gave me a chance to whack the PA up for a change.

I noticed something else that was different about this group. Apart from being younger than 'yer average pub band', they had shorter hair, and Rotten's was a mess of orange spikes. They wore tight trousers, ripped t-shirts and teddy boy boots (this was, remember, at a time when virtually everyone from street kids to TV news-readers wore flared denim baggies, patterned shirts and long hair, me included). Joe Strummer and the 101ers looked a bit edgy too but not as wild as the Sex Pistols did.

We got the sound-check out of the way and then grabbed a few beers before heading backstage for a pre-gig chat. There we found Malcolm winding the band up – telling them how the audience were a bunch of apathetic old farts who needed shocking into some sort of response. He was also passing round a bottle of Remy Martin, which became a sort of ritual at those early gigs. Once the Pistol had been loaded, it was herded on stage accompanied by much jeering from the audience, who seemed to take great exception to their age and appearance. The band returned the compliments and told the audience that if they "didn't like it, they could fuck off!"

They were loud, manic and loose. When they performed 'Substitute' it was as if they played it as badly as they possibly could, just to annoy people. Then Rotten said ..." That's an improvement, ain't it?"

At this point some of the audience got up and walked out while others started shouting.

"Turn down! Turn the volume down!"

"No!"

"Turn it off and go home!"

"You go home if you don't like it!" Rotten snarled.

Fortunately some could see the humour in all this, but the band were treading a fine line. If things did turn ugly who was gonna bail them out? Not me, I was a 'stoned hippy' (whatever that meant) Peace And Love Man was my mantra. I couldn't bear to see violence, although I've seen my share over the years. It's hard to avoid when you've done as many gigs as I have, but in these early days the Sex Pistols gigs rarely turned violent.

Should push come to a shove I was no fighter, although my Dad's cousin or second cousin (they rarely talked about it) was boxer Henry Cooper.

Cooper was my Gran's maiden name and Grandad Goodman had been a prize fighter and was once the Middlesex Bantam Weight Champion ... I, on the other hand, had never really had a fight in my life. I knew I was strong though, after all I'd been humping all that equipment around for many years. Roadies were virtually unheard of in the 60s, so you had to carry your own gear and run up and down fire escapes with Hammond organs and Marshall stacks ... Any road – let's get back to the gig.

"You should start your own bands," advised Rotten. "You don't have to rehearse for five years in yer bedroom before you're allowed to play."

"There's a lack of good young bands, the world needs some decent new groups." Steve joined in.

"Like who?" shouted some heckler.

"Like us!" the Pistols fired back.

The band got louder, more out of tune and more abusive. They even did an encore, just because no one asked for it. How they ever managed to get out alive I'll never know, but I guess it did show just how apathetic the audience really were. I fear that most of what John said – about starting new groups – fell on deaf ears, but a few young guns down at the front enquired later whether they had any more gigs lined-up?

Throughout the Sex Pistols' set, Joe Strummer sat transfixed in front of the stage and never took his eyes off them. You could tell he was amazed and inspired. I was experiencing similar feelings behind the mixing desk at the back of the hall above the crowd. I kept myself busy by adding psychedelic effects to their sound and being a sort of invisible cheer leader (people want to clap really, they just need leading). Kim kept the joints rolling while also being ready to leap on stage should the need arise. I noticed John was quick to pick up on the dubby type echoes I was introducing and use them creatively. I even added square wave type distortion – that's very, very distorted – to Steve's guitar, by heavily overloading his input on the mixer. This I would use to enhance his guitar sound in between John's vocals. It was a very punkadelic full sound and made them more than just another Pub Rock band. It enhanced their presence no end. Just check out recordings from this period!

After the Pistols' set I went backstage and waffled on about the atmosphere they created and asked what other gigs they had. Did they want to hire my PA? "Fuck Me," said John, "someone's actually offering to help us for a change." Anyway, something clicked and I was to do virtually all their gigs from then on, in England, Wales, Scotland and Holland – right up until their Swedish and American tours. And most enjoyable they were too!

When the 101ers went on, Strummer went really crazy and kicked ten shades of shit out of our monitor speakers. The next day, Kim and I tracked him down to his squat and kidnapped his roadie (I guess the roadie must have been Boogie who, would you believe, later took over part of my job with the Pistols).

Maybe kidnapped is a slight exaggeration. It was more like persuading him into Kim's old Jag and driving him round the corner for a drink. Once there, we phoned Strummer – squats can have phones too, you know – and demanded the £18 to repair the speaker cones he put his foot through last night. If they wanted Boogie back then they'd better pay up.

"Ring us back in half an hour," Joe said, "I'll try and get some cash together."

Half an hour and several beers later I get Joe back on the phone.

"Look I've got your money here, Dave, but..." he paused for maximum effect, "... for an extra £20 will you keep, Boogie?" It was tempting but he looked like he had a big appetite, so I declined the offer.

Anyway, Strummer saw his wrong and made it right. Hopefully, he respected me for my actions – we certainly became friends ... Shortly after this gig, Joe Strummer left the 101ers and started the Clash – "yesterday I was a crud then I saw the Sex Pistols and I became a king and moved into the future," he was quoted as saying.

There was something else very special about the Sex Pistols, apart from youth, fashion and attitude. They had ... Malcolm McLaren! With all his anarchic wit, charm and creative imagination. He was one mighty fine manager who any band should have been proud of. His aloofness was annoying at times – and why did he keep calling me 'boy'? – but he was great company and he amused me, as did the band as a whole.

The other great thing about Malcolm was that he didn't know the meaning of the word 'No'. His dogged determination, along with his belief in his work and skill at manipulating events to create a 'GRAND GESTURE' – his words – were, in my mind, second to none, despite what others may have said since! 'BE REALISTIC AND DEMAND THE IMPOSSIBLE' was one soundbite he emblazoned on his attire – and lived!

Probably because of Malcolm's pushy charm, the band were taken on by Ron Watts, promoter of Tuesday's rock nights at the 100 Club. Ron had already seen the band perform in St Albans and liked what he saw. The 100 Club was ideal, smack bang in the heart of the capital city, on the east side of Oxford Street. They started a once fortnightly residency there that built up over a period of several months, culminating in an ill-fated 'festival'.

By this time Nils Stevenson and his brother Ray, the photographer, had become involved on a pretty regular basis – they were present almost every night from April onwards. Nils, who was dating Marc Bolan's ex-wife at the time, did much of the legwork for Malcolm. He was under the impression that he was a co-manager of the Pistols but when the band finally signed their management contract with Malcolm and his Glitterbest company this was shown to be a bit of an illusion.

Ray, his brother, was the band's official photographer and copyright owner of many of the photos in this book (you should check out his excellent Sex Pistols File book). He was at most of the early gigs, snapping away at the band. He would always come up to me just as the band were due on stage, screaming "Quick, give me some gaffa tape, I've gotta get me flash guns stuck in place!" and I'd run around looking for the fucking gaffa tape – which never seems to stay where you leave it! (I've just sussed it – I should have gaffered it down!) There's nothing like some last minute tension to get the adrenaline going!

His pictures were always pretty good and I don't know what else I can say about Ray Stevenson ... except to say he's an extremely nice bloke – oh yeah, and he once built a 20 foot catamaran in his back garden (which was within spitting distance of the house where Andy Blade of Eater lived). Ray intended to sail around the world in this boat – and it looked good enough to make the trip – but it was vandalised whilst in dock.

CHAPTER TWO

APRIL 1976

IF YOU WANT TO BE NOTICED, THEN YOU'D BETTER EXPOSE YOURSELF!

In these early days, regular gigs for the Sex Pistols were hard to find – I mean, who'd book a band with a name like that? But unperturbed they found their way into a seedy strip joint in London's Soho called El Paradiso (I understand that Nils was given the task of finding 'interesting' places for them to play and came up with this one). They took along whatever friends and followers they could muster. The club was no bigger than your average front room, but the main thing was they were performing. A truly fitting place for the Pistols. I wasn't needed for this one although I was invited along.

At another Nashville date, a long-haired guy tried to have a go at Rotten after Vivienne Westwood had apparently abused the guy's girlfriend, but I dunno if I believe it. Vivienne has always come across as a charming lady to me. A big fight broke out and a photo of this got into NME and, months later, made the front page of Melody Maker. Which was a mixed blessing for all concerned …

Anyhow, the Tuesday night 100 Club residency became great fun. One week we staged a Retro-Event with lots of obscure Sixties records including stuff by the Creation, the Action, and the English Birds (featuring one Ronnie Wood on bass). Malcolm pulled a few stops out on this one and press-ganged his many friends and acquaintances into coming along dressed for the occasion. It was a bit too Rocky Horror Show for my liking, but once the band started playing we were all brought back to Earth.

The Sex Pistols soon attracted a following and in the space of three or four months, it went from people walking out, to people being locked out.

18

Some would come and see what all the fuss was about, hang around for a few numbers then leave, but most were there to stay.

Each early London gig was an 'event'. There was a growing family, easily identifiable by their looks, i.e. torn clothes, safety pins and coloured spiky hair. Straights and oldies were welcome to the party too, the fact you were there was enough. At the end of a gig nearly everyone looked elated and left arranging to meet at the next one. Fans would bring friends along. You could spot the newcomers by their initial apprehension and reluctance to join the pulsating mass in front of the stage but, once they did, they experienced something that was really a new form of self-expression. The next week they would be back with a marked change in appearance and attitude, often bringing more friends with them.

EARLY DEDICATED FOLLOWERS OF FASHION

As I remember it, the following in order of appearance, went something like this. 'The Bromley Contingent' with Simon Barker, Jordan, Susan 'Siouxsie Sue', Ballon and Steve 'Two Tone' Severin, Sue Catwoman, Marco Pirroni, Debbie 'Juvenile' Wilson, Tracy O'Keefe RIP, Afro-Caribbean Simone. Then S&M mistress Linda, Sid Vicious, Sarah and Joe (Sarah became our secretary when old friend Caruzo and I started the 'Label' indie label in the spring of '77).

Then there was the Finchley mob, which started with Andy Blade and Brian Chevette of Eater and swelled to a considerable size. Not forgetting Rat Scabies, Joe Strummer and Micky Jones. These were some of the more familiar faces, most of whom took the Sex Pistols' advice and actually started their own bands.

From the amount of people who claim they were at those early gigs I'd say a lot of them would have to be lying. Up until the Anarchy Tour, the band could only have played to a few hundred people. I know that anyone who saw the Pistols in the early days was witnessing something very special indeed and is probably still talking about it to this day. Without those early followers the Sex Pistols and hence Punk Rock, and the whole New Wave that followed, would never have gained momentum. The Pistols changed many people's lives and as Malcolm once remarked to me – "If at the end of the day the Sex Pistols mean that people become more aware of themselves and their situation, then it's all been worthwhile."

The majority present at a punk gig in those days were in their teens. Many fans were still at school. They had probably come without even enough money to get home, but they had got there and whilst walking home, I'm sure they felt good about that fact. Imagine getting into bed at three in the morning, high on whatever, then having to get up again for school at eight, sitting in the classroom with the crash of the Sex Pistols still ringing in your ears! The teacher can't hold your attention and you can't make your friends appreciate what you experienced the night before (unless you can get them to go along next time).

Malcolm knew how vitally important it was to get in the music press in those early days and he set about obtaining maximum coverage. Whatever tactics were needed, he would usually deliver. Such as 'reverse psychology' – writing to the press pretending to be some nerd who hates the band and slags the press for covering them. Or challenging other up and coming artists like Dr Feelgood or Johnny Wotsit and the Whoweretheys. He also encouraged the band to take on established artists like The Stones and The Beatles – I don't think Glen ever swallowed that one – and give them a run for their money.

His research into the media was impeccable and he knew the sales figures for each editorial. He told me once that, "at the end of the day it didn't matter if the likes of the Melody Maker or NME were not on our side, because their circulation wasn't that big" (100,000 to 250,000 maybe). But it was a start and he set about priming journalists with his visions of a new youth culture based on rebellion and chaos, rather than servitude and order. He virtually handpicked journalists John Ingham and Caroline Coon, whilst others like Tony Parsons were eventually rejected.

WHEN YOU KNOW YOU'RE RECORDING HISTORY, MAKE SURE YOU DON'T ERASE IT!

I started recording these early gigs on my trusty old 4 track Teac. I took it along to create the tape echo effect and often captured the band in stereo on the spare two tracks. Sadly to say, I recorded over most of them, wiping out history and never allowing myself enough time to copy the good bits first. You see, a reel of blank tape in those days cost an incredible £10 – maybe £90 or more now – and I was only making about £11 a gig after expenses. Occasionally, I'd get a new reel and keep some bits, but apart from those few fans with hand-held cassette recorders, most of these performances now only exist in memory. I'd be a very rich man indeed if I had managed to keep the recordings of all those early punk gigs. Doh!!

Once the gigs started getting reviews you found people coming into London from far-off towns, such as Birmingham, Manchester, Bristol and Glasgow. Although I doubt they would have experienced anything like this before, the mere description of a Sex Pistols gig would have been enough to attract them. They must have returned home with wild tales of this crazed young, brash band who performed as if there was no tomorrow and who's attitude was to burn down the empires of the established rock artists, the dinosaurs who John labelled 'boring old farts'(or was that Malcolm's description?).

The kids returned with a new attitude and no wonder, when you stop and think about the other musical entertainment being offered to them. Kenny, Sweet, The Bay City Rollers. Or how about queuing up for two days to buy a £6 ticket to see Yes at Earls Court and then getting there and finding you needed binoculars to see self-conscious musical heroes play 25 minute solos. Here – in the Pistols – you had the live act that spoke out about all this bullshit. Here was the band you could get to see every week for less than a pound and who were talking about you. Here was the live act that truly was ALIVE.

Soon the Sex Pistols acquired a rehearsal gaff in Denmark Street, the old Tin Pan Alley of yesteryear where the Stones, Hendrix, Kinks and I had once recorded (not all at once you understand – though what a fun day that would have been!)

I believe Glen spotted the ad in the back of Melody Maker and persuaded Malcolm to rent it for them. Number Six, Denmark Street was an ideal base camp, right in the heart of London's West End. It used to belong to Pete Ham of Badfinger, the one who had hanged himself ... apparently in Number Six (Badfinger, incidentally, were also the first band signed to The Beatles' Apple Corps label).

The rehearsal place came equipped with a small Electro Voice PA, a few mics and a bit of soundproofing, all left over from the Badfinger days.

Steve Jones moved into the room upstairs with all the mod cons – an electric fire and kettle. Oh! Yeah! It also had a disgusting loo outside, that everyone was afraid to use let alone clean. Can't you just smell that anal retention? I believe Malcolm found a few loopholes in the lease and managed to avoid paying any rent until Glen finally took it over in his Rich Kid days.

Despite enjoying the 100 Club residency every other Tuesday, the group needed to play out of London, so a sort of mini-expedition was set up, to the North. Back then, a typical day for me would be to make a ten mile bus journey to hire a single wheelbase transit van – we couldn't afford anything bigger – drive it back home, load it up with my PA then drive to our usual meeting point in Denmark Street (where, hopefully, the whole motley crew had assembled).

After I'd get bollocked for being late – I always was but, hey, we never missed a gig – we'd load our hire vehicle to the brim with the equipment and then we'd squeeze the band in. We'd position a row of seats at the back and leave the doors slightly open, for their feet to stick out.

Off we went – usually with barely enough money to get there. We had little idea what to expect when we arrived and I'm sure the clubs were none the wiser. You must remember that, at this point, the band only had two or three write-ups and had probably played to less than a thousand people in all.

They needed to spread further afield to expand their audience. Their (un)popularity had to rise! So if there was a half decent gig to be had they would take it! Whenever they played they shocked the audience into some kind of response … be it for or against.

A cabaret club in Northallerton was another odd venue for the group – being a right chicken-in-a-basket place. The compere announced them – "Tonight ladies and gentlemen, in cabaret, all the way from the Big Smoke, the amazing Sex Pistols!" How did they ever manage to get a gig like that with a name like theirs? Anyway, there was at least one person that night who was inspired by the band. Pauline Murray, later of the group Penetration, was there to witness the Pistols fire off in this bizarre setting. I can remember her calling me over to her table and asking questions about the boys. You have to appreciate that the band had no real following outside of London at this point. By gatecrashing the cabaret circuit, they were taking real chances and making very real music. Their honesty was a threat to the safe, tried and tested attitudes of these working folk (not that all of them still had jobs mind you).

Next was Scarborough's Penthouse, an old favourite of mine. It was situated on four floors with various styles of disco on each floor. At about 1.00 a.m. curtains would pull back to reveal whatever live music was happening. You had to work hard to keep the audience and that night was no exception – but we did it and the spoils of war were ours.

In May '76 Malcolm and 'co-manager' Nils approached promoter John Curd about supporting New York's Ramones at their forthcoming Roundhouse gig – their first outside America. Curd said 'no' from the next room and his wife passed on this refusal. And she was then told, by Malcolm, that her husband must be an 'arsehole' for saying no to the Pistols. Curd was eating in the next room and, on hearing this, he threw his food aside – and then threw Malcolm down the stairs of his houseboat before ripping Nils' Pistols t-shirt into several pieces …

One day around this time the Pistols came to check out my eight piece psychedelic, jazz-funk band, Polecat (previously known as Orange Rainbow). We were playing at the old Marquee Club in London's Wardour Street. The Pistols had already played there, supporting Eddie and the Hotrods (they got their first ever review for it, by Neil Spencer in NME, and Eddie and his band didn't even get a mention. "We're not into music." the Pistols told Neil, "We're into chaos …").

The Pistols should have been gigging somewhere else that night but, as we both used the same PA, they decided to cancel and come and watch me play for a change. Glen, Steve & Paul sat right at the front scrutinising us funkadelics closely. After the show, Paul and Steve complimented me and drummer Graham Broad on our groovaciousness (my word not theirs). Glen also got into it and later asked me to show him some basslines he'd heard me play. John seemed vaguely amused by it all, he wasn't that rude but his smirk said what he couldn't be bothered to articulate himself: i.e. this funky, jazzy, rockadelic dance rubbish was a bit beneath him. Ironically, in years to come he would be making similar music himself, but that page has yet to be turned ...

The other band performing that night were the Fabulous Poodles. Somehow they recognised the Sex Pistols and did some parody of 'Anarchy' from the stage. 'I Wanna Be Bourgeoisie In NW3' or something like that. Now you have to remember that the Pistols hadn't even been signed yet, let alone released any records. It actually turned out that the Poodles' publishers had played them some Pistols' demos for feedback and something must have stuck with the Fab Poos. Weird shit eh?

CHAPTER FOUR

JUNE 1976

LESSER FREE TRADE HALL
TO WALTHAMSTOW

Malcolm felt that the time was right to take on the next major satellite city in his never-ending quest for mass recognition. He simply researched some venues, picked the Free Trade Hall, booked it and advertised it. When we arrived outside we were greeted by a gang of scruffy 'erberts offering to help us carry in the equipment (so they wouldn't have to pay on the door of course). Soon we all got chatting and it turned out that they had taken the Pistols' advice and were on the verge of starting their own bands. Howard Devoto, Pete Shelly, Diggle (Buzzcocks), Mike Rossi (Slaughter and the Dogs), I think they were all there. The turnout was so poor that Malcolm made everyone take turns standing outside persuading people to come in – even Kim had to leave the mixing desk and try to hustle up some punters. "It's only 60p mate, come on in, they're the future of rock'n'roll …"

I can't recall anything else about the first gig in this small hall, only that the low balcony made the acoustics very weird – everything sounded three times louder than normal, i.e. really fucking loud. The place was plagued with bad acoustics – so I laid down traps in the hope of catching them! We still got soaked in standing sound waves though.

Next they played the midsummer music festival in Walthamstow. A sort of coincidental, complementary line-up this one. I remember Kilburn & The High Roads because I got a really good recording of them on my 4 track (yup! that one got rubbed out too). But the Stranglers I don't recall, although I do remember some greasy pub rockers sticking their collective penis in my ear. 'No More Heroes'? The Sex Pistols were bloody heroes alright. And that Malcolm, he's a bit of a Shakespearo, doncha think?

The Summer of 1976 was a scorcher. The hottest for decades. We did a few more 100 Club dates to an ever-growing audience There was still an extremely pleasant side to the whole scene back then, one of comradeship between the bands and their fans. The unpleasant side I initially didn't notice, though it became more obvious in 1977 when lots of idiots began to gob (spit) at the bands. But that era was many months away and we still have the good old-fashioned rotten eggs and tomatoes yet to come ...

The Sex Pistols were angry at the Establishment and not the individual. True, they wanted to shock, but how strange it was that some people found clothes and words far more shocking than massacres and famines.

"Hi fans, peace and love!" Johnny used to say more than a few times when he came on stage flashing peace signs. It wasn't all sarcastic – I expect he would have loved it if his fans had thrown flowers. The Sex Pistols' preaching of anarchy I took to mean freedom for the individual to do as he pleases, while still showing compassion for his fellow beings. Music is a non-violent form of expression. It can provoke violence, but is non-violent in itself – unless you count wear'n'tear on the eardrums. There was growing concern from the medical profession about the damage to the hearing from the sheer volume of punk bands and in Leeds, where they impose a maximum volume level on live music, Paul Cook managed to shut down the power just by giving a quick blast on his unamplified drum kit. That's why there were never many punk gigs in Leeds. When we did eventually play there, the shut-off system had to be cleverly bypassed in order to continue.

CHAPTER FIVE

JULY 1976

SUMMER OF DISCOMFORT

We played The Black Swan in Sheffield with the Clash supporting (with Keith Levine on guitar). I had to help them tune up! I was no stranger to the Swan as I'd been gigging there regularly for the past five years. It was a real live music house with a good size crowd each night, made up mostly of students and local hairies. Local lad Joe Cocker used to play here a lot when he was in town. This crowd did not accept shit and tonight was no exception. I doubt if anyone in the audience had any idea they were witnessing the birth of the next musical phenomenon. To them it was just another Sunday night's entertainment and it had better be bloody good. It may have been free to get in but the ale was two pence more expensive and with the amount that's downed up here, it could put another twenty pence on your night's expenses and make the difference as to whether or not you treated your bird to that ribbed condom!

This gig happened right in the middle of a heatwave. Virtually everyone was sweating buckets and all the doors and windows were opened to let some air in and smell out. The Clash performed a chaotic discordant set and considering it was their first public airing, managed to hold their own despite shouts of disapproval from the crowd. When the Sex Pistols came on a lot of people got up and walked out. Some couldn't take the heat and the pure volume – I wonder if sound is louder in hot air? – and went to experience the spectacle from outside. With all the windows open you could hear them from miles away, which must be why people started arriving in droves to check out what all the noise was about. Even some of those that I thought had walked out in disgust earlier, had in fact gone off to get some friends to enjoy this event. By the end of the evening, Rotten's dry wit had well and truly won over most of the audience and the joint was rocking. 500 punters squeezed inside with another 200 outside still able to see and hear the show. Punk had walked right in on the most established rock venue in Sheffield and taken over.

That July the band somehow got a booking at the Sundown Club, a sort of trendy disco in Tottenham Court Road and in spitting distance of their Tin Pan Alley rehearsal studios. Sid (Vicious) came down sporting his new look, spiky hair, punky shades and all. For some reason there were only about ten fans at this gig and obviously the club didn't know what they were getting. Some prat of a DJ wanted them off after only two numbers. The set degenerated into a barrage of abuse between the band and DJ until the bouncers decided to sort it out. After much arguing backstage over principles, the band tried to perform again, but as most of the crowd seemed to prefer listening to the disco we were asked to leave – or be thrown out.

As we were carrying the last piece of equipment out the back door, I remember seeing Rotten standing there with a rusty nine inch nail clutched in the palm of his hand.

"What's up?" I asked.

"It's that bouncer," he explained. "He don't like me, he wants to have a go, and if he comes out here I'll fuckin' let him have it with this".

"Are you kidding? He's three times your size!"

"So? He's a fucker, ain't he?"

"Yeah, but what's the point, people like that aren't worth bothering about."

"God Dave, you wouldn't last ten minutes round my way with that attitude."

"Maybe not, but let's forget about him all the same. Let's go and have a beer or something."

I could see then that my upbringing had been very different from his. Johnny lived near Stoke Newington in north London, whilst I lived in Feltham in Middlesex, west London. Steve and Paul came from Shepherds Bush and Glen was from somewhere in North West London near Harrow. He got nicknamed 'Posh boy' because of his so-called middle class roots. All of which makes him sound like a bit of a toff – which he wasn't. His background was just a bit more ordinary than, say, John or Steve – the latter came from a broken home and he'd been skiving school and ducking 'n' diving since the age of 14.

John struck me as a forthright character with an extremely interesting personality and a great sense of humour. We used to muck around together a lot before gigs – doing silly dances mostly.

Earlier in June, Malcolm played me three tracks the Pistols had cut with Chris Spedding in Majestic Studios – a fair-sized 24 track. They were 'Pretty Vacant', 'Problems' and 'No Feelings'. I knew immediately I could do better in my home studio, The Four Track Shack. Working with the band live, I was aware of what they were capable of energy wise and felt it hadn't really been captured on the recordings. Malcolm felt the same. He told me, "It was like playing in an aircraft hangar" (or words to that effect).

So I invited them to my studio to re-cut these songs and maybe do a few more. I felt pretty confident as I'd spent the last four or five years honing my skills by recording my own and friends' bands, not to mention all the session work I'd been doing playing bass on various projects.

After a bit of discussion, it was decided it would be better if I brought my recording gear up to Sex Pistols Central i.e. their Denmark Street gaff.

I wasn't just gonna record them, I decided, I was going to PRODUCE them (not that any of them seemed to know what a producer did back then – as at least one of them later admitted). I suppose it never really occurred to them how bleeding lucky they were to be hiring a PA from me. With me they also got a musician, arranger, bassist, sound engineer and producer. Listen – I don't wanna sound like I'm boasting but my work has bee dissed big time lately, mainly through people's ignorance and arrogance – not to mention piss poor journalism and ghost writing – so I'm surely entitled to put the record straight once and for all.

I had done session work before and befriended a few name producers so I knew a bit about copyright and royalties. I negotiated with Malcolm and settled for an agreement that was basically this: I would supply all the recording equipment and tape plus give my services as Producer, Engineer, and Musical Arranger. In return, Malcolm would make sure all my travelling and food expenses were covered, and I would get a producer's royalty if any of my tapes were commercially exploited. I think I got about £60 in exes for about eight long days' graft. I also supplied an assistant – Kim Thraves (he was joint roller, tea boy and – occasionally – a blinding ideas man).

The Pistols' Denmark Street den was an ideal location – with Steve's flat upstairs swiftly being turned into the 'studio' control room. The only effects available were the echo obtained from one track of the tape recorder, a bit of reverb, Steve's phase pedal and my famous square wave distortion.

The rehearsal room downstairs was about 20' x 12' with cork tiles on the walls and ceiling. When the band played at their normal volume they really saturated the room with sound. I experimented for quite a while as

29

to the best positioning of mics. Steve's guitar wasn't easy to record as it was always at deafening volume. As is usually the case, it sounds wonderful in the same room but loses its bollocks when it comes back through the monitor speakers. If I'd turned the speakers up to the same level as Steve's amp it would've sounded mega, but the speakers would probably have blown after a few seconds.

I discovered that if you put a flight case in front of the amp, around seven feet away, and had one mic pointing at the amp and another pointing at the flight case, then position them hard left and right in the stereo, this would open the sound up no end. With a bit of equalizing you could regain some of the power lost by having to monitor it at a lower level. The drum kit had stereo overhead mics, one in front of the bass drum – not in it – and one on the all important snare drum. I tried miking up every drum but it gave too dry a sound. By using just stereo mics overhead you don't get any phase problems, which can cancel out the sound. It also makes the kit sound more powerful without having to be so high up in the mix. The bass sounded better through an amp and 15" bass bin and not directly injected into the mixing desk (as was the fashion of the time).

The sound had taken shape and now it was up to the band to lay down some rhythm tracks with the right feeling and atmosphere. This is not always easy to do when you keep going over the same song again and again.

It's usually advisable to try and capture it in a few takes. To get, in other words, a real performance down on tape. This is not always possible as the recording level might need adjusting or someone breaks a string or drops a stick or something.

As the drums, bass and guitar were all being recorded onto a stereo pair of tracks, there could be no dropping in if someone fucked up. I had a talk-back system run down to the studio and gave cues and advice on how the tracks were shaping up. The band must have felt at home in these familiar surroundings and it showed in their playing. Most tracks were put down in two or three takes and some in just one. We had a whole week to record seven songs which is OK for demos – there wasn't too much of that 'clock-watching' pressure which a big expensive studio would have induced.

Every decent take was kept and at the end we listened to them all and the magic ones were selected to be worked on and completed.

In the evenings, when the rest of the band had headed home, I stayed around with Steve experimenting with different guitar sounds til two or three in the morning. I suggested he should try some overdubs to strengthen the tracks.

"What's an overdub?" asked Steve innocently.

"You know, you can put another guitar over the top of the original."

"Oh, sounds great," he said, "any ideas?"

"Well, you could go kerrang on the beginning of the chorus or put some fuzzy lead on here ..." I enthused.

"Yeah, sounds interesting," he replied, "lets have a go!"

And we did. Steve was quick to catch on and in no time at all came up with some brilliant ideas of his own. The tracks started to sound even more exciting. One effect we used quite a bit was the desk overload distortion. You can hear this on 'I Wanna Be Me'. I used to use this live quite a lot and it gave the guitar the appearance of being played at ten million watts. What you do is start with a heated old valve overload sound from the amp – no distortion pedals please – and make sure the channel fader is right down, then you put the mic gain on the mixer to full. You also boost the treble and then when you bring the channel fader up slightly ... and there you have it! A sort of square wave distortion. A lot of engineers are afraid of doing this as they imagine it will damage the mixer but I've never had any problems

When the rest of the band heard this sound the next day they loved it, so did Malcolm. And this is the version on the B-side of the 'Anarchy in the UK' 45 that EMI later issued. The whole track cost them under £50 to record and ended up selling millions.

Another trick of mine which I used on 'Satellite', was to have John whispering the words over his lead vocal. It added a surreal intimate quality and I noticed that John used it on a few PiL tracks years later. 'No Feelings', with its wall-of-noise phased guitars in the verses, also got recorded that week. A great performance that became the B-side of the never released A&M single 'God Save the Queen'.

Most of the tracks recorded at this session Malcolm would have liked released as masters, but some people at record companies, and some members of the band, saw it differently.

I also had the idea for the overdubbed riffs on the 'Pretty Vacant' intro. It was one of Glen's songs – and a great one at that – but I thought the start could be even better so I suggested to Steve that, for a change, he could pick out the notes in the chord he was gonna play. It was something we used to do a lot in my band Polecat. For good measure I got him to double track it. Finally I got him to play it once more, but this time up the octave and then finally an octave above that, ping-ponging all the way (bouncing from track to track). A dynamite hook if ever there was one.

We tried out many different techniques, some silly, but mostly interesting – like handclaps on 'Anarchy' and backing harmony vocals. At the end of the week we had seven happening backing tracks, screaming out for a lead vocal.

We'd recorded some vocals at Denmark Street but to get the best out of John's voice, more sophisticated equipment was needed. It was left up to me to find a studio that could transfer the 4-track to 8-track and overdub the voice and a few extra guitars. After many phone calls I hit on Riverside Studios, Chiswick. The engineer for this session was Neal Richmond, whom I knew of previously by reputation, for his excellently produced Sci-Fi album by Seventh Wave. Also sitting in on this session was studio manageress Ruth (we all knew she was named 'Ruth' because she had it printed on the back of her silver jump suit). Later on she and I became lovers and even lived together – until she threw me out as Glen stepped in (but that's another story).

Malcolm was pushing me to take over the mixing desk on this particular session but I shied away from it on the premise that it was in capable hands. I felt that I had the session in control and if I heard anything unsatisfactory, I would act accordingly. I now realise that he was goading me – pushing me forward – for my own good but my reaction was stubborn.

Johnny knocked out seven excellent vocals in under four hours, leaving Steve time to do a few more overdubs. The tapes were nearing completion and all that was needed was for me to go MIX THE FUCKERS!

"The Sex Pistols played well, really well. It was down to the sound guy – it's really the sound guy that's responsible for me thinking I could start a band." Peter Hook (Joy Division, New Order)

This time when we got back to Manchester, we were being invited to headline a July concert organised by the two new bands that were inspired by the Sex Pistols' first performance there. Namely The Buzzcocks and Slaughter and the Dogs. We had three separate PA's between us, none of them really good enough individually, so Kim and I quickly set about wiring them all together for maximum effect. Journo John Ingham noticed this and referred to us in his review as 'Sound Wizards'. I liked that and it kinda stuck for a while. Johnny offered to lend me his famous striped peg trousers – his baggy zoot suit pants – probably because he was getting embarrassed by my wearing denim flares. I graciously accepted his offer and wore them with pride.

The place was pretty packed and I positioned the mixer up in the circle right next to the bar. It was hot, I was thirsty and the sound was manic.

Another seminal gig that was to change many people's lives. Come to think of it, Malcolm must have organised this gig through The Buzzcocks & Slaughter, because he collected the money from the door and at the end divided it up fairly equally between all involved. Later, when I talked to him about money, he said that it was the best way, "spread the cash around, keep it flowing."

That night he had us all line up for payment while he meticulously counted out the copper, silver and paper into our palms. Everyone seemed delighted by this gesture, except I got less than my normal fee. When I complained to him he just shrugged it off with the comment – "We're part of a tribe now, we have to make sacrifices for the cause." All well and good I thought, but I still have my overheads. I let it go that time, putting it down to experience.

I decided to go to Decibel Studios in Stoke Newington north London to do the final mix on the Denmark Street demos, as I'd worked there before and got good results. I arrived early and when Rob the engineer asked "Shall I put the kettle on?" a wacky idea presented itself to me. I'd been pondering over what effects to use on 'Submission'. I wanted it to have a sub-aqua atmosphere to complement John's lyrics. So I grabbed the kettle, got the track lined up, then stood in front of a mic, headphones on, and started speaking down the spout. If I got the angle right, my words would emerge through the water, all bubbly and marine-like. If the angle was wrong, I would get a mouthful of water and be choking half-to-death. Once we got the track running and the mic balanced with a canyon of reverb on it, it was great – just the effect I was looking for.

John walked in during this and the sight of me with a kettle in my mouth made him smile. "What the fuck are you doing, Dave?" he asked. I just ushered him into the control room to hear the results. He promptly gave me the Rotten seal of approval (I've since come across a photo of Steve playing a kettle and can't remember if I got him to try it out before I took over).

It was a lovely warm day, and … you've guessed it, we were stoned again. This time on some killer Thai grass. Kim was rolling joints and putting his oar in as usual. One idea of his we used was on 'Satellite', where John sings about the song's subject looking like they'd just come out of hell. I'd already got John to overdub a whisper vocal all the way through to give it a kinda eerie effect. Kim's idea was just to make the word HELL emphasized. I did – and it worked a treat. I was firmly in control of the mixing desk and it all went pretty smoothly. The tracks sounded great to me in my state of heightened consciousness. It was a full sound yet you could also hear the lyrics, which I deemed to be all-important. Look, if you've got anything worth saying you should at least make the effort to ensure that people can hear it! Everyone seemed satisfied with my work and now Malcolm had some decent demos to hawk round the record companies. These recordings – but not these first mixes, which in my opinion are better – eventually became the A side of the infamous Spunk bootleg. Stay tuned for further revelations.

CHAPTER SIX

SHE WAS A GIRL
FROM BIRMINGHAM

Barbarellas in Birmingham was always a good place to play. Flashy lights, a real stage and a large dressing room. These are the small pleasures in life that can make a band real happy. Before the show we sat back stage enjoying the booze and food the manager had laid on.

Now, I'd never seen John with a girl before and was having my doubts. I know he saw himself as one ugly fucker but I think he had an attraction of his own. Or, to put it another way, I would give him one if I were gay, I reckon. He had asked me, only half-jokingly, on the start of the tour, "now we're a real touring band, Dave, when do the groupies show up?"

Anyway, that afternoon there was a knock at the Barbarellas door and Steve looked outside. There stood several girls wanting to meet the band. One in particular requested to see Rotten.

"Cor, John here's your big chance – you've scored at last, mate." the band joked.

"What's she like Steve?" asked John.

"Just your type John, real punky." We decided to let her in, and slip out the back and leave them to it (I knew my way round as I'd played there before). John's eyes nearly popped out of his head when he saw her. She had coloured hair, safety pins, ripped clothing and a fair-sized plastic bag with some coloured liquid in it pinned to her jacket (similar in style to Johnny's syringe and tubes). She also looked a little crazy.

"Where are you going boys? I'll come with you," John said in a panic.

"We're just off to check out the talent, we'll be back in 30 minutes," Paul said with a wink. Before Johnny had time to follow us, she had cornered him and started asking about the burns on his arms (these were the cigarette burns he'd peppered himself with when bored onstage at the Lyceum).

"If John don't give it one, I will," said Steve gallantly as we started to move away. We gave John just enough time to do the business and then swiftly went back in (secretly hoping to catch them at it). Instead we found John sitting alone in the corner, looking wide-eyed and shell-shocked.

"What's up?" we asked when we saw John's face – now even paler than usual.

"God, I feel sick ..." he said.

"Why?"

"It was that bird you bastards left me with. You know that plastic bag on her jacket?"

"Yeah?"

"Yeah, well, inside it ... inside it was her abortion ..."

In Birmingham, we were joined on the bill by a glam rock outfit called The Suburban Studs. They weren't exactly a punk band having both flares and a sax player, but they were a bit different, being loud, obnoxious and dressing in home-made glittering clothes. I think Malcolm liked the name and invited them down to play with the Pistols at the 100 Club. The fact that they got this gig shows just how few compatible bands there were at the beginning. Soon though, new groups were to be springing up all over, almost all inspired by the Sex Pistols. Some bands had only been together three or four weeks before they took to the stage. I won't bore myself with a long list of names. You know who you were anyway!

We arrived in West Runton about 6.00 pm. It was a small seaside resort situated on a cliff overlooking the bay. I remember there was this force nine gale and it was bucketing down. We quickly ran into the club to be greeted by all these old age pensioners fox-trotting to some record.

"Oh, the band's arrived at last".

"We didn't think you would make it because of the rain – the stage is over there."

"You're much younger than we expected, would you like some tea and Dundee cake?"

We stood there looking at one another in disbelief. "That bastard Malcolm," someone said, "I bet he's having a right laugh back in London".

We had no choice, we had to go through with it. We needed to get paid to get to the next gig. Besides, there were all these dear old folk waiting to be entertained.

We started getting the gear in when some rain-sodden chap ran up and cried, "What are you doing? The club's round the back ..." There was a sigh of relief, although John reckoned he would have preferred to play to the Doris and Alberts he'd already been befriending.

Inside the real club, rain was pouring in through holes in the roof and much of it was landing on the stage. "Can't someone do something about that?" I asked, "The band could get electrocuted". Some buckets were eventually brought out and put into place.

"Right, forty minutes to opening time boys, snap to it" said the manager of the club. Who's gonna turn up on a night like this we wondered? During the sound-check the manager started freaking out about the volume. He threatened not to pay us unless we turned it down. As he was also paying the bouncers, we decided not to make too much of an issue out of it and did the deed. "Still too loud!" shouted the manager. We turned down again, "Too loud!" and again and so on. In the end I suggested to the band to play as quietly as possible and make a joke out of the whole event. It was hilarious, with Paul just tapping his drums and Steve still doing his guitar hero poses but with a dinky little sound. They just took the piss and I don't think anyone really cared or noticed. The venue's manager was happy at last and we did get paid. At one point, I even saw Steve stick his bare arse out of the dressing room door to the audience, to much giggling and laughter.

As expected, not many people came, although a few came up afterwards and said how much they liked it and how different it was. We were even offered a few floors to sleep on. We declined the offers and with the money from the gig, about £75, we checked into the nearest vacant bed and breakfast. I had already lined this up earlier by running up and down the sea front in a torrential gale, knocking on doors till I found someone who would take us in (at the right price). The best I could do was four to a room with nylon sheets ... but you did get a full fried breakfast. Up in the morning to the plate of grease and goodbye to our friendly landlady. She was very motherly towards us and thought we all needed fattening up. I think Steve was the only one to take these thoughts seriously.

Nottingham Boat Club was one happening Rock Venue with a mega juke box to match. It was right on the river front and was usually packed with an enthusiastic crowd of students and locals. They had previously been spoilt with the likes of Thin Lizzy and local heroes, the Steve Gibbons Band.

But the Pistols were playing so well now that they were a match for any legend, local or international. They still managed to cause a rift amongst the audience with some of the older hairy hippos walking out – but the majority were soon sold on the Pistols and they wouldn't let them leave the stage. Afterwards, a big crowd gathered in the dressing room and John held court as usual. Gigs like this were always the most rewarding.

One night around this time, we were travelling back from somewhere when something very strange happened. We were on the motorway and Kim was driving the van, Nils was co-pilot and the rest of us were asleep. Apparently Nils was the first to see these strange lights hovering on the horizon to the left of the van.

"Can you see those three white lights Kim?" he asked, "they look like they're suspended in mid-air."

"It's probably the floodlights at that brick factory," Kim replied. But the lights were still hovering there after four miles or so.

"What's that?" screamed Nils, amazed by the sudden blue flashes he saw.

Everyone woke up with the commotion – all apart from me and Glen that is.

Apparently we seemed comatose. The others all had their own theories as to what the lights were.

"It must be some electric pylons that are down and sparking," someone said.

"It's probably the electric train rails," said another. They carried on watching the sight with amazement. Knowing that I wouldn't want to miss this, they tried to wake me. It was no good. I appeared to be in a deep coma. They hit me, screamed in my ear but I didn't move. "Fuck me!" everyone cried. They couldn't believe their eyes. The lights had now changed colour and they were giving off very precise patterned flashes. It was as if they were signalling to each other. One gave an (H) sign, but sideways on, another gave off two blue lines (=) and the third a vee shape (V). As quick as a flash they turned from green to red and in formation, zapped off over the van and disappeared into space after making several elegant loops. Kim stopped the van and they sat there looking at each other. "Did we really see that?" they all asked one another. Sure enough they all had.

They had one more attempt at waking me before giving up and spending the rest of the journey talking about what they had seen. When we got back to London, I woke up outside Steve's pad, to the sound of much chatter.

"We saw flying saucers!" I was told, "real UFOs!"

"Yeah, yeah, yeah – why didn't you wake me then?"

"We tried to for hours – we thought you was dead …" At first I thought it was one big wind-up but they seemed so convincing and still stick to the story to this day. Strange!

The first, now legendary, Screen on the Green gig was a 'Midnight Special' put on at the end of August. Malcolm knew the Screen's manager Roger Austin.

The Buzzcocks, Clash and Pistols were fixed to play after the movies had finished. Through word of mouth and some hand-out leaflets that Jamie Reid designed, they managed to pack the place out. Malcolm brought along some so-called underground movies – Kenneth Anger & some other arty film-makers – which he projected in the intervals.

The Bromley Contingent were there, with Siouxsie daringly exposing her boobs through a peep-hole bra and dancing onstage with some of her mates.

Everything went off well, but by the time the Pistols were due on it was so late that people started falling asleep. Malcolm, being the canny bugger he is, had foreseen this and asked me to organise some surprise stage explosives to go off at the start of the Sex Pistols. It did the trick and at 3.00 am on that magic morning there were three or four hundred euphoric kids pogoing to their hearts' delight as the Pistols did their thing. The rest of the world had been locked outside and even the police, when they arrived following noise complaints, couldn't find any way in. I've read somewhere that Joe Strummer accused me of sabotaging their sound to make the Sex Pistols sound even better, but that's bollocks. I loved the Clash and worked hard at making them sound good. It may well have been their own backline that let them down. Anyway, how would he know what they sounded like out front when he was up on stage?

It was such a good feeling leaving there at dawn, after you've seen your current favourite bands play their hearts out.

Soon Malcy was doing the rounds of the music industry. He's the kind of guy that goes straight to the top, then works his way down. He told me more than twice to "broaden my horizons". He also told me that some people choose several dozen doors to go round knocking on, he on the other hand only chose one, then kicked it down. And he did – EMI was the first port, and he attacked with a vengeance. As soon as he had them hooked and while they were umming and aahing he'd be straight off to CBS or Polydor etc, honing his act on the way. The band – at this point – were virtually unheard of in this industry, although Malcolm had already done some preliminary web weaving.

One day he called and asked me to meet him at a café in South Molton Street. EMI had liked my tapes and wanted to meet the guy who produced them. I arrived to see him exuding his debonair charm, sitting outside reading a big newspaper and joking with the waiters. He was in a great mood and offered me refreshments. He then gave me the run down. "Your tapes done the trick, play your cards right and your name could be on the records of the biggest musical phenomenon since Gene Vincent." He stared at me as if he was expecting me to fall over with excitement (now if he had said the Kinks or the Who!).

"Dave, I'm gonna take you to meet Terry Slater & Nick Mobbs up in the Ivory Tower, they're real decision makers those two …"

Wow! I thought … Malcolm's stopped calling me 'boy' … We got to EMI where we found Terry & Nick already listening to Malcolm's copy of my tape. They asked me some questions about my production techniques and once satisfied I was the real thing, indicated that if the deal went through, then I was on the cards for producing. They told me my tapes showed that the band could play despite rumours to the contrary. They also asked me if I thought 'I'm so Pretty' (Pretty Vacant) would make a great first single? "No", I replied "'Anarchy' is the obvious choice, it's their strongest statement, maybe Vacant's the follow-up." They looked worried but who cared? I was becoming an Anarchist and proud of it.

Malcolm and I carried on our double act, telling them all sorts of stories and visions about the coming of a 'New Music & Fashion' and left them almost as excited as we were.

"Well it looks like the cat's in the bag, Malcolm, you can stop looking now." I commented on the way down in the lift.

"Are you kidding?" he bounced back, "the work's just started. Now I need more offers to play them off against each other – that will up the stakes, you mark my words." He left me on the south side of Oxford Street and headed north to some other record company to work his magic.

CHAPTER SEVEN

SEPTEMBER 1976

SO IT GOES

So It Goes was the TV show – the Granada studios in Manchester was the venue. Malcolm had somehow managed to get the Pistols top billing on this show at the start of September 1976. This was before they had a record or music publishing deal signed. I took the whole of my PA up there on the insistence of Malcolm. He wanted to recreate their live sound in the studio.

TV studios are renowned for their ability to fuck up a band's sound and there was no way this band were going to make any compromises. As it turned out in the end we had to, cos the sound technicians went on strike when they saw us erecting our own equipment. After several hours of negotiation a compromise was finally struck. They would use their mics and mixer and we could take a feed from them into our Mega PA and do our own live mix.

Tony Wilson was the presenter. He was hanging around asking lots of questions about this new punk scene, while still trying to argue the worth of bands like Steely Dan and Genesis. I'm not kidding, people may believe that he fell completely in love with 'Punk' the first time he slapped eyes on 'it', but I could definitely sense his reluctance to accept the Sex Pistols outright. He did become interested enough to study the development of the movement … and when it became obvious that it wasn't going away he capitalised on it. Maybe I'm being a bit cynical, at least Wilson was the first to put the band on British TV …

The SIG team were recording three shows in one night and there were various other artists and guests on the bill. Peter Cook was there (pissed, of course) and two other bands, Gentleman and the Bowles Brothers. One of these groups was local and sounded like a third rate Genesis. They got really annoyed because the Sex Pistols were allocated a larger stage. They argued that as they had more effects pedals, they should get the big stage. "Piss off!" was the heartfelt reply.

At the run-through, Malcolm told the band to be very cool and just go along with it all. Crosses were marked on the stage where the band were supposed to stand and cameras were wheeled in front. Sound-check over, we retired to the dressing rooms for refreshments. Kim and I were given several complimentary Sex Pistol t-shirts. These were the ones with the multicoloured guitar shapes printed over a photo of a naked lad smoking a cigarette – Shock! Horror!

"Will you really wear those t-shirts?" asked John.

"Of course we will," I replied and put mine on there and then. I thought it looked rather groovy with my maroon crushed velvet flares.

I decided that it was now time to confront Malcolm over the producer's royalties I was currently negotiating. I'd been offered one percent of retail for the UK and half a percent for the rest of the world. Having no idea what this meant in cash terms, I had consulted Johnny Goodison, a producer friend of mine who'd produced the Bay City Rollers and various other chart bands. He said he wouldn't even produce his own son for less than 2%.

I repeated this to Malcolm in front of the rest of the guys and, after some haggling, he agreed to 2%. With that little matter out of the way, and with a TV show still to do, Malcolm started giving the band one of his little pep talks in his usual 'undogmatic' way.

"If I was you, I wouldn't stand on those little crosses they've made," he said, referring to the camera marks. "Make it difficult for them! Jump all over the place!"

The band were good at adopting and adapting Malcolm's ideas – probably because he made them feel as if they were their own (come to think of it, they sometimes were!)

He also thought that it was a good idea for the band not to stop playing after their allotted time, but to carry on regardless. As they were the last act on the show there was no way they wanted Wilson coming up after their number and standing in front of them while he signed off the series. So the plan was hatched that they were gonna leap all over the place to confuse the cameramen and carry on playing well past the cut-off time. There were a few more surprises as well.

Fortunately for us we could hang around in the staff bar waiting for our turn to come. That meant that we had about three or four hours from the sound-check to the real thing. This was plenty of time to get well and truly psyched up. It's plenty of time to get pissed and stoned as well. It's not an awful lot of time to lay crazy paving, but enough for, say, ten caterpillars to completely devour an average-sized cabbage …

Jordan and Nils were with us that day. Pete Shelly of the Buzzcocks and Peter Hook – later of Joy Division/New Order – turned up too for the Pistols' TV debut. Malcolm had fixed it so that Jordan could announce the band, but the producer insisted she had to remove her swastika armband first. She refused and the whole gig seemed in doubt. Someone – I think it was me – came up with the idea of putting a circle of paper over the emblem marked 'Censored'. In the end, just the white paper was agreed upon, now all she had to do was think of something to say as an introduction for the Pistols.

There was no shortage of ideas but, in the end, she accepted Kim's suggestion of; "The Sex Pistols are, if possible, even better than the lovely Joni Mitchell!" Kim was on form that night, it must have been all that Thai dope he smoked.

About 150 punters filed in and took up the tiered seating at the back. Clive James, the Australian media celeb was the warm-up comedian. His job was to make sure the audience didn't fall asleep, by telling them funny stories and jokes. Just before the Pistols started warming up, Rotten got on the mike and started slagging James off. The comic cobra was taken aback. He sized Rotten up, then attempted to ridicule him. But this scruffy upstart was too quick and ended up with the audience on his side laughing at this balding Aussie. For someone who makes their living out of piss-taking, you'd have expected him to take it much better but, before he had time to retaliate, the band were off bashing out a few warm-up numbers.

I was viewing all this from the second control room high above the studio. Not being part of the TV technicians' union I wasn't allowed to touch any equipment, but I could make suggestions and did. The man at the controls was about 65 and he looked at me in disgust.

"Your band are much too loud!" he barked. "The singer's going to swallow that mike if he's not careful." He insisted on putting the sound through a limiter to compress the level. I told him it sounded better without it.

"I can't do that," he snapped, "you could blow up people's TV speakers!"

Now you're talking, I thought to myself and when they finally came round to doing 'Anarchy In The UK', I grabbed both his wrists and kicked the compression switch off with my foot. I thought the guy was gonna have a heart attack the way he carried on, struggling and swearing at me. The band stuck to their scheme of leaping all over the shop and the cameras were bumping into each other and desperately zooming all over the place, trying to focus on the boys. Nils followed instructions and threw a chair onstage towards Jordan, who was dancing on the side. Steve kicked it off, hitting a camera after John had given it 'the finger'. When their three minutes were up, they carried on playing regardless. Glen kicked the mikes over and Steve smashed up his guitar. Glen threw his bass down and it started feeding back loudly. "What the fuck are they doing?" mouthed an engineer in the control room next door.

"Cut!" the producer said.

"No, don't!" said his assistant.

"I said cut!" the producer demanded again.

"No, keep running!" ordered Mr Big Wig from the back. The tape was stopped and restarted several times. When the band had finally finished playing – and smashing – Rotten just stood there, surrounded by demolished equipment, giving a piercing stare at the frozen audience and then walked off in disgust. This was one of their best ever performances and they knew it, but instead of the thunderous applause they deserved, the audience just sat there dumbfounded, in complete silence, until the silence was broken by a few Mancunians – "Fucking brilliant!" they shouted "Play some more!" The audience agreed and more and more of them clapped and cheered.

The technicians were most upset about their precious mikes being kicked over though. "Don't worry if they're broken, we'll get ya some new ones," said Malcolm casually, "how much do they cost? About forty quid each or something?" He took the wind right out of their sails.

We made for the bar and more free drinks and food, only to encounter either irate or congratulating individuals. The mob that sounded like a second-rate Genesis were anxious to tell the Pistols that they couldn't play. But who cared what they thought? Peter Cook wanted to know if the Pistols were doing any more gigs, as he was sure some friends of his would love them as he much as he did. "No respect for convention, that's the attitude," he said before asking John, "do you always abuse your audience that much?"

Everyone seemed to have something to say about the Pistols one way or another. Pete Shelly got into a raging argument with someone in one of the support bands, and was trying to argue his worth by the fact that his bands' guitars only cost £20 each, whereas theirs cost hundreds. A non-starter argument if ever I heard one. I decided to give the support band a break and lifted up Mr Shelly and carried him to the bar. We continued drinking until we were eventually invited to leave. Glen had decided to stay up in Manchester for a few days on an invite from The Buzzcocks. While saying his goodbyes to the boys in the van, he started acting in a way that might have been seen as a bit camp.

"I'm getting a bit worried about Glen. He's been doing a lot of that lately." said John on the way home in the van ... "emmm", came the consensus reply, but were any of us wishing the invitation had been extended to them as well?

A new club, the Club Chalet Du Lac, was opening in Paris and the Pistols were booked as the first act to play there. They were going to do three free shows and for the Parisians to get anything for nothing is unusual, so quite a crowd was expected. The band were still relatively unknown abroad and I couldn't figure out how Malcolm got this gig – Roxy Music were booked to play the following week and we were getting more money than them. I guess Malcolm must have sold the band on the buzz they'd caused in London and the amount of similar publicity they would attract in Paris.

As my parents lived right next to Heathrow, I was asked to put the group up for the night to avoid missing the plane in the morning. I missed my chance to show them any real hospitality. I don't think I even offered to feed them. My mum had a bit of a shock getting up in the morning to find Steve asleep on our sofa, but once they got chatting she thought he was a decent lad. Malcolm was given a child's bed at my trumpet player Martyn Hayles' flat. We insisted on playing our new Polecat LP *Money Talking* to Malcolm and whoever else was there. He listened intently then commented "I don't understand it."

As it turned out, we missed the plane anyway although Malcolm sorted things out ...

Once on French soil, things felt a bit uncomfortable. The Customs wouldn't let our gear through for some reason and so I was sent ahead to make sure the club's PA was working, while Malcolm and the band waited for the equipment. It was touch-and-go whether we would get it in time for the gig.

The Chalet Du Lac was in a beautiful setting on the side of a lake, right in the middle of the woods that are the Bois De Boulogne (or is it the Bois De Vincenne? All these Parisian woods look alike to me). There were posters everywhere. 'Opening Tonight – Sex Pistols from London; Free Admission!' It had been on the radio all day and the cab driver informed me that everyone was talking about it. When I arrived there about midday,

45

there was already a crowd growing outside. The security was strict and everyone was kept out by a high metal gate and fence. The Bromley Contingent was there but I was unable to get them in early. Once I got inside the club I had a shock. They were still building it! Literally! Workmen were everywhere. They were building the stage, painting the walls, fixing bar stools and installing the sound equipment. My immediate concern was that the PA system was working and that we had enough mikes. Armed with a soldering iron I set about the problem. I kept looking around and couldn't believe this club would be open that night. The magic time was 9.00 p.m. or so it said on the posters. It was 6.30 when Malcolm finally rang from the airport. "Don't panic, I've sorted it with the officials and the gear should be there soon. What's happening down there?"

"Well, you won't believe this Malcolm, but there's a club being built in front of my eyes."

"Is the P.A. working yet?"

"Just about!"

"Well that's the main thing. Smell you later!" And he hung up.

I sat down on a chair to smoke a joint but was quickly removed so they could varnish it! Two hours to opening time and the furniture was getting a coat of varnish! Mirrors were being stuck on the walls and lights hung from the ceiling. The activity all about me was intense. The paint started to dry. The lights were dimmed and the lasers switched on. A crew of about ten started bringing out ready-made bars from the back somewhere – they were immediately stacked with drinks. Suddenly there was the sparkle of glass everywhere, the tables were covered in lace cloths and candles were placed upon them. The disco was now working and had quite a decent sound to it. All the workers put their tools away, filed out the back, then re-emerged ten minutes later neatly dressed as waiters and barmen. It was five past nine when the doors finally opened and the crowds were let in.

Everyone made a dash to the still tacky seats and tables. The staff continued to bring out pots of flowers and palms to decorate the place. I suddenly realised I had been sitting there for a few hours. Imagine seeing it for yourself – a nightclub had been built around me. The stage looked great. It came right out into the audience and had lines of mirrors and lights in strips under the floor. Seeing it all had been like a trip, especially as I was stoned on this beautifully strong Thai grass – yet again! There was still no sign of the gear though. I looked outside and was relieved to see the police helping a van through, loaded with the Pistols and their equipment. There were thousands of people out there, no way were they all gonna get in. We'd been given an old gypsy-type caravan out the back as a changing room. It was full up with booze. Vivienne had had some natty clothes knocked up for this occasion, which she loaned to the band. Johnny looked quite a sight in his black bondage suit and beret. Siouxsie had arrived in her see-through bra and mac. Apparently some French guy had been offended and attacked her. Caroline Coon was there too, wearing a t-shirt cut down the front with a safety pin in the middle – she was thrown across a table by some incensed French chappie.

There was a barrage of liggers trying to get into the dressing room to help drink the booze.

"No-one's allowed in apart from our friends." John told a security bloke.

"Unless they've got drugs," Steve added helpfully.

For some reason I can't remember much about the actual performance, except that it was fairly average. No one was struck by lightning or burst into flames. I think a few total strangers might have disappeared but how do you prove that? What I do recall is the excellent restaurant Malcolm invited us to afterwards. You should have tasted that food! Oysters, frogs' legs, snails, the whole bit …

The next day the band paraded around the trendiest coffee shops and bars. They caused quite a stir. Some people were disgusted with their look and let them know it. Standing on the opposite platform from us on the Metro, a pin-striped man dropped his pants and showed us his cock. We all laughed – this Parisian business suit had out-punked us something rotten.

Word came through that there had been near riots outside the club the night before. Hundreds of police had been called to handle the 2,000 or so punters who couldn't get in. The next night even more people were expected. The French capital was both outraged and intrigued by the publicity the Pistols had generated. In the end, some recruits from the French Army were called out to control the crowds.

The only way we could get to the club was by helicopter. A staggering crowd of nearly 200,000 had descended on the place. It looked a truly awesome sight from the air. The club resembled a matchbox surrounded by an ever growing mass of people – ants. They were being held back by armed police and soldiers. As we got nearer we could hear a mass hysterical roar of joy mixed with anger. A petrol bomb was thrown at the guards and tear gas was fired back. Real bullets began to fly – then I woke up …

I looked out of the window, then at my watch. It was actually three in the afternoon. I must have fallen asleep. I glanced over at the empty egg boxes still littering the windowsill and chuckled at the memory of the game Nils invented last night. Kim, Jordan and I had been barracked in an attic room together.

Later that afternoon, after I'd finally got up, we did a gig for over a thousand 10 to 16 year old French kids, where ice cream and soda were the main refreshments. Later we played for the 18s and over where alcohol was the main refreshment. I felt sorry for the 17 year olds! Considering there was no proper sound-check, both gigs were so-so.

The Pistols had set Paris alight and knew it. To celebrate further, I suggested we should visit one of Paris' top night clubs, (Les Crazy Horse or something). At this venue I knew we would find several members of my old band Polecat. They were the resident band there and were sorta trapped there due to the lack of money to get home. They had originally been invited to Paris to do some recording and somehow became embroiled in the music scene.

Although it was well after midnight when we arrived, the place was empty except for the band, who were both pleased and surprised to see me. When they took a break, they came over to our table and struck up conversation with various members of the Sex Pistols. My old guitarist – who was so thin that we nicknamed him Twiggy – got on well with John and when they went back on stage I was invited up to play bass on some of our old songs that they were still doing. Fortunately I remembered them and didn't make a total prat of myself. That night developed into a drunken blur and the next thing I remember is arriving back in England.

Malcolm looked like he was in a total daze, staring around and mumbling incoherently.

"What's up, Malcolm?" someone asked. "Was the strain too much for you?"

"The food was good wasn't it?" he responded. We left him walking off into the sunset and made our way towards the comfort of our own homes.

We next did a gig somewhere on the east coast, Whitby I think it was. It was still the hottest summer in decades and all the girls were strolling around on the prom. We were supported that night by a band not too dissimilar to the Incredible String Band. They had previously visited me at my '4 Track Shack' studios down in London and I really liked some of their material. Although the hall could hold over 900 people, less than 30 turned up. And they all just sat around the edge looking mildly amused.

To liven things up a little, Kim and I took turns to go and stand in front of the stage and indulge in some silly dancing … When we came to depart the van wouldn't start, so we arranged to leave our gear in the club until we could shift it later. I rang the van hire company to report the problem and was amazed when they said they would send another one up immediately. Just one chap would drive the 200 odd miles to us, towing a replacement van. This delay meant we could hang around 'Holidayville' for a bit longer and enjoy the local hospitality. Steve steamed straight in and shagged three birds before teatime. Paul persuaded several of us to help him carry his drums from the club back to the hotel for safety. We had to march along the top of the sand dunes and must have made a strange sight. I remember picking up one of those plastic traffic cones and shouting shark warnings through it to the general public on the beach. Despite drawing some attention, no one really panicked (Jaws was a big hit at the time) It was like the band had never been on holiday before – maybe they hadn't, come to think of it – and were trying to cram it all in, in one day. I had to ration what little money we had left to make sure they all got their fair share of toffee apples, whelks and shandies. Eventually we got kicked out of the hotel and ended up sitting in the van, waiting for its replacement to arrive. Rotten soon got bored and thoughtfully scribbled all over the van ('Fucking Naff Vans! Go fucking fuck yourselves!' and other good luck Lydon slogans). He then offered to cut my hair but I bottled out (again). Finally a very tired looking Jaf Vans man arrived and we exchanged keys. On seeing the graffiti he flipped a bit until someone pointed out that they were lucky we hadn't set fire to it. I attempted to laugh the whole thing off, thanked him for coming and in no time at all, we'd collected our gear and were on the road to our next adventure.

As I mentioned earlier, Leeds council had imposed a restrictive maximum decibel level upon the live music establishments in the district. It's been there since the early 70s and makes it bloody difficult to perform. They have sound meters installed in the clubs that switch off the power if you cross the threshold. At the sound-check, Cookie's unamplified drums managed to shut it down, so I couldn't see how we were going to do our normal show that night. Some quick thinking was needed. I'd nobbled one of these volume vultures before just by ripping it out, but this one was placed high up on the back wall, way out of reach. The only way we could get to it was by hanging Kim over the balcony by his feet. We then passed him the jump leads from the van which he cleverly attached and bypassed the system. No one in the club seemed bothered and in fact they complimented us on our clear, full sound ...

We arrived in Chester very early and set about exploring the town. I was already familiar with the locality, so with me at the helm we trundled off round the streets. Our first port of call was the supermarket, to pick up some booze. Chester's a very quaint Tudor-style town. The new shopping precincts have been cleverly hidden away behind a façade of old buildings.

By venturing up alleyways and small flights of stairs, you suddenly enter the modern shopping centres. Staggering around, we were attracting strange looks and comments. As soon as the pubs opened we got down to some serious drinking. After being chucked out of several drinking establishments, we took to the streets again. In our drunken state we revelled in engaging the passers-by. I also remember some of us racing each other round the racecourse before some irate jobsworth steeple-chased us away! We soon headed back to the van – this was a larger box transit version – to sleep it off until show time.

In the back of the van we got into a lengthy drunken debate about the pros and cons of writers' royalties. You see, the band were due to sign their contract with Malcolm when they got back to London and I was pumped for advice. They seemed to agree with me about the fairness of splitting it equally i.e. four ways.

I'd once had a chat with Queen's bass player at the bus stop at the end of my road (Freddie Mercury lived in the next street to me, at 22 Gladstone Road, Feltham Middlesex – I lived at 32 Buckingham Ave and Freddie and I both went to Isleworth Polytechnic around 1967). Anyway, Queen's bassist – John Deacon, I believe – started complaining to me that because he wasn't credited as a writer, he wasn't getting anywhere near the kind of money that Mercury and May were. He felt as if he'd written the bass lines and put a few of his own ideas in and deserved more. I agreed! Jagger and Richards, McCartney and Lennon, got more than their fair share in my opinion.

So after my little pep talk, the Pistols decided to cut the crap and do the sociable thing. After all, it's usually the drummer who writes the drums and the bass player who writes the bass part to a song etc. In the cold light of day, I wish I hadn't got involved with this side of their affairs, because this one decision alone later caused many problems within the band.

They were brilliant that night though! I remember leaning across in front of Steve's amp to replace a mic that got knocked over and the sheer volume of his amp nearly blew my head off. My ears didn't stop ringing for three days afterwards and for a long time it sounded as if I had a permanent distortion pedal on my left ear. Eventually it healed.

Somehow, after the gig, four crates of beer got packed into our van by mistake. We did our best to finish them off, but by the third crate nearly everyone was asleep.

The Lodestar pub in Blackburn was our next port of call. The band played to a packed house in a large hall out the back. It wasn't packed because the Pistols were there – I doubt if many of the audience had even heard of them – it was just like that every night. The Pistols managed to upset everyone before even playing a note – by taking a helluva long time to start, so when they first wandered on there were only a few people at the front of the stage. Anyway, once the stage light – singular – had gone on, the crowd had to take notice.

The stage was only about two foot off the floor so the punters were right up against it, eye to eye with the Pistols. "Come on! Bloody get on with it! Show us what you can do!" shouted someone in the audience. Rotten just stared back grinning sinisterly. Steve, who seemed paralytic, spent over ten minutes tuning his guitar at ear-splitting volume. The crowd grew more and more uneasy. "Get off, if you can't play!" The mob were turning ugly, the shouts of abuse were only silenced when the band eventually steamed into 'Anarchy'. Fuck me – they were loud! Soon a large amount of drunken jostling was taking place (not surprising once you'd sampled their rather intoxicating brand of beer). Everyone was swilling with gusto, including the band.

They stood their ground against the crowd and gave as good as they got. Crashing from song to song, their energy seemed endless. They started to win over certain members of the audience. You could see some people moving around in time to the music, although there was still a lot of booing and shouting from those opposed to the band's appearance and behaviour.

The manager of the pub came over to me at the mixing desk. He asked me to tell them to cool it, but I knew there was no point, this was the type of reaction they enjoyed. Then someone called Rotten an 'arsehole'.

"You paid to get in here mate," John instantly shot back, "and we're taking your money – so who's the arsehole?" This amused the audience and annoyed the heckler, who stood up and punched the air with his fist in defiance. He was so drunk that he fell back in his chair to much laughter.

They carried on to finish what I thought was a great set and left the stage with Rotten advising the audience that if they wanted more, they could ask for it.

There was a certain amount of conflict as to whether they did or not. This nearly erupted into a fight. The only thing that stopped it was the band's uninvited reappearance. John said that as they'd liked them so much, they would do the entire set again. This almost caused a riot. The manager, who'd been standing next to me all this time biting his nails, nearly fainted. There were only twenty minutes left till closing time and the band tried to cram as many songs in as they could. Ten minutes after closing time the power was switched off. The crowd seemed to enjoy their act of defiance though. The manager was still convinced there would be a lynching however. I headed to the dressing room for some much-needed refreshment. I had to push my way through the mob gathered there.

"Oi, you! We wanna see the band, especially that singer!" one of them said to me angrily. The bloke who had called Rotten an arsehole was there too.

"Here mate, tell them to come out now!" Not bloody likely, I thought. I went inside slamming the door behind me and the mob took to banging on it.

"Do you think they liked us, Dave?" John quizzed sarcastically. Steve and Paul were flexing up for a knuckle, whilst Glen was busy trying to pack himself into his guitar-case. Just then the door flew open and the mob poured in. The sheer weight of them pushed me back against the side wall.

The 'arsehole' had now become their leader and he came straight over to Johnny and looked him straight in the eye. There was a deathly hush.

"What do you want?" said a pale Johnny, as defiantly as he could, while staring back at the chief arsehole.

"I've come to tell you something ..."

"Yeah? Like what?"

"You're fucking brilliant, you don't take no shit from no one and we like that up here."

There was a big sigh of relief and everyone made friends. They said we were welcome there any time and should come back and play soon.

When we got back to the digs, we were all in high spirits. John had insisted on a room of his own and sulked until he got it. Me and Kim were sharing a room, whilst the other three had been barracked together. After much bedroom boisterousness – you know, burping, farting and pillow fighting – Steve, Paul and Glen finally fell asleep.

Kim and I stayed up getting stoned and discussing the meaning of life. We had been flicking through some pages of an early translation of the Old Testament that my Mum had got for me. I found some accounts of what sounded like flying saucer encounters. Just then there was a knock at the door. It was John, who wanted to know what we were doing and could he come in? We sat up for hours talking, mostly about religion. John is no fool when it comes to such things. He can see through the bullshit and reminded us how the original meaning of the scriptures had been lost and changed through misinterpretation. Each time they had been rewritten, distortions were added. Being brought up in a Catholic school, John claimed to have detested the 'bigoted, dogmatic' words of his teachers. Apparently he used to get into a lot of trouble questioning his religious instructors.

Anyway, that night the three of us had a good chat and a laugh.

John had apparently dropped some acid earlier and it had started to take effect. He eventually went off to his room and told us the next day that he'd heard noises all night. It didn't seem as if he'd enjoyed his trip.

Not surprising really – being on your own, in a bed with nylon sheets in some B & B isn't exactly the ideal place when you've dropped acid. I think John used to do a lot of LSD, although even when he was straight you would think he was tripping.

Another little outing Malcolm organised was an afternoon gig at Chelmsford Prison. We had to arrive at 2.00 p.m. and play for an hour.

Paul arranged to meet us there as this was his last day working as an electrician at the Watneys brewery. He arrived totally pissed. We sat outside the main gates looking up at the huge walls. There were no openings of any sort and one could only imagine what went on behind them.

At 2.00pm sharp, the doors slid open to reveal an inner cage. They waved us in. To my surprise we were not searched. The doors slammed shut behind us and we proceeded into the exercise yard, surrounded by high walls peppered with hundreds of tiny cell windows. All you could see was a small patch of sky overhead. Once you were in, this was to be your only view of the outside world. Standing there looking up at the grey walls and tiny patch of sky, the reality of being locked up suddenly hit me. I shuddered at the thought.

We were to play to about 500 prisoners. Some were lifers, some murderers and some – who the hell knew what – but we were about to meet them and they were about to witness a Pistols gig. One prisoner was allowed to help us in with the gear. We pumped him with questions about life inside. He was a right Jack the Lad and was already planning his escape in the back of our van. We couldn't see the point as he was coming out in three weeks for 'good behaviour'. One thing he said was how it was a real achievement to get the prison officers to look you in the eye and if they ever smiled at you then it must be your birthday.

Once the gear was set up we were taken to the officers' canteen for tea and sandwiches. There was a really strange atmosphere. It was staffed by prisoners and we noticed most of them had nasty scars across their faces.

The show was to start at 4.00pm. We were taken back to the hall down a corridor which was a series of cages, each one unlocked and locked as you passed through. John Ingham, the journalist, was with us, but unfortunately for him he had to remain backstage. I did the mixing from the back of the hall and had truncheon-wielding screws on either side of me.

The prisoners filed in and as they passed I was bombarded with various requests, "Give us a fag", "Could you get a message out?" etc. I was advised to ignore them. The prisoners were ordered to sit in their seats.

There seemed to be a sort of unspoken seating hierarchy, with the strongest built chap sitting in the front row dead centre. He was the head of the prisoners, or at least the head of the white ones. On either side were his henchmen. Sitting close behind grouped together was the black faction.

Slouching around the back were the dregs who no one seemed to want near them.

The band deliberately took their time coming on just to annoy the prisoners. The guard next to me said, "Don't be surprised if they get booed off, these boys are hard to please."

One band that had gone down well previously was Hawkwind. Apparently they were allowed to play for five hours, for fear that if they were stopped there would have been a riot. Some prisoners were tripping for days after the Hawkwind concert and it was suspected that the band had somehow distributed acid to the inmates.

After what seemed an age, Rotten walked on making wanking gestures.

"Alright! you load of tossers, the Queen sends her regards", he said. The band didn't start playing immediately and the guards looked very nervous and began patting their palms with their truncheons. The opening number was 'Anarchy' and John had cleverly changed the words to be more directed at the prisoners. At the end of the number there was a barrage of catcalls, boos and screaming. John continued his insults. "Why don't you go home if you don't like it then?" The guard next to me looked alarmed as he jabbed me with his elbow saying, "Is he bloody kidding or what?"

Just then, the leader of the black contingent stood up and waved to one of the guards. They had seen enough and wanted to be taken back to their cells. There was much laughter and comments after they were led away. The show was suspended until they were back in their cells. I personally couldn't understand it, I mean, surely any entertainment must be better than sitting in a cell? The atmosphere became more relaxed when the band continued, especially when Paul – who was still pissed – fell off his drums.

I think that was when they really won the crowd over. Rotten asked why no one was standing up dancing.

"We can't," they all shouted, "it's the rules."

"I can't see the rules," replied Rotten, "let's smash the fucking place up, let's have a riot!"

The prison officers stepped forward brandishing their truncheons and ordered everyone to remain in their seats. They said they would cancel the concert if they didn't. The Pistols carried on playing anyway and during the next song the head prisoner stood up in defiance of the screws. He had long blond hair and looked like Thor. The officer who I was getting matey with told me it was no use hitting him over the head, as it was so hard it would break the truncheon. He commented that he thought the band were going down really well and the gig would probably keep the prisoners content for quite some time. The band were really enjoying themselves and Rotten carried on winding up the audience. Thor had, by now, stripped off and thrown his clothes on the stage. No one else dared stand up. Thor seemed to relish the fact he could get away with it and did a kind of tribal war dance to emphasise it.

The group ended to thunderous applause and the prisoners were led back to their boxes through the corridor of cages. Until their next concert the cons would probably only be let out in the exercise yard for a mere hour a day. They would see nothing of the outside world but that tiny patch of blue sky.

We had only been in there for three hours but were already eager to get out. It was a strange feeling, a sense of claustrophobia, and paranoia that the familiar scenes outside might disappear. This feeling finally vanished as the last door slid back and there were all the people going about their business. Cars, buses and pubs, what a welcome sight! A sight the inmates of Chelmsford prison would not see until their release.

We went straight to the nearest pub to celebrate our freedom and spent the rest of the evening discussing our shared experience. One thing we all seemed to agree upon was that we never wanted to end up in prison.

I think the 'captive audience' crowd in the prison may have been one of the best the band ever played to. If it was Malcolm's idea then hats off to the man! The head of the prison actually wrote to the band and thanked them for their brilliant performance.

John Ingham wrote a review of this gig, but neither Sounds nor NME would publish it for some reason – NME might still have been annoyed about Sid's barny with Nick Kent.

The two day Punk Festival was to be the next great event. On the bill were The Clash, The Subway Sect, The Banshees and from France, The Stinky Toys who had a girl singer named Ellie.

They were great and surprised me, I hadn't considered that the French were already this hip to the punk scene. Maybe they'd seen the Pistols in Paris a few weeks before. I know Malcolm had connections in France and may have had something to do with the styling of the band. I wonder whatever happened to them?

The first night was also to be The Banshees' first ever gig. I think it was quite impromptu with little or no rehearsals. Sid Vicious banged the drums, Marco Pirroni – later of the Ants – played guitar and Steve Severin was on bass. Siouxsie sang 'The Lord's Prayer', 'Knockin' On Heaven's Door' and 'Germany, Germany Over All' adding a few of her own lines over a pounding improvised backing. I swamped the sound in effects and the performance lasted 20 minutes or so. For a first gig it was brilliant. They proved how easy it was to break into the scene. Just get up and do it!

Mind you, Siouxsie always looked the part. From that night on there was to be no looking back for the band. Clash manager Bernie Rhodes was very upset about their swastika armbands and refused to let them use the Clash's gear.

He did have a point and being Jewish, a sharp one at that.

The Clash themselves put in a great performance that night. They still had problems tuning and playing together but who cared, here was another group who had a similar attitude to the Pistols and that's what the movement needed! In the silence that followed someone breaking a string, Joe Strummer pulled a tranny out of his pocket and held it up to the mike while he spun through the airwaves. I think he was trying to prove that there was nothing but crap on, while the guitar was being re-strung. To add depth to the moment, I quickly added long echo and other psychedelic effects. As fate would have it, Joe hit on some radio chat show where they were discussing the bombs in Northern Ireland. "Bombs! Bombs! Bombs!" went echoing round the room. Another sublime moment of improvised audio!

The place was packed to capacity that evening (I think some latecomers even got turned away). When the Pistols came on it was real mayhem, with the crowd jumping and gyrating in time, or not, to the music.

They were surging right up to the band and spilling onto the stage. And no wonder, the Sex Pistols were devastating! People stood on tables at the side too, which collapsed or fell over causing a few scuffles, but that sounds worse than it really was. There was a line of people at the back standing on chairs, looking very out of place and uncomfortable. They were journalists and music business hacks, invited or sent down to check the band out.

The music business was now taking notice of the Sex Pistols, and things were starting to move. My recordings of the band had been toted around the record companies and certainly dispelled any notions that the band couldn't play. Just for the record, despite many rumours, Chris Spedding didn't play on any of the Pistols' releases that I produced. I reckon he may have played the solo bits on his demo version of 'Problems' as they're so slick and high in the mix. I confronted him about this but he denied it. Anyway, on all the stuff I did with them, Steve played all the guitars himself and didn't need the help of anyone else. I blasted these Denmark Street recordings over the P.A. for about twenty minutes before the band came on – right after tapes of Mahavishnu Orchestra, *Return to Forever* and Edgar Winter's *White Trash* that I happened to have with me. It certainly set the mood and familiarised the audience with the Pistols' songs. Due to a lack of time, Stinky Toys didn't get a chance to perform, apart from the sound-check, and were rescheduled instead for the following night. A couple of our mics and stands got kicked into the audience and when they were returned to the stage, the mics had been swiped. At the end of that evening the debris was unbelievable. Piles of empty cans littered the floor, along with ripped pieces of clothing, discarded underwear and even clumps of hair.

I found a pair of scissors and was moved to cut Nils Stevenson's suede tie in half – he was wearing it at the time. I never really got the 'punks in ties' thing, to me a tie represents a division between your head and your dick! Anyway, I started to cut it when Nils exploded with rage – apparently it was a present from his mum. He grabbed hold of my neck chain and we stood there staring each other out. I tried to explain my actions but it was no use, he had the shits and ended up breaking my chain.

Getting the gear out that night proved almost impossible. You see, earlier that day I purchased two huge 'W' speaker bins that had once belonged to The Who. They were difficult enough to get in, but to get them out we had to go up the stairs. Bernie and Malcolm stayed around to help us.

It was a hot, clammy night and every ounce of strength was needed to shift these giant speakers back out. It seemed impossible and eventually Bernie gave up, but to Malcolm's credit he stayed. After an hour or so of puffing and panting, they were out and we never used them again. They eventually ended up being used as a stage for some alternative Jubilee Party in one of the backstreets of Fulham near where I lived.

Day two of the Punk Festival saw the Damned, the Buzzcocks, the Vibrators and Stinky Toys play (I missed it because I was in Wales doing a gig with the Pistols). At the 100 Club, a girl got broken glass in her eye.

Sid Vicious apparently threw a glass at The Damned, although some witnesses disputed this, so, after a few weeks in Ashford Remand Centre, Sid was released. It was remarkable how members of the band and Malcolm rallied round to support Sid at this time and visited him in Ashford.

Anyway the festival got big press coverage, six pages in NME, the Maker and Sounds and half a page in the Evening Standard. Kids had come from all over the country – the scene was no longer confined to London. Now you had bands springing up in the provinces.

At the Pistols' Welsh gig, I was approached at the bar by two members of Bad Company. They'd been high in the charts that year and I hadn't really expected to see them in Swansea. They said they'd cut short a recording session in France to fly over and see the Pistols, as they were intrigued by the group's growing reputation. After the show, they told me they definitely wanted the Pistols to have the support slot on their next UK tour. It felt like a real compliment and Malcolm smiled when I broke the news to him back in London. He seemed interested in the prospect, but said he already had something better planned (I later discovered that this alternative was the 'Anarchy in the UK Tour').

After the gig, the Bad Company boys came backstage to announce their tour offer.

"Fucking hell!" said John, smiling with just a touch of unexpected enthusiasm.

"Yeah? A whole tour?" said Steve, looking up from some girl's cleavage.

"Yeah," said one of the Bad Company, "we really do like your band. That was some great kick-ass rock 'n' roll you played out there tonight!"

"We were shit ..." said Rotten deadpan, regaining his cool as he spoke in his usual wry tones.

We later joined the Bad Company guys at the bar and listened to their stories of country mansions, studios in the south of France, platinum girls who could be seduced in under two minutes and platinum LPs that took over two years to record, hotel rooms with running champagne bars that never ended ... The Pistols didn't seem overly impressed with any of it. They had just shown their own, greater, wealth on stage. For what the Pistols had was unique and remains so. They were the art of Rock 'n' Roll. They had spirit, the spirit of questioning men who could skilfully vent their anger and energy in their music. They had charisma and were fast becoming aware of it. As the poet once said, 'Precious is he who joys and grieves, Who wears the coat the rainbow weaves, All love around their body ... ' I quote that not to be arty but because I think that, most of the time, the Pistols' attitude towards their fellow men really was one of goodwill. A world away from their public image as portrayed in the musical, and then national, papers. I thought they were loveable and cheeky, but others were to see them differently.

With ever growing confidence, we set off for Burton-on-Trent. The routine was similar to the night before, with plenty of time to work on the sound.

The stage was big enough for the band to leap all over. Every night they were getting tighter and more in control. This concert is on one of the tapes recorded on my old 4-track which never got erased. On the end of the recording you can hear a mixed reaction from the audience. Amongst shouts of "Piss Off!" and "Go back home!", you can hear cries of "More!" This division of crowds was typical and it often created friction within that could sometimes erupt into fighting. Those that liked the band usually offered to carry out the gear. They used to ask the Pistols all sorts of questions. "Why do you dress like that?" and "what are you singing about?" were the two you'd hear the most.

Rotten was the best at holding court. I've seen him gain the attention of twenty or more at a time. He used to enjoy it too! He used to lecture them about how the youth of the country had been thrown in the dustbin and how everyone was so apathetic about it. How all the established rock stars had deserted their audiences and how they should form bands themselves in order to get heard. It was never his intention for bands to copy them, in fact he used to stress the point that they should do their own thing. I guess most weren't that imaginative at first ... mind you, the Sex Pistols were so bleeding good, if you were an 18 year-old, you'd want to copy them, wouldn't you?

That night some bastard slashed one of our tyres ...

Next stop Stoke. We were fortunate to get in early to set up so we had plenty of time to adjust the equipment in that never-ending search for perfection. The club was designed to take the maximum amount of people for its size, with a balcony round each wall and a wide staircase coming down the centre. It looked a lot like the deck of a galleon. The posters on the walls were advertising the week's events. The club was so popular that it had live acts every night. We noticed that the night before they'd had The Groundhogs and the next night it was going to be Geno Washington.

It was unusual in those days to sense an aggressive vibe in the clubs.

After the peace and love message of the Sixties, most people just went out for a good time and the bands were supposed to contribute to the pleasant flow of the evening. Bouncers were still a permanent fixture, but probably a bit rusty as no one seemed to have much to fight about in these apathetic days of post hippydom.

I still had a good supply of Thai grass and most of us got pretty out of it that day. We even had time to take a leisurely stroll around town and visit a few pubs. The town still had many smoke-blackened factories. You could see the pit-shafts and slagheaps silhouetted against the grey sky in the distance.

A far cry from London! In the pub we ran into a couple of girls and one had "I Wanna Be Me" (a Pistols' song title) painted on the back of her jacket. John was amazed. Where did she get the title from? No recordings had been issued yet, not even any bootlegs.

When we got back we were delighted to see a queue of people outside the club. Steve discovered a door in the dressing room which led out to the street. A few girls were let in free for services rendered.

More smoking and boozing went on before the band fell on stage. I made a real effort to get Steve's guitar in tune for once. I was aided by this monster of a strobe tuner which they'd found in a box of assorted goodies that had been left behind by the previous occupants of their Denmark Street base. The problem with the guitar was that you would get it in tune but, because Steve played it so hard, it would soon go out again. The solution I discovered was to tune it, then tug at the strings, then tune it again and so on, until all the slack was taken out. I understand that discordancy and sheer volume can provoke feelings of aggression, but to me, if the Pistols were too out of tune they would sound a bit sad. Not tonight though, tonight everything seemed perfect. I can remember sitting there behind the mixing desk thinking to myself that I was probably witnessing THE BEST FUCKING LIVE BAND IN THE WORLD. Certainly at that point in time. In the past I'd seen the likes of Hendrix, Who, Stones, Floyd and Faces in smallish clubs, but none compared with this bunch, they were real – not posing.

For half the set hardly any of the audience moved or spoke (we're talking about 70 people at the most). They just looked on in amazement.

The atmosphere finally broke when some bouncer started picking on this poor bespectacled student who was jumping up and down with excitement. It was pathetic and John told the bouncer so.

The Sex Pistols were becoming even more powerful and aware of it. If this gig had been filmed and recorded, I'm sure it would have stood out as one of the best gigs in rock 'n' roll history. Unfortunately, I hadn't had the foresight to invest in a cine camera and no one put one in my hands.

I understand that discordancy and sheer volume can provoke feelings of aggression, but to me, if the Pistols were too out of tune they would sound a bit sad. Not tonight though, tonight everything seemed perfect. I can remember sitting there behind the mixing desk thinking to myself that I was probably witnessing THE BEST FUCKING LIVE BAND IN THE WORLD

OPEN DOOR, POLYDOR, CLOSE DOOR

As contrasts go, Sex Pistols and folk group Griffin were pretty extreme, but at Didsbury College they complemented each other superbly. To see the stage littered with electrified harmoniums, tubas and bassoons next to the Pistols graffitied amps was hilarious, but it worked a treat. I guess Griffin were a kinda 'punk/folk/rock' band anyway, just posing as hippies with their long hair and colourful rags. Both bands seemed to respect each other's music and when Griffin played, after witnessing the Sex Pistols' sound-check, they had a new-found gusto to their performance and I'm sure I heard some feedback from that harmonium.

Anyway, backstage it was all rather friendly between the two bands and I even heard several intellectual conversations about music developing between them. I reckon Griffin would have made a better support band for the 'Anarchy Tour' than, say, The Heartbreakers, but wot do I know?

After the Punk Festival press interest had reached fever pitch and Malcolm had several interested parties in the pipeline. It came down to a toss up between Polydor and EMI. He had his heart set on EMI, as he wanted the 'dog listening to a gramophone' logo on his boys' records (although the EMI/HMV label connection had, I think, lapsed by then). Malcolm really knew the value of playing one record company against the other, and had no scruples about doing this. It certainly helped them to focus on the deal and come to a concrete decision. Other punk bands were already preparing record releases, he had to move fast and take the best offer. Polydor were very interested though and were talking about paying £20,000 (maybe £190,000 or so now).

Chris Parry, Polydor's head of A&R, became really set on signing the band. He'd booked a studio for us even before the contract was signed. We were all set to go into Deep Purple's De Lane Lea studio in Holborn at the coming weekend. Late the night before EMI came across with a better deal and snatched the band. It was reported as being the fastest deal ever made in the music biz.

To cushion the blow to Polydor we had to go through this whole charade of turning up at the studio, as if we were going to record, then find some excuse for why we couldn't. On the way in Malcolm started complaining about some half-eaten takeaways that littered the reception. "My band can't work in this mess," he told the studio engineer, "we at least expect the studio to be cleaned before we enter it." But before the poor old engineer could clean up the mess we had all walked out. We hung around on the steps of the studio for a while waiting for Chris Parry to turn up, so he could be given the news that the Polydor deal was off. He was late, and as the band and Malcolm wanted to visit Sid in borstal, it was left up to me and Kim to drop the bombshell on him. He finally arrived ...

"Hey Dave, the band not arrived yet?"

"Er, well, they were here but Malcolm wasn't happy with the studio and John's voice is shot, and they needed to visit Sid in borstal – and by the way, they signed with EMI last night!" He was so upset that he broke down in tears. We tried to console him by telling him not to worry as there'd be other punk bands to sign, but he really wanted the Sex Pistols and felt he had been betrayed. I also believe he was left with the bill for the studio but hey, that's the way it goes I guess. I mean, they were offering less advance, and where was the dog on their label?

As EMI were now dealing with this fairly unknown commodity, they were a bit apprehensive to say the least. As a producer I had no track record to speak of, although I had gained lots of experience over the years and was very confident I could deliver the goods. I'd also had one meeting with Malcolm and EMI when they'd first been approached by him. I assured them that if they just left us alone, then they would be delivered the heaviest piece of rock music EVER – 'Anarchy in the UK'. They didn't seem convinced and kept going on about 'Pretty Vacant'. They thought this should be the band's first single, as did Glen, but without any reservations I told them they would get the band's strongest statement – 'Anarchy'. They would have to like it or lump it. They weren't used to this kind of behaviour and appeared uneasy, but this was the exact kind of behaviour Malcolm was cultivating.

"EMI are the enemy," he kept telling us, "keep them at arm's reach, boys" and we did (for a while at least). Once again, it was left to me to find a studio to record the single. One place we checked out was Konk Studios in Hornsey, owned by Kinks' Ray Davies and yes, there was a giant nose hanging outside. I loved the idea of the Pistols cutting stuff there as the Kinks were one of my favourite bands and still are. So we all went down to Konk one afternoon to play my tapes and see what reaction we got. We'd heard they had their own bar and billiard room upstairs, where many a star-studded drinking session went on. We felt sure Ray would be aware of the band and welcome us with open arms.

When we arrived we were greeted by a very apprehensive engineer. He told us everyone was out, then made us sit downstairs for what seemed like an age while he did something upstairs. Malcolm must have even more acute hearing than me, because he claimed that he could hear much shuffling of feet upstairs, but when we were finally allowed up, mysteriously, no-one was there apart from the engineer. All the equipment had been covered up and Mr Soundman was reluctant to play our tape. When he did, it was so quiet I immediately insisted that he turn it up, "to check out your monitors, man." Reluctantly he obliged. We watched his feet but they weren't exactly tapping. This wasn't the place for us! We asked about the bar out the back.

"It's all locked up," he said nervously.

We left disappointed and fell into the pub next door.

"I'm sure they're all in there hiding in the bar," said Malcolm, "They didn't want to see us, they must be afraid of us. Here, phone them up Dave," he went on, "ask to speak to Ray, tell 'im it's his buddy Dick Emery, camp it up a bit." I've learnt by now that if Malcolm asks you to do something you may just as well go for it there and then, it's a lot simpler in the long run, believe me.

"Hello, is Ray there?" I said into the phone receiver.

"Who is it?" came the reply,

"It's his buddy Dick ... Dick Emery."

"Hold on," said the voice on the other end, "I'll just get him for you."

"See? He is there, give us the phone." said Malcolm.

"Davies, you dumb deviant!" Malcolm barked down the line, "Malcolm McLaren here, Sex Pistols' manager. Call yourself a rock'n'roller? You just missed out on the biggest break of your retirement." And with that he hung up and we all had a laugh.

We had a good old chat that night Malcolm and I, as we staggered round the streets of Hornsey Rise making our way home. We passed a little shop on the bend of the main road. "I used to sell old records out of there," he said, "78's mostly."

Now I have some knowledge of old 78's, being a bit of a collector myself, inheriting old Elvis, Buddy Holly, Bill Hayley etc records from my older sister Val and her friends, when they became redundant due to the much more portable and durable 45's. But Malcolm's knowledge of early recording artists was very impressive indeed. He rattled off a huge list of his favourite recordings from this bygone era, some I'd heard of, but most were obscure. He also had an extensive knowledge of vaudeville acts and music hall comedians, especially those that had risen up out of the poorer parts of the East End. "Anarchists of their time" he said, "politics through humour." Hmm! This sounds familiar, I thought.

THE MADCAP FORGETS TO LAUGH ...

I was still on the lookout for a suitable studio and, as EMI were picking up the tab, the sky was the limit, or that's what I thought at the time. I was pleased the band had stuck with me as their producer as they could have easily obtained the services of someone with bigger knobs, although whether they would know how to use them properly in this situation is anyone's guess. Malcolm actually tried to get Syd Barrett of Pink Floyd to produce some demos during the early days. He told me a funny story about the time he had a meeting with Syd at the hotel where he lived (Syd's room was being paid for out of Pink Floyd royalties).

Malcolm turned up and sat in reception expecting to meet some long-haired old hippy, when in walks this guy with a crew-cut and an American business suit, carrying a copy of the Guardian newspaper. Malcolm instinctively knew this was Syd by the psychedelic gleam in his eyes.

Malcolm approached him and reminded him of their arranged meeting, but Syd seemed to have trouble recalling it. Malcolm tried to interest him in the subject of producing the band.

"Well Syd, I've got this band called the Sex Pistols."

"Yes, isn't it terrible the problem in Angola?"

"You'd really love them Syd, they can't play and the singer can't sing."

"I think it's criminal, all the things that are still going on in Chile – excuse me, I must go to the loo."

Malcolm watched as Syd, who'd been staying in the hotel for some two years, then asked the porter where the toilets were.

"What was it you wanted?" Syd asked on his return.

"My band, the Sex Pistols, I want you to record them."

"Oh yes, could you leave the details in my cubby hole at the desk? I must fly now. I've got to stop a war in the Middle East …"

That was the last Malcolm heard from him. A brilliant idea, Barrett and the Pistols – I wonder whose loss was the greater?

Here I was producing what was poised to become the greatest, most explosive band since the Beatles. I'd chosen to record in Lansdowne Studios in Holland Park as I had worked there before. This was a fair sized 24-track which was conveniently located between Hammersmith and Notting Hill Gate.

Malcolm had asked Kim to get some cocaine for the big event (he did, but when Malcolm tried it he complained about the quality). The band were called over one by one and offered a snort of the white powder, before steaming into the recording session. The control room was about 30 feet above the studio floor with a small window looking down upon it. A few people had been invited along to add a bit of atmosphere, notably John Ingham and the small girl, Helen Wellington-Lloyd. We spent a bit of time getting a sound while everyone sat huddled around the mixing room. The band were below, poised to go.

"OK, 'Anarchy in the UK', take one!" Paul let out an almighty "One! Two! Three! Four!" Malcolm then leapt up brandishing a can of crazy foam and proceeded to spray 'Anarchy' over the control room window. This was supposed to incite the band to play with even more fervour. As the window was so high up and so small, I doubt if they even noticed it. The rest of us though fell about in hysterics, except for the engineer who mumbled something about who was gonna clean it all up … ?

They put down two or three almost note perfect takes, but to me they were lacking in sheer energy and atmosphere. They were too clinical and staid. To set my foot tapping wasn't enough, it had to make me want to bang my head on the mixing desk. The band came in to listen to the play-back.

"What's wrong with that?" asked Paul.

"Yeah, there's no mistakes," said Glen. But no, I wasn't gonna give up that easily. I knew what they were capable of. In my book the Sex Pistols were the heaviest band of all time at that point, 'Anarchy in the UK' was the most controversial song of all time and therefore I wanted the performance to be both. There was a bit of confusion in the band as to what was expected of them. I said we just had to keep going until it happened.

When it did we would all know. Disgruntled, they carried on. At that point Mike Thorne of EMI walked in – uninvited I may add. Malcolm leapt up and sprayed "EMI's here!" on the window, and pissed off the engineer again. It's getting mighty crowded, I thought. Johnny had been busy decorating the studio with slogans using his felt tip. When the engineer saw them he flipped (and EMI were later billed for the damage). After a few days, we decided we would go elsewhere and try again – put some distance between us and the busybodies at EMI.

Why we ended up doing a gig in Scotland right in the middle of a recording session I'll never know, but I guess it was a prior commitment that we were honouring. The venue was Dundee Technical College, the only Scottish gig the Pistols were to do – well, the first time round anyway. We had a nice leisurely drive up, getting stoned on this really, really strong Thai grass – surprise, surprise. The countryside was beautiful and the people really friendly. Nils came along carrying the gig contract on a clipboard – he was ribbed for his efforts. I think the consensus of opinion was that Nils was often a 'waste of space' (he wasn't allowed in the office when the Pistols signed and a row broke out between him and Malcolm – Nils soon went off to manage the Banshees and I got the impression that Malcolm sort of set that up for him, giving him some money to help him on his way).

The audience seemed to accept the band's appearance without question. The gig itself was packed and the crowd were won over very quickly. John put so much into this set that he almost sung himself hoarse. You could see the pain he was in but he just kept going. I thought that at any moment he would be coughing up blood and, in fact, he did later. Everyone was very pissed (which is not surprising as the booze was only 10 pence a pint – a real bargain, even back then). After one long amazing set, the band just wanted to collapse from exhaustion, but the crowd wouldn't have it and kept shouting for more. They bombarded the dressing room door with empty beer cans and plastic glasses until, after ten minutes of mayhem, the boys finally gave in and went back on. The Pistols were treated as heroes that night and nearly everybody wanted to talk to them and buy them drinks. They made many friends, especially the hotel owner with whom we stayed up drinking all night. He insisted on giving us free rounds and told us it was a real pleasure to meet people almost as outrageous as himself!

We then booked ourselves into Wessex Studios in North London near where John was brought up. This was a massive studio complex in an old church. It had a kind of fairground feel about it with brightly coloured plastic tubing and neon lights everywhere. It wasn't exactly cheap, costing £50 or £60 an hour – I suppose that's about £400 an hour or more in today's money – but EMI had already agreed to give us ten days in a studio of our choice so who cared? I took their equipment down the night before and erected it in position and gave the drums a much-needed, in my opinion, tuning. The studio was so large you could get an orchestra in it, so I spent the rest of the evening moving screens around and making rostrums for the band to play on.

It was important to make them feel comfortable. Also, we insisted that EMI should supply us with refreshments too – in order to help the session along, you understand. We even had to threaten to go on strike until they arrived. And when they did we ordered some more. I think we got through 1,000 cans in the end – though it was pretty weak stuff and some of that went to friends, relatives and hangers-on ...

The next day we were able to launch pretty much straight into it. Each band member was lifted off the ground on their own kind of stage. They were facing one another, apart from John who was in a vocal booth on his own, in almost total darkness. It seemed to work. They were playing much more confidently.

Converting the engineers to this 'New Sound' was often a problem, as they were not too aware of what was going on. If you'd let them, they'd try to clean it up too much.

"Let's go for the Cat Stevens drum sound," they would say.

"Oh I think the bass would sound better if we plugged it straight into the desk."

"I think the guitar is a trifle too distorted, don't you?"

"No! No! No!"

"But why don't you at least use our new sessionette modulated Guitar Hero Cube?"

"Has it got valves?"

"No, but it cost nearly £2,000".

"Oh, no valves eh? I think we'll stick with our trusty Fender Twin."

Sometimes you could see the studio hacks sniggering at the band. We didn't expect them to like it. The engineer was there to help work the gear, and whoever he was we were more or less stuck with him. If they did offer any genuine help that was a bonus. Most did the job they were paid to do adequately, although sometimes reluctantly. I used to notice how they would leave the room on our mega-loud playbacks. I couldn't understand that at all, I mean, imagine the Pistols blasting out over four huge studio monitors, one in each corner, with it all so loud the woofers are shaking!

It was blissful. Still, everything was under control – well nearly – and we weren't taking any shit from anyone.

EMI kept ringing up to see what was going on. They couldn't understand how a three minute rock song could take so long to record. When they asked to speak to us, they were told to 'piss off' and stop causing a disturbance. They would get their product I said, and it would be the ultimate rocker. EMI ignored all this and started sending down spies to see how the session was progressing, but they were kept out. One bloke they sent down was so persistent about getting in, Steve and Paul had to douse him with water on the steps before he graciously agreed to leave.

As far as the single was concerned, it was still proving a bit of a problem to get the right backing track. The band were playing all their other songs magnificently, but when it came to 'Anarchy', they seemed to become too self-conscious. It didn't sound as if they enjoyed playing it any more. I resorted to tricks like putting it in the middle of their set and getting them to perform like they would live. I made sure everything they played was recorded and these tapes still exist somewhere. Every song sounded great, until it came to 'Anarchy'. The same problems occurred. I tried smashing bottles in front of them and setting light to wastepaper bins, but they still never delivered the magic backing track. I just kept driving them on and on, hoping they would get so frustrated and angry they would take it out on their instruments.

After playing over their whole set two or three times, we still didn't have it. The track kept slowing down slightly in places. Sometimes this came from Paul, whose drums were always pretty tight live, but who tended to slow down very slightly in less exciting settings. In a way this made him the perfect drummer for the band, as he was able to pull them back from becoming too frenzied, unlike a lot of other punk bands that followed. It was a very subtle thing, but it made all the difference in the world to the final feel of the track. I felt it was OK if the track was speeding up, but allowing it to slow down just made it sound sickly and it lost all sense of excitement. I had no doubt though, that most of the versions of 'Anarchy' we had, once they had been overdubbed and mixed, would have sounded great and would be revered and raved over now. But I felt it could be stronger and I had a powerful idea of what it could be – and was directing this session to my own satisfaction and vision.

Malcolm turned up the next day to see how we were getting along. He hadn't bothered coming down all week, preferring to let us just get on with it. He was pleased the way things were shaping up. We'd managed to upset EMI, we'd been banned from one studio and we were being sued for damages and had already spent over £7,000 of the record company's money, yet still hadn't handed over a single minute of finished product. Apparently EMI were still waiting for 'I'm So Pretty' and had been sending down people all week to make sure that we cut a take of it. By some bizarre coincidence, that was the only song we did not manage to record.

After getting bored with going over and over the same songs, I suggested that they should play all the covers they knew. This would add a bit of light relief and thus reduce the tension. 'Substitute', 'Doncha Gimme No Lip', 'Stepping Stone', 'Whatcha Gonna Do About It?' were all knocked out in great form. This was a good thing as they were to be the only studio versions committed to tape (at the time the band were unaware that all this was being recorded).

The engineers there thought I was crazy however, wasting all this tape. As the reels piled higher and higher, I just kept shouting

"Bring more tape, we mustn't run out!"

"What shall we do now, Dave? We don't know any more fucking songs," said John.

"Just play anything, make something up."

"I know," says Paul, "tell John to sing 'Road Runner' while we play 'Johnny B Goode'.

"God!" says John, "sounds like an awful idea." But they tried it and for me it was one of those rare moments of classic spontaneity. John forgot the words and had to be cued in by Paul, who was bashing away at his drums like crazy. It was a mad idea but it worked. The band were now enjoying themselves and the ice had been broken. This seemed a great time to attempt 'Anarchy' – and there we had it! A great pounding take, full of all the energy and gusto that made it worthy of its title. They still hadn't gone all the way for me, but it was good enough.

Suddenly its 7.00 a.m. and time to go home. I'd been operating on pure adrenaline for over 20 hours and was still buzzing from all the whizz and booze I'd been consuming. To burn up some excess energy, I went round binning the many empty beer cans we'd left scattered around, downing the half empties for good measure. I must have put away gallons of the stuff. Breaker was the make of this particular beer, although "Piss" would have been more appropriate. It came courtesy of EMI, who'd probably sussed not to send us anything too strong. Anyway, there I was at dawn in this converted church trying my hardest to come down.

As we all walked out into the cold drizzly morning air I offered, or was asked, to give Malcolm and the boys a lift to Highbury & Islington tube station. By now the rush hour traffic was building up and while I was letting them out on the double yellow lines outside the station, some car started beeping from behind. The windows were all steamed up and I couldn't see who it was, so I just beeped back. It turned out to be the Old Bill. Once they'd smelt my breath they had me in the back of their car blowing into a breathalyzer within seconds. The band had become spectators to my plight and their jeering and leering wasn't helping. I attempted to explain the situation, but stopped short when the test miraculously proved negative. A second test was performed which was again negative, so they had to let me go. I guess the cocktail of substances in my blood must have cancelled each other out. It also proves just what piss this Breaker beer really was.

The next afternoon we returned and apprehensively stuck on yesterday's take of 'Anarchy'. Fortunately it still sounded thrilling, so we set about overdubbing it. Steve and I worked out some great guitar parts and by the time we had six or more layers on, it sounded very powerful. The engineers objected to me overloading their mixer again to obtain that over-the-top distortion I so liked. I assured them that EMI would pay for any damage that might occur, so they reluctantly agreed. When it came round to doing the vocals, John, who'd been singing his heart out all week, was nearly hoarse. He didn't let that stop him and he delivered what I consider to be one of the raunchiest vocals of all time, quite fitting for the song. Glen, however, wasn't convinced and, though I hardly noticed it at the time, the seeds of discontentment had been sown ...

'No Fun' was also recorded at this session as the possible B-side. a full seven-minute version that ended with Johnny screaming after the group had finished playing. It too had the immediacy that 'Anarchy' had. You can hear Johnny advising the rest of the band to "Go mad! Go like we go live!" over Paul's pounding drum intro. You can also notice the same hoarseness on John's voice. I gave him some really long reverb to inspire him, and he remarked "Cor! Sounds like I'm singing in a cathedral!" before delivering another spine-chilling vocal.

The next day we were to move into Studio Two to carry on overdubbing and mixing. When we arrived it was pouring with rain. Coincidentally we all got there at the same time. We stood huddled together in an arched doorway looking for a way in. The door we usually used was locked and we couldn't get any reply.

"Here, this door is open," someone said.

"What about that red light up there, doesn't that mean they're recording inside?"

"Well I ain't standing here getting wet." said John, so taking no notice of the red light, we went through the door and found ourselves in Studio One, which we'd been using the previous day. We made for the EXIT sign on the other side of the studio. The room was in almost total darkness, so we followed one another in single file to avoid tripping over any obstacles. As we approached the far side of the studio we noticed a voice coming out of the darkness. It was someone singing in an almost operatic tone. It had a familiar ring to it. We strained to see where it came from and noticed a candlelit face in the distance, behind this large wooden music stand. The singer was clutching a pair of headphones to his ears and singing with closed eyes.

"Hey, isn't that Freddie Mercury!" cried someone.

"Yeah! Hi Freddie!" Just then he threw off his headphones and looked over to see the Sex Pistols and me waving at him. A crowd of red faces appeared at the control room window, their arms flapping in unison. Their mouths were going up and down but we couldn't hear what they said. We carried on through the exit door and collapsed with laughter on the other side.

Apparently our intrusion had ruined the best vocal take of the day. Freddie had lost his concentration and wouldn't even contemplate any more vocals until the next afternoon. Later on we kept noticing him hanging around outside the door of Studio Two. He was probably taking a closer listen to 'Anarchy', which had been echoing around the corridors all day. Every time we poked our heads round to say hello, he made out he was reading the notice board. Glen caught him taking a peep round the corner.

"Can I help you, Freddie?" he asked.

"Oh, I was just looking for the toilet," said Mister Mercury.

"It's behind you," said Glen, "it's that door marked 'toilet' ..."

This was probably Mercury's first encounter with the band and the music that was to knock him and many more superstars off their pedestals. Even though Queen managed a comeback, they did disappear for a good while and some other rock dinosaurs went forever – in most cases deservedly.

I didn't mention to anyone all the hours of material that I had managed to record at those sessions. It was a closely guarded secret until long after the band broke up. It was also a pleasant surprise for Malcolm, who was in short supply of material at that time – I wonder if EMI realize that they also contributed towards the Great Rock 'n' Roll Swindle soundtrack?

Malcolm appeared again later that day and was keen to feast his ears on our musical achievements. We were just as keen for him to do so. Before getting under way we rolled the ceremonial joint. These were usually seven skinners packed with half-Thai grass and half tobacco. Malcolm had, up until now, refused the stuff, claiming that it made you lazy. Well, today was different.

"Cor, that smells good," he said, "pass it over."

"Are you absolutely sure, Malcolm?" I teased.

"Oh yeah, I might as well get into the mood." He gave about three hard puffs on it and then, after a few coughs and splutters, sat there completely motionless. After the cloud engulfing his head eventually drifted away, one could see a very queasy-looking Malcy staring out into thin air.

"Eh, Ah, c-c-could someone get me a tea?" he finally managed to say as we all burst out laughing.

"Right on, Malcolm, be one of the boys for the day, eh?" said Steve.

A call went out for a tea for Malcolm, but Paul had already slipped out to make it. This was probably to avoid the embarrassment of refusing the joint (he virtually always did). Once it got to John, though, no one else would get it anyway. Not unless you prised it out of his hand by sheer brute force. He was a great one for disappearing into a cupboard or somewhere with it. Not today though, for once he was more keen on handing it to back to Malcolm.

At this point, Paul returned with the tea for Malcolm, who seemed desperate for it. Next, the tea boy walked in and handed him another. Before Malcolm had a chance to put one down, John shoved the joint back in his mouth. He looked a sight with a cup of tea in each hand and the joint sticking out of his mouth. He tried to hand a tea to someone, but no one would take it from him. Instead, Steve and Paul took to tickling him trying to make him spill it. He started twitching nervously, then let the joint fall from his lips.

"Don't touch me." he groaned.

"Why not?"

"I'll fucking scream!" he snapped back and he nearly did too. This little fracas gave us much enjoyment and no doubt caused a similar degree of embarrassment to Malcolm. He reminded me a bit of the accountant Gene Wilder played in that Producers movie, especially that scene when him and the Zero Mostel character are wrestling over his security blanket ...

There was one finishing touch I felt the 'Anarchy' track needed. It was on the end, where Rotten says "D-e-s-t-r-o-y". It needed something to actually be destroyed – audibly. A likely candidate was one of Steve's much-cherished Les Paul guitars. Steve obviously wasn't too keen on that idea and suggested just whacking it about. It didn't sound right. He tried hitting his amp with it. That wasn't right either. Then I suggested that if he played it and we hit the guitar with drumsticks and things, that might do the trick. Suddenly everyone was keen to join in, including Malcolm, who was probably trying to get his own back for the tea and joint prank. It's a shame no one had a camera. It did look completely bloody ridiculous.

"Ok, let's have a run-through for a sound level, just a bit more ..."

"Come on Dave!" said Steve, "I'm getting bruised out here, not so hard Rotten, you fucker!"

"OK, let's do it then!"

Crank! Thwack! Boing! Smash!

"Oh dear! Sorry Steve, I forgot to record any of it!"

"You fucker, Goodman!"

"Only joking! Let's have a listen!"

"... Nope, still not right, I think there's nothing left but to smash it up!"

"Yeah, go on Steve! Smash it up!" cried Rotten. Suddenly we were all carried away with shouts of 'Smash it up!' 'Wreck the fucker!"' and so on.

Steve said he would allow it to be trashed but only on one condition – that Malcolm would buy him a new one. All eyes were on Malcolm.

"Well ... if it's in the name of art... I suppose I could."

"One of those gold top anniversary models with the gold-plated bridge and knobs and everything?" asked Steve.

"Eh, well, lemme think ... ".

"Go on, Mal! Don't be so bleedin' tight!"

"Oh, all right then," he said, mumbling something about art coming before material wealth.

Steve was no longer apprehensive about destroying his old Gibbo and probably already had his eyes on the new gold top Gibson he'd been promised. We sat with bated breath as Steve stood there poised, guitar held above his head ready to bring it crashing down onto the floor in an explosion of chordant metal and wood. We had one chance to get it right.

'Here we go then!' We ran the end of 'Anarchy' through again and just as Rotten sang the closing lines 'Anarchist! Get Pissed! Destroy!', Steve brought his guitar crashing to the floor. He looked like an axeman carrying out an execution. We thought the monitor speakers were about to blow up. The Gibbo's neck snapped off and bits of guitar went flying through the air. It was marvellous, just what the track needed. When the dust had settled and the reverb died I said – deadpan again –

"Sorry Steve, we'll have to do that again."

"Yeah? Why? Don't tell me you didn't record it?"

"Oh no, I recorded it alright … but it was out of tune." Big laughs all round.

"OK, let's double-track it!" More laughter …

We spent the next half-hour just listening to the end. We tried playing around with reverb and echo to enhance it, then realized Malcolm was still waiting to hear the rest of the song. We played it through at ear-splitting level. It did sound good. Malcolm was smiling. We played it through again on the small speakers. Malcolm was still smiling. Then he asked for a pair of headphones to listen to it. He started singing along with it in every possible key except the right one. We played it through again and again and it didn't seem possible to get bored with it. There were still a few dodgy bits that bugged me, but no one else seemed to notice. Just then we heard a "Hi Gang!" from the doorway. We looked round to see the entire Queen band standing there, in all of their shiny, satin finery.

"That sounds great man!" said Brian May,

"Yeah! Real heads-down!" someone else exclaimed.

"What type of music do you call it then?" asked Freddie.

"REAL," sneered Rotten.

"Oh …" and they all stood there embarrassed, not knowing know what else to say.

We still had a few more days left on the budget so I decided to try and record the song all over again. As we had this version to fall back on, the pressure was off. I announced this decision to disbelieving ears.

"That was a good demo," I joked, "but tomorrow we're gonna do it for real.

"You fucking what?" they all choroused.

"We all know what we're doing now," I explained, "it will be worth the effort, trust me, I'm your producer."

Everyone looked a bit glum, but the next day the first take was the very best one without a doubt. The energy didn't ease off for a second. We had the whole song with its multitude of overdubs, finished in less than eight hours, whereas it had taken over eight days to record the previous version. For the manic ending we thought twice about smashing up another of Steve's guitars, so a compromise was struck whereby, on the last chord where Rotten passionately yells "Destroy!", I got Paul to start whacking the guitar with his drumsticks. As Steve was still playing it he had to be careful not to hit his hands but they soon got into the spirit of it. It was now almost complete, apart from the final lead vocal, which we needed to come back in and redo once John's voice had had time to heal, although I liked the honesty of the earlier one with all its roughness.

Then I heard arguments breaking out at the back of the control room between Glen and John. Something about harmonies and handclaps. The row began to get nasty so Malcolm intervened and managed to calm things down for a while. Glen still seemed put out because we hadn't recorded 'Pretty Vacant', (which, while great, was also their least offensive song). Malcolm finally sent them all home and said to me, "Just do a good rough mix and we'll listen to it in the light of day to see what we've got." People had been getting so tired it was hard to tell exactly what was working and what wasn't. But I was confident we had recorded a blinding version that any band should have been proud of, with or without a new vocal.

Johnny secretly asked if he could come back later to listen to the track with a friend. When he returned, he'd just left a party and was really off his face, totally stoned. He put on headphones and rolled about on the floor screaming "This is brilliant! fucking brilliant!" This rough mix is the version that came out on the Swindle vinyl LP in 1980 and on the French release etc ...

I took the 15 ips (Inches Per Second) master tape home with me (and I still have it). Then I biked a 7.5 ips. version over to Malc, knowing that this was the fastest speed his home machine could play. Later he gave me a bollocking for not sending him the higher quality one, but my reasons were innocent, honest! I'd also mixed the seven minute 'No Fun' from these sessions and that sounded very complete to me. And still does.

I was looking forward to finishing 'Anarchy' properly, but things were about to go drastically wrong for me. I'm not entirely sure exactly what happened next, but I gather that Mike Thorne, EMI rep, had secretly gone in over the weekend to do his own mix of my production – behind my fucking back. How dare he? Thorne had been itching to produce the band and thought this was his big chance. I was in bed recuperating from the past eight and a half days of madness, totally oblivious to these back-room happenings.

Basically, I reckon Thorne might have just fancied himself as a producer and tried to muscle in on my act.

Despite the fact I hadn't actually finished it yet, come Monday, I was summoned to EMI for a midday meeting with Thorne about the fate of the single. Boy was I tired that morning! Sophie, from Malcolm's office, called and woke me. I was late for the meeting and when I finally got there, I found Kim and Thorne having what seemed like a friendly chat in the foyer.

But I was too late apparently, and Mike was far too busy to see me, so taking out his diary, he managed to squeeze me in several days later. I made some crass comment to him about "living his life out of a diary," and walked out.

At the following meeting I had to listen to Mike Thorne moan on about how he wasn't happy with 'Anarchy'. He thought the vocals were too rough and it didn't sound like a chart record to him. But as this was a whole new genre and a whole new sound – coming from an original new group – I couldn't see how he could compare it with anything he had ever heard before. It definitely wasn't supposed to sound like anything else and I attempted to explain this. My idea of having the guitars and drums mixed up with the vocals gave it the powerful feel. Alright – so how many singles do you hear where the singer is really singing at the top of his voice? Up until then, precious few, but this is the way it came out, and to me it sounded important and honest.

Thorne then had the cheek to play me his mix of my production. My production that I'd sweated blood over. He got it all wrong in my opinion, the toms were too loud, he'd missed out a lot of Steve's overdubs, and the vocals were swimming in reverb. I was so pissed off with his unprofessional behaviour that I took the acetate off the record player and threatened to smash it (I didn't trash it, in the end, but wish I had)

I stormed out of the meeting with these words, "When I finally finish it, you will be getting the heaviest, most exciting rock'n'roll record of all time and if you can't hear it, then you don't deserve to work here." I stormed out kicking over a cardboard cut-out of Cliff Richard on the way.

The sad thing is, it was probably the Mike Thorne mix that was spun around the EMI offices and hence rejected by the high-ups, damaging my career in the process.

I was never given the chance to finish the record I'd started. Someone threw a spanner in the works and the band switched producers (for a while at least). Can you imagine how amazing it would have been if my wild version of 'Anarchy' had come out on a 12" vinyl, with my full length, seven minute 'No Fun' on the flip side? Possibly the heaviest 45 ever released up to that point!

But no, others thought they knew best, but I tell you this, get hold of my unfinished mix of 'Anarchy', (it's the one that starts 'Bible quotation number one' – another idea of mine). Then compare it to the later Chris Thomas version and tell me I'm wrong. It was my mix not Thorne's that later got released by Virgin which surely goes to show something.

I've always been a big fan of Pete Townsend, ever since I first saw him at a High Numbers rehearsal in the back room of my Dad's works' clubhouse in Osterly, where my Dad used to play football at weekends. He would ask if I could sit and watch the rehearsal, and watch I did. It only happened a few times, but what a lucky boy I was. The next time I witnessed Pete in action was a gig in 1964. My older cousin John Greenwood took me there on the back of his scooter to see them in Southall Town Hall. I had never seen anything like it. It was amazing.

That is the feeling I got when I first witnessed the Sex Pistols way back in early 76. Just for the record, apparently when Pete heard my 'Anarchy' version, he actually said that he thought it was the "heaviest piece of rock'n'roll" he'd ever heard. Now there's a compliment!

COUNTDOWN TO ANARCHY

By late October '76 the Pistols were being booked into bigger and bigger venues as the countdown began to the release of 'Anarchy in the UK'.

On the 21st they played Queensway Hall, Dunstable, where they were supported by Paul Weller's first band, The Jam. Both bands claimed not to have heard of one another at this point. It was a pleasant surprise seeing two young bands on the same bill. You could have squeezed at least a thousand into that hall but only 70 or so turned up. ("I thought you lot were supposed to be big and famous," Weller said, inadvertently revealing that he'd been reading the music press a lot more than he'd admitted to).

Unperturbed by the low turnout, both groups put in their best. They also made a point of watching each other play. Glen seemed the most impressed with The Jam, who were mainly playing pretty tight versions of old Tamla and Soul songs, a bit different from the style they became renowned for. Paul Weller's dad was the roadie and probably more talkative than the rest put together. He was invited to visit Malcolm's office to get some advice on getting a deal. I think the reason they finally obtained such a good one from Polydor owes a lot to this meeting.

Siouxsie was "nothing if
not magnificent", wrote Caroline Coon. "She'll
wear black plastic non-existent bras, one mesh and one rubber
stocking and suspender belt all covered by a polka dotted transparent mac."
Dave Goodman, on the other hand, was still wearing flared jeans.

CUM ON AND JOIN US WE'RE A YOUNG NATION

After the national press had begun to write a few articles about the band, Pistol fever finally infected the boys and girls in television. Young Nation was the youth slot of the BBC's Nationwide evening news'n'views show (the Beeb's version of Thames TV's Today programme). It was the band's first brush with the BBC – evidence of the lads' growing power. We arrived at BBC's Shepherds Bush studios at around four that day, bringing my 3,000 watts of PA with us to play in a studio that was less than 24 feet square.

"It's the only way to get a decent sound on TV," said Malcolm with a knowing smile, "Set the lot up, let's wake 'em up."

And then he went into this lecture about how the TV crew were all boring old farts etc... until someone said, "Not that old chestnut. Leave it out, Malcolm, we've 'eard it all before – go and get some drinks or something." I think it was the whole band in unison.

Once we'd set up and started making some noise the BBC boys wanted to mike everything up separately into their own mixer, but as it was already sounding good coming out of our speakers, I advised them to just stick up the best two mikes they had in the room and leave it at that.

"Alright mate, if you say so," one techie said "makes my job easier."

"Can you turn down in there, we're getting too much level," came a voice from the control room.

"Why?"

"Well, er, it's..."

"Can't all that equipment handle us then?" said John over the microphone, "we sound great down 'ere."

The band just carried on playing for the two mikes.

Someone had organized some fans to come down and amongst them were Sid and Siouxsie. It was a welcome sight to see their faces, especially as they had brought some booze with them. It was a strange scenario, to see the familiar BBC Nationwide News Desk on one side of the studio and this colourful, outlandish-looking mob lurking on the other.

Giovanni Dadamo, a one-time music staffer at Sounds magazine, was to interview the band, along with the rather straight girl who was the show's co-presenter. He was led from the make-up room to the studio looking so ponced-up that he caught everyone's eye and someone remarked "Cor, look at that prat!" The make-up girl spent another ten minutes or so making sure his bouffant hairdo was in place, while the band messed theirs up and got ready to play. Their followers stood next to them and they all looked wonderfully bizarre. They were sneering at the cameramen and generally taking the piss out of the presenters.

The band did a few warm-up numbers then 'Anarchy' was recorded for the show. It was loud and chaotic – just right for their image. Some of the followers got carried away and fell over the equipment. One of the speaker cones got ripped out and after the show I placed it on Malcolm's head like a hat, to make him realize the full extent of the damage. "I suppose we'll have to replace that for you one day," he laughed sadly.

Transcript of show:
Starts with four young 'jet-setters' clad in Omo-white denim flares riding around the Houses of Parliament in an open-top beach buggy. Draped across Big Ben is a huge banner saying 'Young Nation' – what a contrast the Pistols made to this outdated spectacle. The show continued with some snatches of the band performing 'Anarchy' followed by this dialogue.

Presenter: "Well, it may not be the greatest rock and roll in the world but it's certainly the most controversial. One London newspaper called them the most aggressive, nasty band ever – they're the Sex Pistols and they're led by Johnny Rotten. And they've already been barred from most of the leading London clubs, both because of their music and because of the violence they bring with them. And yet this group are leaders of a whole new teenage cult that seems to be on the way to being as big as Mods and Rockers were in the Sixties."

Girl Presenter: "The cult is called Punk. The music Punk Rock. Basic rock music, raw, outrageous and crude. Like their foul fan magazine (sniff) Sniffing Glue, which is produced and stapled together by two young

Punks from Deptford."

Presenter: "Punks have multicoloured hair, vampire make-up, ripped t-shirts held together with safety pins, swastika arm bands, pink plastic trousers and tight leather jeans. You can't buy this sort of gear in Marks'n'Sparks, so you have to go to shops like Sex in the Kings Road ."

Girl: "Finding places to play is becoming harder, thanks to the reputation punks are getting as trouble-makers. The 100 Club in Oxford Street banned all punk groups after an incident at a punk gig where a girl was nearly blinded by a broken bottle."

Presenter: "And at the I.C.A. two weeks ago a boy (Shane of the Pogues) had his ear lobe bitten off by his girlfriend, driven to frenzy by a punk group appropriately called 'Clash'."

Girl: "And the Sex Pistols themselves even had to hire a strip club to get themselves heard. No one else would take them ... What about the word 'Punk'? It means worthless, nasty. Johnny Rotten, are you happy with this word?"

JR: "No the press gave us it. It's their problem not ours. We never called ourselves Punk."

Girl: "Which bands do you think are old hat now? Are you against the Stones and the Who – sounds like that?"

JR: "Yes, of course, because they're established."

Girl: "With us also is Giovanni Dadamo. Now I know you're very worried by the Sex Pistols. Why?"

GD: "Well, not very worried, but there are aspects of what they do or what they provoke that worry me. You know, I think that if you go all out to provoke people like they've done, people react, right? Now it's all very well for Malcolm to say it's good for bottles to fly through the air or mugs, but if they hit you in the head or if they hit Johnny in the head ..."

Cut-away to Rotten giggling as he raises a dismissive hand.

Girl: "You've heard them, they're angry and they're frustrated. Now do you think their music's worthwhile?"

GD: "Erm, I've enjoyed it at times, there's times when it strikes me as being a bit derivative. I mean the great danger with the Pistols is that they can be boring, you know their attitude can be boring. It can become boring. I mean it's not, like say ... just destruction for its own sake, is ... is dull ultimately. You know it doesn't offer any hope, it doesn't really wanna change things, it's just saying, 'you know, we don't like this, we, we're different, look at us'. You know, that's just attracting attention to

85

yourself. I think it should be constructive revolution if there's gonna be revolution, only like ..."

Johnny: "You mean established ..."

Malcolm: "You have to destroy in order to create, you know that."

No one warned me that the following Notre Dame Hall gig was to be filmed for TV. Suddenly I was besieged by a sound crew demanding to plug this in here, that in there and could I make separate monitor mixes routed to their cameras etc ... Well, my main concern was to make sure the band sounded good on stage and out front. They were so loud that it was impossible to tell what the TV mix would come out like. It was dire! If only they'd just recorded the out front sound they would have had some very useable footage.

It was a semi-secret free gig for the fans. Rotten made a grand entrance wearing the long, blonde wig he'd bought to wear for the upcoming Talk of The Town gig, but took it off after a while. Vivienne Westwood was there and after a few drinks took to dancing on stage, apparently unaware of the cameras around her.

Glen had been on at Malcolm for a new bass amp and cab to replace his old Fender Bassman. Tired of repeating himself, Glen decided some direct action was necessary. Before he went on stage, Glen made a final plea to Malcolm, who managed to avoid the issue. During the last number, Glen kicked his amp over and proceeded to put his guitar through the speakers. He had made his point, but now he had no amp for the encore. I quickly leapt on stage, plugged him into the PA and he bodged his way through the rest of the set. They ended with a great version of 'No Fun'. Steve over-used his P45 phaser effects pedal and when you stuck a bit of echo on top of it, it sounded like a 747 jet taking off.

There were quite a few interesting people present including Shane MacGowan (Pogues), Joe Strummer (Clash), Keith Levine (ex-Clash,) Toyah Wilcox, Andy Blade (Eater), Don Letts (Big Audio Dynamite), Jeanette Lee (PiL), Poly Styrene (X Ray Spex), TV Smith (The Adverts), Siouxsie, Glitterbest staffers Jamie Reid, Sophie Richmond and Boogie, plus Sid, Phil the co-editor of this book, his brother Jay Strongman ... in addition there was the ever-growing crowd of record company personnel and journalists, including Tony Parsons and John Savage. Everyone seemed to be having a good time, (even the 'Cambridge Rapist' who was present in the crowd – black leather mask and all). The strange thing was the 'Cambridge Rapist' never arrived until after Malcolm had slipped out the back somewhere, and Malcolm only returned a few minutes after the 'Rapist' left. Who was the man behind the leather mask? Perhaps this will remain one of the great-unsolved mysteries of our time …

Following this gig, I headed off to my old mate Caruzo's flat in Muswell Hill, where we sat in two armchairs for three days, talking about the whole new scene and its potential for new record labels – and how we were going to set one up ourselves. My idea was to get Johnny Rotten involved in our company as a partner, talent scout and who knows what else? I was convinced he had the taste to discover the type of acts I'd be interested in. We planned to develop not just punky bands, but new young psychedelic, dubby, acoustic bands – maybe something extremely original in a futuristic kinda way. I approached John later and he seemed flattered, although somewhat dubious.

"What you gonna call this label then?" he quizzed.

"Dunno, we thought maybe Rotten Records." I replied.

"And I'd get paid and be able to choose the music?" he further enquired.

"Yeah! Sure," I replied – stroking his breadhead.

"Well, I'll have to give it some thought and maybe talk to Malcolm about it."

He did – Malcolm apparently didn't think it was such a good idea. The next time we saw John he explained that Malcolm said he wouldn't have time to get involved. So this brilliant idea of mine – well I thought so anyway – was thwarted from the outset. I wondered at the time if Malcolm was jealous, or if he just couldn't stand the thought of John entering another camp, or maybe he just didn't have the confidence in me with my flared dungarees and beads, or Caruzo in his bri-nylon shirts and gold medallion …

As John wasn't able to get involved with our record company there was no point naming it 'Rotten Records', instead we christened it 'The Label'.

Original don't ya think? This idea was supposed to make the bands seem more important than their record company. Don't ask me why, it's just that it seemed a good idea at the time. A sort of reverse attitude to Stiff, who were probably our main competition. We went further and named our publishing company 'The Publishers' and the first album by 'Eater' we simply named 'The Album', an idea that John Lydon would copy later with PiL.

Caruzo Herbert Owen Fuller (to use his full name), was the twin brother of my childhood sweetheart Camelia. He was also an ex-

Royal/Merchant Seaman who'd just come back to London after living for some time with his Japanese wife Naomi in Tokyo. While he was over there he did quite well as a club DJ and stuntman-actor. I used to send him over all the good stuff in the charts, until he couldn't be bothered to pay me for them. He had this Steve McQueen type persona and was well up for the stunt man act.

I guess he got a bit homesick and wanted to check out what was happening back in London. He had about £20,000 to invest in the project and loads of energy. We'd already been on the lookout for potential bands to record. I'd been sniffing around the small ads in the Melody Maker and I'd check out any ad that looked interesting, i.e. 'Young band into Stooges, Alice Cooper and West Coast garage looking for manic singer to take on the world', or 'Teenage velvets meet Motorhead looking for Animal drummer' etc ...

I'd made a few calls – the most interesting one being to some former members of the London SS (their past line-ups had included Mick Jones, Tony James, Brian James and Billy Idol, before they morphed into Chelsea, Generation X, Sigue Sigue Sputnik and the Billy Idol Band). In the end we settled for schoolboy band Eater. Their drummer Dee Generate was only 13 when we first met him and considering his age, he was brilliant. I bet the lessons he got from Rat Scabies helped a lot. Singer Andy Blade and guitarist Brian Chevette were just 15 and a great double act who often reduced me and Caruzo to hysterics. The old man of the group was bass player Ian 'Grumpie' Woodcock, a sprightly 17 years young.

The band had been together for about three months and were inspired mainly by Bowie, Alice Cooper, Marc Bolan and Lou Reed. They did covers of 'Queen Bitch', 'Jeepster', 'Waiting for my Man' and their own version of Alice Cooper's 'Eighteen', re-titled 'Fifteen' to correspond to their average age. The formation of Eater is a hilarious story and if you're sitting comfortably, I'll begin.

Andy, real name Andy Radwan, didn't like going to school. He wasn't very popular with the other kids and found solace in his classmate Brian Chevette. To obtain popularity with the girls, they perpetuated the myth that they were in a rock band. It seemed to work and rumours flew around the local schools and youth clubs. Now Andy was from a large family, seven kids in all, and lived in a big house in Finchley. He shared an attic room with his older brother Hass and younger brother Luffie. It was a large room and one got the feeling you could make a lot of noise there without annoying anybody too much. And indeed, that's what they did.

They used to have regular gatherings, with friends, (including Brian) and called it the Bedroom Club. With an old Spanish guitar, a fake microphone and some pots and pans they started miming along to their favourite records. Word of their performances soon spread and they were contacted by the local paper, who arranged an interview and photo shoot.

"By the way, can you make sure you bring your guitars with you for the photo?" the man at the newspaper said, before hanging up. "Shit, we've only got this poxy acoustic guitar and that won't look any good in the picture," someone said.

Not wanting to miss out on this golden opportunity for self-promotion, they hatched a plan to steal 2 guitars from the local music shop, which they passed every day en route to and from school. They spent several days just looking in the window, observing the activities of the shopkeeper and noticed that immediately before he locked up each evening, he went out the back to get his coat. This would give them just enough time to run in, grab the guitars and leg it, before the shopkeeper returned. They planned to escape down a side alley and leave the guitars hidden in some bushes in a garden, until they could go back under cover of darkness and retrieve them.

They did the dastardly deed and it worked a treat.

They looked great in the photo, really professional, and the kids at school were mightily impressed. The photo appeared in the same edition as the news about the music shop robbery, but amazingly no one put two and two together.

Armed with their newly acquired axes, they soon found a drummer and bass player and in November of '76 they were in Decibel Studios cutting their first single, 'Outside View' coupled with 'You' – with me at the helm (I'd been working there recently, finishing off some Pistols tracks)

Caruzo and I got busy setting the wheels of manufacturing in motion, and a short time and a few grand later we had a batch of white label promos to distribute to the press etc. I remember having to trundle down to the pressing plant in Hayes, Middlesex and bring as many boxes as I could carry home with me on the train. We spent the whole evening with Eater, who were encouraged to write personal messages on the records for the intended recipients, i.e. John Peel, Janis Long, Malcolm, Sid, Fluff, Wogan, Saville, Jonathan King, Tommy Vance, Nick Kent, Parsons, Ingham, Coon, etc … We just blitzed the lot. It seemed to work 'cause we had instant feedback.

Peelie loved Eater and came down to Dingwalls especially to see them.

This first single 'Outside View' might only have had a white label on it when we sent it out in Dec 1976, but it still makes it the third UK Punk single to be released! We would have preferred to release it on a major label, but we just couldn't find a sympathetic ear – believe me we tried! We developed a network of independent distributors and bucket record shops and in no time we sold out and re-pressed and so on. We must have met with just about every major label licensing manager in town. Most were middle-aged and virtually unaware of this new musical phenomenon. One thing we did discover was that, at this point in time, the majors were having trouble shifting singles of new artists, despite expensive promotion budgets. When we informed them that we had already sold nearly 10,000 Eater singles, they looked at us in disbelief. 'Outside View' clocked up sales of over 17,000 – a number which would get us into the Top Ten nowadays. It should have at least gone Top 40 even back then, but it wasn't selling in the right shops to qualify for a chart entry, so 'Outside View' stayed outside. That's how unfair it was then and in some ways it's still the same, no matter what the industry spin doctors tell you. We were asked by the industry why we needed them if we were doing so well? They went on to tell us that we could never make it without them! That was it – now we were even more determined to make it alone. Malcolm loved the Eater single, and whilst we were sharing a hotel room on the Anarchy tour, he would ask me to play it to him again and again.

The Hendon Poly gig we played that month was mayhem. I don't know what they put in the water in this part of north London but it certainly isn't ginseng. The actual performance was eclipsed for me by the after show aggro. The bouncers on the door threw a load of yobs out and refused entry to a load more, who were all hanging around outside. In their lustful wisdom, Steve and Paul slipped outside to chat up some birds. They got involved in a slagging match with some of the expelled yobs, who chased them inside. A kinda Keystone Cops escapade unfolds. I first encountered it while carrying some gear down a corridor. I turned the corner and saw Steve and Paul dash past and leap up some stairs. Round the next corner came about half a dozen youths, hot on their tail. I pointed them down the stairs in the wrong direction. This cat and mouse chase went on and on and soon the yobs were being chased by the bouncers. I rounded yet another corner to see Steve and Paul shoot into one of the classrooms. Next came the yobs who went straight by, except the last one who ventured into the classroom, only to be jumped on by Paul who was standing behind the door. Steve joined in and eventually they ran off before the bouncers arrived.

Finally, the Aged William materialized – you know the Old Bill? – and things got even more complicated. The police were looking for Steve and Paul, who they'd been told, were the instigators of this little show of madness. During all this kerfuffle, the mob outside had taken to throwing abuse and stones at the   Steve & Paul swung up onto the pipes above a doorway just as the boys in blue came round the corner. Amazingly, no one noticed them and the coppers chased their ghosts outside and disappeared into the night …

"THEY'RE GREAT, RELEASE THEM, WHO NEEDS ME?" SAYS CHRIS THOMAS." Chris Thomas' alleged words on the subject of Dave Goodman's Spunk tapes. The premature rejection – by EMI and then the Pistols – of my version of 'Anarchy' delayed the single's launch by seven days. Chris Thomas was now the producer with whom Malcolm and the boys hurriedly agreed to re-record 'Anarchy'. He had apparently been tipped-off by EMI that they were looking for a new producer (maybe one they might have a bit more control over?). Paul was also keen on the idea as he liked Roxy Music and Chris had produced them.

Mr Thomas had suddenly appeared on the scene with Air Studios dangling as a carrot. "Hello boys, I've got Air waiting down the road for you, for free, how would you like to come in there with me?" With the Beatles, Pink Floyd and Roxy Music under Thomas' belt, it was, I'll admit, a fairly tempting offer. But the band in general didn't appreciate what I had done for them musically, both in the studio and on the road. Glen later apologised to me about this and said, "At that point Dave, I really didn't know what the producer's role actually was." Anyway EMI were glad to see the back of me, although they didn't mind capitalising on my work.

Although its incredibly hard for some to understand this, I did carry on working with the band as their live soundman. They never really talked much about how it was going with Thomas. Malcolm described him as a real 'cool-hand Luke', who mostly sat at the back of the studio giving instructions on what to do next and relying on the engineers to make it so. I, on the other hand, would get my hands dirty and didn't need an engineer, (except when I wanted the occasional cup of tea or takeaway). I first heard the Thomas version of 'Anarchy' when the band went to record a video for it with Mike Mansfield. They mimed to the record as Rotten ruffled his newly dyed blonde hair. It wasn't bad but I wasn't overly impressed. I later played both versions back to back and still couldn't see why mine hadn't been released. Paul kept going on about the repeat echo Thomas had put on the snare drum. "It's great, ain't it? Great!" Hmmm.

Some people are easily impressed I thought to myself, but I didn't bother to say it out loud – whatever I said it would simply have been written off as sour grapes.

To add insult to injury, when the record did finally come out, Chris Thomas had been credited with producing the B-side 'I Wanna Be Me', which came from my 'Denmark Street' sessions. When EMI found out about the boob they didn't even have the decency to tell me – I had to find out from Malcolm and immediately rang EMI who mumbled a half-hearted apology but offered no compensation. They just put me through to the guy responsible – one Frank Brunger. He said he'd been told that the producer had been switched and assumed that the new label credit was for both sides. He hadn't bothered to check and he wasn't very apologetic about it. How on earth thousands of copies got pressed without anyone noticing I'll never understand.

I felt I had no alternative but to go to a solicitor about this mistake and seek an injunction to stop production until things got sorted out. Kim knew of a solicitor at the end of his road near Manor House, who happened to be Jewish. I don't know if traditionally Jewish guys make good lawyers but he was amazing. Once we gave him several hundred pounds, he arranged an immediate hearing in the Strand's High Courts. We hurriedly drove down there in his little Mini car, jumping red lights on the way. We managed to get an injunction to stop EMI releasing the record until they had corrected their mistake. The last words the judge said to me were – "However, if there are any damages or losses arising from this injunction, and should the said injunction then be dismissed, any such damages will then plainly rest upon the plaintiff's shoulders ... ". This frightened me, the record was already late and any further delay could lose the band and EMI valuable Christmas sales. I was in a real quandary as to what was the best action to take. I came out of the High Court clutching the injunction with the judge's last words still ringing in my ears.

We had fixed a meeting with EMI in three hour's time and they had already agreed to re-press future records with the correct credits. They had also agreed to my demand to notify the music papers as to their mistake. But they refused to scrap the records already pressed or to further advertise their error. Another meeting was arranged.

I held Malcolm somewhat responsible and felt he should have spotted the mistake himself, so stupidly I turned to him for compensation. I rang him and mentioned the injunction, saying I was coming around to his office with my lawyer to discuss the matter before going to EMI. When we arrived members of the band were there with him. I said I wouldn't serve the injunction if he paid me £500 compensation (what a cheapskate I was!). I was immediately ordered out of the office while my lawyer attempted to negotiate a suitable solution. After a few moments of pointless conversation – he followed me.

Off we went to meet one of EMI's A&R guys and his corporate legal adviser. By now my solicitor was itching to serve the injunction, but he agreed not to use it until I gave him the nod. The EMI suits meanwhile accused me of trying to blackmail them. They must have thought we were bluffing but they eventually went along with it all and promised me lots of concessions, so I backed down. Unfortunately I was naive and nothing was put in writing at that meeting – and, as is often the case, they simply didn't keep their word.

There must have been plenty of people around who would have loved to have been in my position and stop the first Sex Pistols record being released, but all I wanted was fair play. Though I wasn't going to get it from the likes of EMI. Malcolm commented to me later that he respected me for what I did – or rather, what I didn't do. But the whole mix-up did cost me – it cost me plenty.

When Lou Reed first heard 'I Wanna Be Me', my B-side, he apparently said, "I want that producer!" but Chris Thomas got the job because of that bloody miscredit. I met Lou some time later when he came down to Dingwalls to see Eater. He told me to my face that it was the B-side that most impressed him. i.e. my version. If I had produced Lou – and at the time I would have been well up for it – who knows what would have happened to me? Maybe I'd have ended up a junkie feeding a habit from whatever royalties were tossed my way. Either that or a millionaire? Who knows?

The above mix-up was and still is quite frustrating for me, but the fact that the likes of Pete Townshend, Lou Reed and Tony Parsons rated my productions above the official releases remains a testament to my work.

Anyway as I bottled out of launching the injunction, the band got their record out for Christmas and, to the surprise of many doubters, it went straight into the charts, making the Top 40 despite receiving no daytime air play from the main radio stations.

The most prestigious Talk of The Town venue almost became host to the most outrageous band in London in late '76 as my studio fiasco was raging. I got a call from Malcolm to meet him there to check out the PA and lights.

I was too busy and sent Kim along instead. Apparently Malcolm arrived in a cab and surprise, surprise, he'd left his wallet at home and blagged the fare off Kim.

This gig was to be very hush hush, so as not to frighten the venue until it had all been already booked. John became quite excited by the prospect of performing there and claimed he would walk out onstage in a dress and wig.

"That will give people something to think about won't it," he joked (by the way, the TOTT is the venue now known as The Hippodrome). Somehow word got out about the event and it was cancelled, so Rotten's satin dress remained firmly in its closet.

One media event that did happen that month was when Janet Street-Porter dedicated the entire hour of her Sunday London Weekend TV show to a punk special on the Pistols, Clash, Siouxsie and other followers. The Pistols had been filmed previously, playing live at Notre Dame Hall, in Leicester Place, Soho.

Janet-Street Porter Show LWT : Interview Transcript.
This takes place in Steve's flat above their rehearsal gaff in Denmark Street. It's about 13 foot square and littered with guitars and clothes. Steve's still in bed while the others sit around.

Janet Street Porter: "Go on, who do you think's a good singer?"

JR: "I don't have any heroes – they're all useless."

JSP: "When you stood up and started singing for the first time, what 'appened.?"

Steve: "Go on John, go on."

JR: "It was wonderful."

JSP: "Oh come on."

JR: "People loved me. They threw flowers."

JSP: "Well look, I saw you the sixth time and people were quite shell-shocked."

JR: "Well then you know yourself, don't ya!"

JSP: "Yeah, but surely by making a record you are in a way becoming part of the system."

Steve: "Is it alright if I get up?" (Steve gets out of bed and walks in front of the camera in his leopard skin undies).

Paul: "Not if ... not if you don't let yourself.

JSP: "But supposin' if your record's a success? Which there is a big chance it will be."

John: "Oh right, yeah, here we go."

JSP: "Supposin' you made a lot of money, what are you? How are you gonna be different from the Stones?"

JR: "I don't need a Rolls Royce, I don't need a house in the country, I don't need to live in the South of France. I'm 'appy as I am and gonna carry on."

Paul: "In Finsbury Park."

Steve: "With his brother."

JR: (irritated) "I don't live in Finsbury Park ..."

CHAPTER TEN

DECEMBER 1976

RUN UP TO THE ANARCHY TOUR

Lancaster Polytechnic was the gig where we tried out the new PA we were hiring for the Anarchy tour. It was about twice the size of mine and came complete with several bearded hairies from Brum. It suited me, I didn't have to shift it and could concentrate more on mixing the sound. It was remarkably cheap considering what you got and the hairies were very friendly as well.

This night saw the debut of 'No Future' and the words 'Fascist Regime' sparked a row with several members of the students union, who refused to pay the band on the grounds that they thought they must be 'ultra right wingers', which couldn't be further from the truth. Anyway, they hadn't bargained coming up against the intellect of Bernie (Rhodes), Malcolm and John and after much heated debate gave in and paid up.

We had a right laugh afterwards, misinterpreting other lyrics like 'Liar', where they go "you're in suspension" well now "you're in suspenders"! And "who wants to be, a hanky?" – you get gobbed in all the time, especially if you're Johnny's.

On the eve of the Anarchy tour, the Pistols were still busy sound-checking in Harlesden, along with The Clash, Heartbreakers and The Damned. The venue was the Roxy Cinema – a Kung Fu flea-pit – where we got to try out the new Mega PA. The previous day, Malcolm had told me that he didn't need my partner Kim on the tour. I was disappointed and told Malcolm that "I would never forget this." Kim was upset and fucked off home. I told him not to worry and to carry on hiring out our PA on his own, but he never really did (the embarrassing bit was, after the rehearsal I shared a cab with Malc – we were going down to Louise's club – and on the way I had to stop off at Kim's to pick up the big piece of hash that he'd got me for the tour). Malcolm waited in the cab while I went in to collect it – in a somewhat leisurely manner.

Kim was clearly upset by Malcolm's blunt decision, although it resulted in him eventually pursuing a career in sound engineering and producing. Back to Harlesden. There was an incredible buzz among the bands. There they were, all grouped together, poised for the coast-to-coast Anarchy tour, about to go out in force and assault the country. Punk music had reached new heights. Who could ignore them now?

During the sound-checks, the Pistols had to go off to Thames TV studios, to do an interview with Bill Grundy and promote their new single. No one really thought that much about it and we just carried on with our business. Several hours later a call came through about the interview. I'm not sure who took the call, but rumours soon started to fly. I think Malcolm was the first to return with more news. He was pale-faced as he said "fucking hell, the band have just sworn on live TV. Everyone's in an uproar and the channel's switchboard is jammed with complaints." Apparently several police vans loaded with SPG (special patrol group) turned up at Thames TV, just as the band 'high-tailed' it round the corner. The Pistols avoided getting arrested by the skins of their teeth! Who knows what would have happened to the band if they had been caught?

Malcolm swore blind that he didn't put them up to it, although he had a mischievous, yet worried look on his face. The story spread round the cinema like wild fire and everyone downed instruments to discuss it. The chatter was broken by the Sex Pistols' noisy return a few minutes later. They were still clutching their drinks and looked exhilarated from their experience.

All eyes were on them and a big cheer went up as they entered.

"Looks like they've heard." said John to the rest of the band.

"They got us pissed, honest." said Steve, seemingly to Malcolm.

"Come on then, tell us all about it," we said as we all gathered round to hear the whole story of TV's biggest swear in.

Bill Grundy Interview. Transcript

Pistols, Siouxsie, Simone, Simon Barker and co. sit and stand next to host Bill Grundy, a middle-aged curmudgeon. As the camera goes over the crowd, Grundy, obviously a bit drunk, begins reading his intro off the autocue, an activity the group begin to copy ...

Bill Grundy: Safety pins? Chains round the neck? And that's just it
   fellas, yeah yeah (momentarily bewildered) Eh ... ? I mean, it is just

the fellas – yeah. They are Punk Rockers, the new craze they tell me. Their heroes?

Steve: Not the nice clean Rolling Stones.

BG: Not the nice clean Rolling Stones – you see, they are as drunk as I am – they are clean by comparison. They are a group called the Sex Pistols and I'm surrounded now by all of them!

Steve: In action!

BG: Just let us see the Sex Pistols – in action! Come on, chicks!

We see 30 seconds of Pistols performing in Mike Mansfield's 'Anarchy in the UK' pop video before we cut back live to the studio.

BG: I'm told that the group have received £40,000 from a record company. Doesn't that seem slightly opposed to their anti-materialistic way of life?

Glen: No, the more the merrier.

BG: Really?

Glen: Oh yeah.

BG: Well, tell me more then –

Steve: We've fucking spent it, ain't we?

BG: I don't know, have you?

Glen: Yep, it's all gone, down the boozer –

BG: Really? Good Lord –

Glen: Golly gosh –

BG: Now I want to know one thing ...

Glen: What?

BG: Are you serious or are you just making things up?

Glen: No, it's –

BG: Really?

Glen: Yeah –

BG: But I mean about what you're doing?

Glen: Oh yeah.

BG: You are serious?

Glen: Mmm.

BG: Beethoven, Mozart, Bach and Brahms have all died –

John: Oh God, they're heroes of ours, ain't they?

BG: Really? What? What are you saying, sir?

John: They're such wonderful people –

BG: Are they?

John: Oh yes! They really turn us on.

BG: Well suppose they turn other people on –

John: (quietly) That's just their tough shit.

BG: It's what?

John: Nothing, a rude word – next question.

BG: No, no. What was the rude word?

John: Shit.

BG: Was it really? Good God, you frighten me to death.

John: Oh alright, Siegfried –

BG: What about you girls behind?

Glen: He's like yer Dad, inni? This geezer –

BG: Are you worried or just enjoying yourself?

Glen: Or yer Grandad –

Siouxsie: Enjoying myself.

BG: Are you?

Siouxsie: Yeah.

BG: That's what I thought you were doing.

Siouxsie: I always wanted to meet you.

BG: Did you really?

Siouxsie: Yeah.

BG: We'll meet afterwards then, shall we?

Steve: You dirty sod! You dirty old man!

BG: Well, keep going, chief, keep going. Go on, you've got another five seconds, say something outrageous –

Steve: You dirty bastard!

BG: Go on, again.

Steve: You dirty fucker!

BG: What a clever boy!

Steve: What a fucking rotter!

BG: Well, that's it for tonight. The other rocker Eammon –

Glen: Eammon!

BG: I'm saying nothing else about him, will be back tomorrow. I'll be seeing you soon – I hope I'll not be seeing you (to Pistols) again. From me though, good night!

That night it was on every news programme and the next day it was front page, with headlines like 'The Filth and the Fury', 'Were The Pistols Loaded?' etc... Bill Grundy was suspended for a fortnight and little more was heard of him until his death ...

   On the day the Anarchy tour began – two days after the Grundy incident – we all gathered at the selected meeting point, outside the

Pistols' rehearsal gaff in Denmark Street. It was a cold, grey morning and we huddled together waiting for the coach to arrive. There was much excitement and story-swapping. Then a coach came round the corner, displaying its destination, appropriately enough – 'Nowhere'. This had to be for us – so, fighting our various hangovers, we all climbed on board.

The Anarchy tour was on and post-Grundy, it was no longer just local or national journos chasing us – there were hacks from all around the planet.

The world's press was in attendance in big numbers. They were all in a feeding frenzy with fleets of cars following us to every venue. Not that there were that many, for council after council banned the gigs – the 'Nowhere' sign started to look more and more ominously prophetic.

The Damned were making their own way around and staying in different hotels from us as well. This didn't feel right and Malcolm criticised Stiff records for allowing it. We were all in the same boat and should stick together. The Damned's exclusiveness was the one of main reasons there was later a great deal of friction (i.e. they got thrown off the tour).

The gigs at Norwich University and Guildford Civic Hall were cancelled – decisions which inspired a student sit-in at the former venue – and the pattern was set. Since bar staff at former Pistols' venues told the gutter press that the band were regularly sick on stage (when the boys weren't kicking dead babies around, of course) – it soon became touch and go whether we would be allowed to play anywhere at all.

History books have claimed that this Norwich gig was cancelled and indeed it was, but what they don't tell you is that an alternative one happened in another venue. Everyone was determined not to let the so-called ban stop them from playing, so if there was a way round it, we would find it.

Malcolm had to join up with us later as he stayed down in London to secure the fate of the tour. Many of us were on tenterhooks awaiting his arrival.

When he did finally turn up, he was surrounded by all and sundry and pumped for answers to the many growing questions. "Has the tour been cancelled?" "Will we get paid?" "Who's been feeding my cat..." etc etc. He seemed to enjoy the attention and appeared very cool in his new fake fur overcoat – Vivienne had sewn strands of shiny silver thread all over it – there was no mistaking who the manager was now!

We were all sitting around in an upstairs bar prior to a sound-check, when in walked this blue-suited gent who gave us all a long hard look, then sloped off to get a drink. "Hey, I bet that's Seymour Stein, the Ramones' manager," Malcolm whispered to me, "I bet he's flown over to check us out.

Here, Dave, go over and tell him he's a total fucker for not letting his band play at such an important event." I did, but not in quite such strong language. Mr. Ramone made some excuse about how his boys were too busy 'recording'. He asked if Malcolm was around for a chat. They went off to a far corner where I could hear Malcolm giving him a good pasting down.

Outside the hall, a fair sized crowd was gathering and we remarked how many of them looked "nothing at all like fans". We were soon to discover why – most had come not to listen, but to jeer and ogle the 'ogres' – the circus was in town and nobody wanted to miss it – particularly a faction of middle aged protestors who seemed to hate "the Sex Pistols and their foul mouths and wot's all this anarchy about then?"

The show was underway and the Damned put in a short, shambolic set. The Clash weren't that much tighter. The Heartbreakers, who'd had a lot more experience, at least sounded like they were all playing the same song. Throughout all this the audience seemed unmoved. It was as if they were holding back all their enthusiasm for the Pistols.

The Pistols came on and the audience flexed up to them. Rotten addressed the crowd. "Come and get your ringside seats, the freaks are on show!" "Fuck off Scum!" came the reply. But 'Anarchy in the UK' was theirs. They let their music speak for them. Those pushing to the front were not the punks and fans – the few fans that had turned up were viewing the event from afar, out of harm's way. Those at the front were the gawpers who wanted a closer look at the 'filth' who'd upset the nation. After the opening number the lighting guy threw the stage into total darkness in his usual artistic fashion. One could hear a barrage of abuse accompanied by the sound of breaking glass.

Above all the noise Rotten was shouting, "Turn the fucking lights up!" They went up, revealing a beer-soaked band covered in eggs, flour and rotten tomatoes. They still looked defiant!

The audience had certainly come well prepared. The band carried on unperturbed, the lights being left on at John's insistence. They managed to complete their set, ducking missiles as they went. They were not in the least put out by the reception – in fact I think they wallowed in it. Once the crowd had let off steam the atmosphere was more relaxed. I think a good time was had by all, although it really brought home what a tightrope the band were walking. With 2,000 or more people present, had the crowd really turned ugly, we weren't equipped to cope. Fortunately a major catastrophe never occurred, although it came pretty close on a few occasions.

After the gig the crowd left without much resistance. Now we could see the full carnage left by the riotous mob. The stage and equipment were covered in a mass of fruit, eggs, flour, beer, beer cans and broken glass. The roadies set about the task of clearing up before heading off to the next venue.

Although this gig gave us all a big laugh, one couldn't help but wonder if it was a taste of what was to come. We quickly escaped the debris and set off to where we were playing the following night. We didn't particularly want to stay in this town and maybe face further hostilities. We thought it would be wiser to head for safer shores. On the tape that I made of this show, you can clearly hear the sound of smashing glass in between songs.

We soon arrived at our hotel, which was a fair and safe distance from the next gig. On checking in, a rather frightened, new-ish, naive Clash drummer approached me and asked where I was staying. I explained that I was sharing a room with Malcolm. He asked if I'd mind swapping as he couldn't get any peace amongst the chaos of the Clash. I felt sorry for him and was up for a bit of chaos, so I gave him my room number. But he soon came scurrying back – Malcolm threw him out.

The hotel bar was still open and seemed to be doing a roaring trade. We suddenly realised that it was full of more journalists and reporters. They had tracked us down and were hungry for a story. "Excuse me, are you a Sex Pistol?" they would keep asking everyone and anyone. We decided to ignore them as much as possible. In general journalists show few scruples when it comes to getting what they want and they were capable of distorting the truth beyond belief. Their eyes had lit up when we all walked in, so all the bands were herded to their rooms and I kept a continual supply of beer flowing to them from the bar.

Malcolm, Bernie Rhodes, Heartbreakers' manager Leee Black Childers and I sat around the hotel bar, having a good chat and getting well sloshed. We were playing Spot-the-Journalist. It was easy, they were the ones making all the noise, knocking drinks over, and passing the joints under the table.

Malcolm had summoned Stiff Records' Jake Riviera to a meeting, and demanded to know why his band, the Damned, were not travelling and staying with us. It seemed that it was something to do with saving money. They were staying in B&B's and had their own van.

The real problem for Malcolm was the fact that they were openly talking to the press, whereas the rest of us had been sworn to virtual silence. They were the only inside link to the media and hence encouraged to tell their own story. Of course this could only be a part of the story Malcolm was intending to tell. I think that Malcolm decided to throw them off the tour there and then, but he waited before making it public. I was getting up to take yet another tray of drinks to the bands upstairs, when the people sitting at the table next to us asked me if I had any skins. Journalists I thought, watch out. There were two guys and a girl. They asked me if I had anything to do with this Sex Pistol lot who everyone was talking about and who were staying there? They claimed they were making a stop-over on their way to a wedding in the south, from somewhere up north. They were very drunk too. The girl gave me her room number and invited me up for a smoke.

First I had to deliver the fresh supply of booze to the boys. They were doubly pleased to see me as I seemed to be the only one with any dope. I can remember sitting on the bed surrounded by 14 or so drunken musicians. I attempted to roll the biggest joint of my life while bedlam broke loose around me. To everyone's amazement, including mine, I managed to get together a super-joint about a foot long. This should have passed round the gathering three or four times, but as soon as it reached Rotten it wasn't being passed anywhere and he had to be held down so we could remove it from him. Just then there was a knock at the door.

"Hey Dave, there's a girl here who reckons you invited her up for a joint"

"I did."

"Don't let her in!" shouted Strummer, "she's a bleeding journalist."

I appealed to the lads to let her in, then thought twice about it as everyone was so drunk. She would have been lucky to get out in one piece. I went out to explain. She then invited me to her friends' room, claiming they had some really good dope. I went with her and as we walked in, she threw the glass she was holding straight through an open window. I heard it hit the ground outside, but her friends didn't seem to notice a thing. In fact they were too busy building a super-joint of their own.

"Hey man, come on in. What sort of dope have you got?"

"I've got some nice black," I said.

"Oh, that's good, we've got grass and Leb." It was decided that the only thing to do was to build a contraption housing the three different types of dope, just to make sure we got really stoned – as if we weren't mashed enough already, but it sounded like a great idea at the time. A few minutes later the hotel's manager came to the door. The mega-joint construction was quickly put away as he came in and walked straight over to the open window and looked down at the cars below. "We've just had a report about a glass being thrown from a window in this vicinity. Is anyone here responsible?"

"No we're not." said one of the lads, "Who do you think we are? Go ask those musicians you've got here, they've probably done it."

"But it came from here!"

"Well it wasn't us, so can you please leave us in peace?"

He left as bewildered as me.

"That was really good," sniggered the girl who was the culprit, "you guys were really convincing."

"What do you mean?" came the collective response, "you don't mean you really did throw a glass out did you?"

"I thought you'd noticed," she muttered in reply, too stoned to lie.

"Silly bitch, are you trying to get us thrown out?"

The atmosphere turned somewhat sour and the girl went off to bed in a huff.

I stayed around to devour the joint, had a bit of a chat then bid them farewell. On the way past the girl's room I gave a light knock. She opened it and invited me in with a sexy smile, but before we could get better acquainted one of her male travelling companions was knocking, with similar intentions no doubt. She tried to ignore it in the hope he would go away, but he started thumping on the door and eventually threatened to break it down unless it was opened. He stormed in and demanded to know what the hell I was doing there? She made some excuses and as she saw me out, whispered that I should come back in an hour, once she'd sorted it out. I went back to the room I was sharing with Malcolm, had another joint and fell fast asleep fully clothed.

Derby was the next town we were supposed to play. That morning the word came through that, due to local complaints, the show would have to be viewed in advance by the Mayor and the Chief Constable to make sure it was suitable.

The 100 Club glass-in-eye story had come up and parents felt their children might be subjected to violence – and obscenity – at the concert.

The time of 3.00 p.m. had been set to view the spectacle. The bands had been milling around outside our room all morning waiting to hear what was happening. I'd been giving this 'censorship scenario' some thought and concluded that it would be a waste of time. It was just a procedure the Mayor had to go through once complaints had been lodged. If his Lordship did give it the go-ahead and someone did get injured or offended the whole problem would come back to haunt him. I couldn't imagine a Mayor putting his office in jeopardy for the entertainment of a few hundred teenagers. So why give him the satisfaction of writing the band off? And what about the domino effect this might have?

I put my theory to Malcolm and he had to agree with me, although if we had gone through with it, we would both have appreciated the absurdity of the spectacle. He made a snap decision, "Alright Dave, get down there and make like it's gonna happen, don't tell a soul and ring me at exactly 3.05 p.m."

I got there at about 2.50 p.m. and was greeted by the roadies who'd been busy all day making sure everything was set up and working. The hall was filled with journalists, all with their note pads and cameras at the ready. Caroline Coon and John Ingham made a marvellous entrance in semi-punk attire.

Finally, at about four minutes to three, the Mayor and Lady Mayoress walked in accompanied by the Chief Constable. They took up seats laid dead centre in the hall. They were wearing their full dress of office – complete with 18th Century hats and silver chains – and made quite a sight. I took up position behind the mixer and a deathly hush fell.

There was a large clock above the stage ticking away the seconds. Everyone was expecting the Sex Pistols to walk on stage at 3 o'clock sharp. At two minutes to, the roadies switched on the amps and the glow of red lights made it seem as if something was definitely about to happen. As the last ten seconds ticked by it was like a silent countdown.

Everyone held their breath until zero, in anticipation of the new phenomenon known as the Sex Pistols. They were to be disappointed. They waited patiently for an embarrassingly long minute or two. The Mayor looked at his watch to make sure he had the time right. People started looking at one another to see if anyone knew what was happening. The Mayor really looked indignant and at four minutes past three he stood up and looked round at me. I smiled then ducked behind the mixing desk and slipped out to the phone. Malcolm answered it straight away and gave a chuckle. "OK Dave, get your arse back here as quick as you can. Don't spare the horses!"

Suddenly everyone realised something was happening – or not, as the case may be – and people began to fall over themselves to get to the phones. As I dived into a taxi, I was pursued by a hoard of journos. They had to stay on my tail to find out where we were off to next. I told the cabbie that there was a good tip in it for him if he could shake off the fleet on my tail. He was game.

As we screeched to a halt in the car park of the hotel, we encountered the 'Nowhere' coach fully loaded, with everyone on board, revving up and primed for action. I quickly switched vehicles and we were off. We made faces at the cameramen who had just caught up with us. You could see the frustration on their faces. They were still unable to talk to us and had to follow us to Leeds for another shot. Banned in the UK!

In fact Derby only objected to the Sex Pistols – other bands would have been allowed to play. Obviously they stuck together, all that is except the Damned, whose management were still busy talking to the press – and offering to play gigs without the nasty Sex Pistols …

When we arrived at Leeds Polytechnic, we encountered a very tired road crew still trying to get things into place and working. I don't think anyone had time for a sound-check that night. The Dean of the Polytechnic went on TV to explain how come the Pistols were playing there when they had been banned almost everywhere else in the country.

Transcript:

Interviewer: "Dr Nashenter, how come that the Sex Pistols with their extraordinary reputation are playing in Leeds Polytechnic tonight when they've been banned virtually everywhere else?"

Dr: "The only people who can really answer that is the Students Union which organises these kind of events. You may think this odd and there are times when I do, but by the constitution and the articles of the government of the Polytechnic, I have no authority over what the Students Union … I mean I am very carefully controlled I may say, but the Students Union is an autonomous body which handles its own affairs and its own money. So if they want these people here – who, er, about whom I know nothing but they sound to me, you know, as puerile and disgusting as most of these people do."

Int.: "By some extraordinary coincidence you're performing the Messiah in Leeds Polytechnic tonight also."

Dr: "Yes, that actually is strange and even more odd is, er, such financing as the Messiah needs, it does in fact come from the Students Union. But the Messiah's being performed actually in another building in the Polytechnic. And the staff and students, there's quite a big crowd, about 80 or 90. It's been rehearsing all yesterday afternoon and, eh, it will do actually rather a good performance of most of the Messiah. The extraordinary thing is that I suppose by the evening, there will be two great sort of streams of prayer going out from Leeds Polytechnic. One upwards and the other, I suppose, down or maybe sideways ..."

As is usual on these occasions, I like to explore the local vicinity to see what action's on offer. I stumbled across a trendy disco and negotiated with the manager for free entrance for our troupe – if we came down later. In these days you could usually get away with this sort of behaviour if you played on the fact that you were touring musicians performing locally.

Later I managed to assemble a fair sized tribe and we marched off to disco-land. What a sight we made, Rotten, Strummer, Mickey Jones and all.

When we got there, the manager had a bit of a shock at our appearance until he realised we were decent folk. Once inside we were having a great time, chatting up the birds and doing silly dances under the mirror ball. The place was pretty packed and seemed fairly friendly. What we didn't know, was that a local gang of hooligans had taken a dislike to our manner and appearance and were planning to start a big fight. Fortunately we were tipped off by a sympathetic female and managed to escape before anything nasty developed. Once again we had avoided violence by the skin of our dicks.

EMI insiders announce that further PISTOLS releases are planned, including a new 45 to be recorded in late December for a February '77 release and an album to be recorded in January for an April launch.

Next stop was Manchester and the Piccadilly Plaza Hotel in the town centre.

We weren't gigging until the next day so had a night off. It wasn't long before the press arrived (even more of the sods). Soon they were walking around saying "Look, I'll give you £50 cash now if you vomit in that rubbish bin – or maybe pretend to – just give me a chance to get the shot in focus." But the bands weren't being bought off that easily and told them all to "fuck off!"

I noticed that long-haired maestro Steve Hillage and band were performing in some theatre nearby. I rang the box office and managed to blag four tickets. I'm not sure now who came with me, but I think it was three Pistols. We arrived late and very drunk and proceeded to cheer and leer as the mood took us. "Come on Hillage, you old hippy, give it some bollocks!" and other supportive words of encouragement.

We were getting some very strange looks and people kept asking us to sit down and be quiet. We couldn't control ourselves and carried on the furore until Hillage looked over in our direction and dedicated the next song to the rowdies at the back. It was George Harrison's 'It's All Too Much'. He played it with such gusto that he broke two strings, but carried on regardless – as indeed we did, until we were eventually thrown out to much cheering from the audience. I think for one night Steve Hillage became a young 'punk' again ...

The next day Malcolm was up early and making general conversation with fellow guests in the bar. He must have enjoyed not being just the Sex Pistols manager for a change. One by one he was joined by various members of the entourage, me included and we drank the afternoon away listening to our favourite records on the jukebox.

Malcolm had a thing about Abba. Why did they sound so commercial? He kept getting me to put them on over and over again, while he scrutinised their sound. He asked me to explain what it was that made them sound so expensive.

"A catchy tune with loads of double tracking and a drum and bass sound that cuts the mustard." was all I could come up with.

"Put it on again Dave, I'm sure there's something else," was his reply. I got the feeling that whatever this 'something else' might be, he certainly wanted some for his band.

That night Granada TV showed an interview they'd recorded with the band earlier that day, fronted by Malcolm.

Interviewer: People say that you're sick on stage, you spit at the audience and so on, I mean how can this be a good example to children?

Malcolm: Well, people are sick everywhere. People are sick and fed up with this country telling them what to do.

Interviewer: But not being paid for it.

Malcolm: Pardon?

Interviewer: But not being paid for putting on that sort of public performance –

Malcolm: Well, nor are we, we ain't even being allowed to play.

Steve: It makes you sick, dunnit?

Interviewer: In fact you're acting as spokesman for the group today.

Malcolm: Yes, indeed.

Interviewer: Have you stopped them from talking to us?

Malcolm: Not at all, they're just so disgusted by having to answer so many questions about something so simple ...

That afternoon we were thrown out of the Piccadilly Plaza Hotel for no other reason than being 'Sex Pistols' and entourage. It was as if we had the plague. The pack of hungry press hacks hounding us had been poisoning our reputation. We managed to find another hotel nearby.

On leaving the Piccadilly Plaza, I noticed my shoulder bag had gone missing. I had put it under the bed for safe keeping as it contained live tapes of the shows so far, including The Damned, Heartbreakers and Clash. I wanted to call the police but Malcolm advised me against it. He said I should call the hotel from our next port of call. He was sure they would turn up. They never did, but years later a certain bootlegger claimed that Malcolm had approached him with several Anarchy tour tapes he was hoping to get £20,000 for. It's possible that's true but I doubt it ...

According to the 'official records' Manchester's main Electric Circus concert happened on a Thursday, but I always remember it as Saturday. The reason being that on the day we did the gig, a football match took place between Manchester City and Manchester United. I suppose this could have been a rematch from a previous draw. Anyway, after the match hoards of angry hooligans descended on the venue. It was the only building left standing in what looked like a recently demolished slum area. The windows had been boarded up and packs of wild dogs roamed the surrounding dusty streets looking for scraps to eat.

The club itself had previously been putting on punk gigs with local acts like the Buzzcocks and Slaughter and the Dogs. It could hold about five to six hundred punters at a squeeze, but with all the recent publicity we were expecting many more.

Sitting around in the dressing room waiting for show time, we heard a barrage of abuse in the distance that seemed to be getting closer. I could just make out "Get the Punks!", "Kill The Bastards!" and other friendly chants. A shudder ran up my spine. I nervously peered out through the cracks in the windows to see thousands of irate football fans laying siege to the club. Mounted police were desperately trying to control them, but it looked to me as if they were fighting a losing battle. The crowd had taken to thumping on the doors, rattling the fire exits and throwing stones up at the boarded windows. It was getting really heavy, to put it mildly.

The poor old punks outside were being harassed by the hooligans army. We realised that they had to be let in for their own safety, so the police and bouncers somehow achieved this, while managing to keep the bulk of the angry mob at bay. Unfortunately, a dozen or two of the more determined thugs sneaked in with them and advanced up the stairs towards us, but they were soon knocked back down by Johnny Thunders, Billy Rath and Jerry Nolan who seemed well up for a ruck. It was like a scene from a punk version of Grease, complete with Steve and Paul lurking behind, ready to join in if the need arose.

Eventually the police miraculously managed to disperse most of the crowd outside and the gig proceeded. The nasties that did get in infiltrated among the fans and proceeded to get drunk. I saw some loonies going round asking people "Are you a punk?" If anyone was unwise enough to say "yes" they would get punched or nutted. Honestly, the hatred stirred up by a few foul words – it was so much more than I could ever have imagined! It was also symbolic of people's resistance to change and fear of the unknown.

The mob had been victims of propaganda. They had been told by the mass media that they – the people! – had been insulted by the 'Sex Pistols' and their evil Punk followers. Now the people were taking their revenge on the culprits. You would think that soccer lads would see punks as heroes but no one had told them to do that yet, so they didn't. They hadn't had time to work things out for themselves.

I kept being approached by nutters and had to talk my way out of several fights, possibly – in the process – turning a few hardnuts on to 'the individual self expression of Punk'. The sensationalist media, as usual, had been irresponsible and were using headlines to promote hatred. One only has to think of the 'Teds versus Punks' battles they encouraged to see them at their worst. It was 'Mods versus Rockers' all over again.

As The Damned had been thrown off the tour, the Buzzcocks stood in for them that night. They were local favourites and put in an amazing set with their £25 Woolworths guitars.

Malcolm seemed to be very worried about the bands' vulnerability whilst on stage – "especially the Pistols". There were no side entrances onto the stage and the only way on was through the crowd. Once on stage, the band could be pinned there. Their only way off was back through the crowd.

Malcolm was totally freaked and kept saying "They could get killed up there tonight!" There was some discussion about pulling out, but the bands were up for playing so it went ahead. Anyway, there would have been an even bigger riot if they didn't play.

Armed with guitars and bodyguards, the other groups went on and managed somehow to complete their sets and retreat to the relative safety of the dressing room. The atmosphere was tense to say the least. We had heard that a crowd had assembled outside and the bouncers were having trouble keeping them out. With all the signs of a massacre brewing, the Pistols' welfare was Malcolm's main concern.

The band refused to bottle out and bravely took to the stage and stood their ground. Missiles were thrown at them but no one was seriously hit. John gave as good as he got verbally. During the whole show, Malcolm was in a panic, expecting his band's blood to fly at any moment. It was a close thing but somehow they got away with it and completed a shortened set with no encores. Miraculously they got back to the dressing room without falling into the clutches of the blood-hungry hounds.

No one wanted to hang around this place for longer than was necessary – apart from Thunders who was having a good time – and a plan was hatched to get us to safety. I had to run the gauntlet outside and go and get our hire car, then back it up to the fire exit at the side of the club. I had no choice, I had to do it! "Don't worry Dave, you look normal, you'll be alright." Apart from a few strange looks and pointed comments I managed to pull it off and then banged on the door – before it opened I was spotted by members of the thuggy mob at the top of the street. They started coming towards me and I noticed some were carrying sticks. This is it, I thought.

Just then, the door burst open and out poured Joe Strummer, John, some Pistols and Mickey Foote, the Clash's sound engineer. Before the crowd had time to get to us we leapt into the limo – Paul Cook couldn't squeeze in and had to get in the boot. As we screeched away we were chased by brick-throwing hoodlums. Bottles and stones were aimed at us but no one scored a direct hit. Some took to cars to chase us but we soon managed to lose them – only to be caught again when we pulled up for petrol. The chase was back on until, after about ten minutes of daredevil driving, they were off our tail again.

I eventually got us to our new three star hotel, only to be told by the manager that we had been thrown out, something to do with the press having spread malicious rumours about our aggressive behaviour … feeling totally despondent – and starving – we headed for the local Chinese restaurant where we hoped to unwind after our ordeal. We ordered our food and reflected on recent events ... I then spotted these geezers sitting in the corner giving us strange looks. I could overhear their conversation.

"That's them, isn't it?"

"Now what would they be doing in here?"

"I bet it is, go over and ask 'em!"

"Scuse me mate, are you the Sex Pistols?"

"What if we are?" quips Rotten.

"You reckon you're hard, don't you?" enquires geezer somewhat menacingly.

It was really hard to tell how this situation would turn out. I mean, these bovver boys may be friendly, but after tonight's ordeal we were feeling somewhat paranoid. Although we outnumbered them, we decided to ring the hotel and see if anyone else was there, so we could inform them about our predicament. Mickey Foote made the call and fortunately Oddjob our security dude was there, along with the 'Nowhere coach'.

"Hold tight," he said, "I'll be there as soon as poss..."

"Then the line went dead." recounted Mickey, back at our table.

It's interesting how a few hours earlier, these punk rock musicians had thrust two fingers up to some of the heaviest crew in Manchester, stood defiantly against the abuse and hail of projectiles and now here we all were, Rotten, Strummer, Mick Jones, Mickey Foote and me, feeling uneasy with our current situation.

We were desperately willing our food to turn up quickly, while trying to ignore the remarks coming from the far corner and avoiding any further eye contact. Suddenly the door flew open. In stalked our bodyguard, who was a pretty mean-looking 18 stone brute. He picked up a chair and fixed his gaze on the contingent in the far corner. Oddjob then ordered us onto the coach and slowly walked backwards out the door, chair in one hand, whilst keeping his eyes fixed firmly on the geezers.

It was at this moment that our food arrived and the waiters couldn't believe their eyes. We scarpered, somewhat relieved but still hungry. You should have seen the looks on the yobs' faces – they were speechless. As we pulled away the waiters came running out, still holding the food, and stood outside looking bewildered as we disappeared into the distance. How bizarre is that then? What a laugh!

We returned to the hotel for our luggage, and found the press pack wallowing in our humiliation at being ejected yet again (thanks largely to them!). There was no reasoning with the manager. He had been shown 'dirt' on the people staying in his establishment and had seen enough. He wanted us off his doorstep, never to return. Realising that he wasn't really to blame, without further fuss we collected our suitcases and hopped back on board the coach to 'Nowhere'.

As we headed back to London, down but not out, the mood on board was somewhat sombre to say the least. I started skinning up and was soon joined by Micky Jones, who'd sort of become my smoking partner on the coach. The main reason I guess, was this huge chunk of hash I had with me. It needed smoking and he was well up for helping me do it. Mick must have felt embarrassed about smoking so much of my dope, because he promised that if he ever became rich and famous he would buy me a huge piece to compensate. Mick old buddy, do you remember that? Fancy a jam? I'm waiting! (he reminded me so much of a young, pre-heroin Keith Richards). 'Keep smoking it and sharing it with friends' was always my motto.

Malcolm kept advising me to go and sit with the main contingent, John, Steve, Strummer etc ... who had settled down round a table for a game of cards. "You should spend more time hanging out with those guys," he would say, "stick with the scene, that's where the action is." But I began to sense a growing 'cliqueyness' amongst the musicians. At the back of the coach it was a bit like the Rotten and Strummer show. Every now and then they would allow guests in, like Bernie or myself, to 'edutain' for a while, before their abstract humour would get the better of us and we'd retire to the wings.

I was starting to feel a bit out of place. I guess the Afghan fur coat and denim flared dungarees didn't help much! Incidentally, the coat mysteriously disappeared at the Electric Circus gig and I was now starting to feel the cold. By the time we arrived back in Denmark Street our spirits had lifted a little, until it hit us that it was three in the morning and freezing. There was no heroes' welcome. The coach driver made sure we were all off, then disappeared into the night.

There was a sudden desperate panic as people realised that they had to make their way home with no money for cabs and – in my case – no warm clothing. It was bitter that night and the streets were deserted apart from this impoverished band of Punk stars all huddled together on the corner.

Without my cherished Afghan, I was turning blue. I just wanted my nice warm bed way out in the suburbs (I was sure mum would have switched the electric blanket on already). I managed to find a cab and once sundry bods had been dropped off along the way, took it back to the family abode in Feltham near Heathrow Airport, a journey of twenty miles or so. Of course the last one gets to pay the fare, but in this instance it was going to have to be my parents – I had virtually nothing left of my meagre wages. Luckily they had enough cash to pay the cabbie. I said my goodnights and lay my weary body out for some much-needed rest. Now my parents had joined Malcolm in becoming financial supporters of the Sex Pistols and their arty anarchistic ways!

The Welsh gig at Caerphilly Castle turned out to be really strange. We were to play in a little cinema adjacent to the age old battlements. The castle itself was centuries old and amazingly battle scarred. It had been blown up during the English Civil War and Cromwell had trashed their monasteries and then informed them they would get their hands cut off if they were found on the wrong side of Offa's Dyke, a 16 ft high ridge that completely cut off Wales from England (just in case you forgot which side of the bed you were lying on!) and to add insult to injury, it was built by Welsh slaves!

The paparazzi gathered there in force, convinced they were about to witness a second English Civil War.

With the sound-check out of the way we went off to explore the town. There was not a single person in sight, the pubs were all closed and many shops in the high street had their shutters up. It's no wonder that folk around there had such a siege mentality when you think of their troubled past.

We'd opened some very old wounds indeed for these borderland folk. They felt the enemy was afoot once more and had decided to lock themselves in until we'd left. So Caerphilly had been turned into a ghost town. It really was like a scene out of some Tales of Mystery play. We wandered around the streets looking for an open pub but we couldn't even find a single living human being. Eventually we rounded a corner and came face to face with two local punks. They gave us the low down.

"There's been such an uproar in the local newspaper," they tell us.

"You lot have been called 'Satan's children'. They've tried to ban the concert but failed. The Council's still threatening to hold back further entertainment licenses from the promoter but he's not local so he don't care. There's gonna be a carol-singing protest outside and local Hells' Angels have threatened to harass any punks that dare turn up."

Wow! We're in for one hell of a night! I thought. We notice trucks of camera crews arriving, BBC, ITN, they were all here. We'd made national news again (you may think it's weird how I often refer to the Sex Pistols and the events as 'we', but at the time that's exactly how it felt. We were a tribe and we knew it!)

Julien Temple arrived accompanied by a very attractive young, female film school student who he was teaching or maybe studying with, I couldn't work out which. I think it was the first time I'd seen him at a Sex Pistols gig – or maybe he came to some earlier gig on the Anarchy Tour – whatever – I chatted with him and his colleague. I don't recall exactly what was said, but I vaguely remember being told that they were on a project for school. Anyway, they had a camera.

Julien had to negotiate with Malcolm to shoot the gig. Malcolm only allowed him to film small portions and never a whole number – the old 'not giving too much away in one go'. "One should always retain a level of mystery," he would announce from time to time. If it looked like they were filming too much, Malcolm – who'd be sitting next to me at the mixing desk, would tell me to go and insist they stopped – so I did. This is why you never see much live footage from early Sex Pistols gigs and rarely a whole song.

The early evening BBC National News: Transcript: The candlelit crowd are singing 'Silent Night'. A fundamentalist preacher is shouting from a platform through a megaphone:

Preacher: "We hope this will get in the Press, to let Wales know, to let the people of this town know, that we do protest and that it's by no fault of ours that this thing has come to Caerphilly. We have done everything humanly possible to ban this thing and to stop it. And as we've not been able to, we have done the last thing possible, to stand here in open protest to let you know that we are responsible, and we are doing all we can to set an example in leadership and every other way, to a clean living, holy living and pure living."

Interviewer talking to band inside club:

Int.: "How do you feel about the crowd opposite?"

John: "They're entitled to do what they want."

Steve: "The thing is they're outside freezin'. We're in 'ere, we're alright."

Commentator: "Caerphilly didn't quite know what to expect so it took no chances. Pubs and cafes were closed before and after the concert. On decibel points the Sex Pistols won. On numbers it was a victory for the carol singers."

Int.: "Excuse me sir, can I ask you why you're here tonight?"

OAP: "Because I'm, er, well … recognised as a Christian."

Middle Aged Lady: "Never mind about Christianity, I think it's dis – well it's degrading and disgusting for our children to hear and see such things."

Middle Aged Man: "Er, I've got teenage daughters and youngsters. I'd let them out to see Rod Stewart but I wouldn't let them go to see this rubbish."

Middle Aged Lady: "If I thought that one of mine was in there, I'd go in there and drag them out. Terrible, I think it is. I think it's disgusting, it's, well, it's lowering the standard of our people in Caerphilly!"

The protesters hadn't realised it yet, but they had made the Pistols even more famous. Only about forty or so punters managed to turn up and the bands put on a marvellous show. Our rather large PA was a bit OTT for the event but that didn't stop us from turning it up full, opening the windows and sharing our wonderful music with the world outside. Anyway, we had to turn it up, there were bloody carol singers and protesters outside, trying to drown us out.

In the end the protesters couldn't take it any longer and went home to their beds and bibles. All that is except the biker-ted-greaser-styley blokes who were still hanging around. Why were they still hanging around…? Were they getting off on the music? Was the rumour that they were planning to start trouble just a myth? Anyway, to my knowledge no fan was attacked when they left and when we all marched out carrying mike stands the local heavies soon dispersed.

At this gig we also encountered the new extremes of punk fashion – a couple of punk chicks from Carlisle – dressed in black dustbin liners with safety pins through their noses and cheeks. It looked more daring than it actually was. Their pins never actually punctured the skin, but were bent and broken to look like they did. Rotten was most impressed and invited them back to the hotel.

The hotel didn't care who we were, as long as we paid our bills. They had laid on a huge banquet in the kitchens below, complete with several kegs of beer. We numbered about 25 as we feasted around one giant table. Mr Rotten ordered an extremely rare steak, and kept returning it until he eventually got a raw one. With blood dripping from his mouth, he ravaged away at it.

After the banquet we all went upstairs where The Heartbreakers set up some amps and kicked off an all-night jam session. We never heard one complaint from the manager and in the morning he bade us all a fond farewell.

Winter Solstice in Plymouth was to be our Grand Finale. We got there early and were greeted by some young enthusiastic chaps starting a local fanzine.

They were quick off the mark and set about interviewing the Clash in the coffee bar next to the club. The Pistols were, for some reason, due to arrive later. It turned out that we played two nights here and they were to be the last of the tour. We had been booked in at the Holiday Inn, complete with swimming pool and sauna. Ah, such luxury. Once again I was sharing a room with Malcolm who, considering the situation he was in, was coping very well.

On the way to the club, I shared a cab with a junior record company rep.

"Hi, I'm from EMI," he said with what I felt was a touch of smugness.

"Oh, right. Well, I'm the sound engineer." I replied.

"The name's Frank Brunger," he said with studied casualness, as if I should be impressed.

"My name's Dave Goodman," I almost growled as my hands involuntarily clenched into fists – Brunger, you might recall, was the man responsible for screwing-up my label credit on the first pressing of 'Anarchy'. He noticed my sudden anger and with concern in his eyes, he tapped on the cabbie's shoulder.

"This'll do for me, driver! This'll do!" he was almost shouting.

"What? Here?" said the cabbie, pointing at the empty park we were next to.

"Yeah, here's perfect, just lemme out!"

He leapt from the cab stuffing a fiver in cabby's hand, and kept out of my way for the rest of his stay.

Despite a fairly poor turnout, the gig was highly rated by most of the audience, so much so that it was decided to do another the next day. The manager got on stage and announced the news to an elated audience who vowed to see us again tomorrow, and bring their friends.

On the morning of the second day, Malcolm made a decision, quite wisely in my opinion, to high-tail it back to the Smoke prior to the last night frolics. He was also concerned about the band's equipment and wanted to make sure it got back safely to town and was not confiscated against some debt or damages. I called my Label mate Caruzo, who'd just bought a secondhand double wheelbase transit, and was up for using it for this very purpose. A deal was struck and, in no time at all, Caruzo had arrived, along with his charming Japanese wife Naomi.

Malcolm was ready to leave and offered them his bed. He then blagged a ride to the station and on the way Caruzo asked him how the tour had gone.

"It's been the most successful tour in musical history to date," he said with a grin, "we've been banned in virtually every town in our own country, they're writing about us all over the world, we make the news at six nearly every night. You just can't buy this amount of exposure. So what if we only played a handful of gigs, we become more mysterious and more and more people will want to see us in the future".

We reached the station before Malc had a jawgasm. He swore us to secrecy about his sudden disappearance, then informed me that fellow Glitterbester Miss Sophie Richmond, was on her way up to take over. He was away – escaping while the band were still sleeping off last night's partying. He was going before anyone had a chance to play practical jokes on him and before people started demanding their final wages. His last words that day were; "There are plenty of hacks up from EMI, get them to sort it out if anything goes wrong, they've got all the money and we're the ones with a record in the charts, have fun!" and with that he dived onto a train.

We headed back to the hotel, then set about devouring some of the elephant tranquillisers – Harley Street-prescribed pills – that Caruzo had brought down with him, along with some good ol' Thai grass. I felt great, really looking forward to the gig that night.

Everything was set up and all we had to do was make our way to the club.

This wasn't all that easy after the pills started to kick in – they made you feel totally uninhibited, you believed you could take on the whole world.

After visiting a few pubs we eventually found ourselves at the club where the bands had assembled in drunken 'last day of the tour' merriment – now ... aren't we supposed to sound-check?

With the second Plymouth sound-check over, we all sat around sinking a few more jars and waiting for the crowd to arrive. Looking at the state of some musicians, I figured that they too must have been dipping into Caruzo's magic medicine cabinet.

Word must have spread about the previous night's sensational gig as quite a crowd was building up outside. Some people had travelled hundreds of miles to be there. John arrived and almost started a riot by insisting that everyone should get in free, and the drinks were on EMI. The crowd that had already assembled took him at his word and followed him in. "EMI are paying!" said John to the bemused staff. John's guest list returned his generosity in drinks and drugs – this was gonna be one mutha of a night!

There was a newly painted dressing room which had been completely graffitti'd with quotes from Chairman Strummer. Someone had kindly laid on 12 crates of beer in the corner – as if anyone really needed any more (it was a little warm but the boys were much too polite to refuse it).

The evening began with EMI's new signing Wire, who'd been posted up from London to join the bill. They certainly introduced a level of musical intellectualism to the event. The Clash then put in one hell of a set and refused to end it. They only stopped when Thunders enticed them off by waving a huge joint at them from backstage.

The Heartbreakers were on form too, I think they managed to play three numbers in between tuning-up, falling over and swearing at the audience.

There was quite a delay before the Pistols came on and this drove the audience to fever pitch in anticipation. Rotten eventually appeared, to much cheering and jeering. He said something about the crowd not making enough noise and the rest of the band wouldn't come on until they did. This was the crowd's cue to go wild, and wild they went. The band eventually came on and roared into 'Anarchy'. All hell broke loose. In my drug-crazed state, they sounded brilliant.

It was a different story that was reported back to Malcolm by Sophie. I later got bollocked for getting too 'out of it' and fucking up the sound.

Anyway, the boys did about three encores that night. I was at the back of the hall behind the mixing desk and had appointed myself cheerleader.

Equipped with a mic that ran to the stage monitors I had great fun hurling abuse at the band and the audience. I managed to keep the applause going for ages with chants of "Come on, you fuckers, play!" and "Call yourselves an audience? I can't hear you at all!"

Caruzo, a one time DJ, muscled in on the mike and gave his Emperor Rosko impression, "Come on now, brothers and sisters, lets hear it for those groovy cats, the Sex Pistols!" Just then the guy who owned the PA spotted Caruzo and ,not knowing who he was, tried to push him away. Before there was time to explain, they were at each other's throats. They were interrupted by the band coming back on for yet another encore. "I'll see you later" they mumbled threateningly at each other. Later, after the show, they locked horns again backstage. Caruzo was looking for an apology.

"Your mate might as well apologise," I advised one of his helpers, "my mate used to be in the Navy."

That's nothing" said the helper, the bloke who owns the PA used to be a commando."

To prove it, Mr PA held Caruzo's throat in a vice-like grip up against the wall. This soon cooled Caruzo down and one hoped that was the end of it.

But an hour later the PA guy came to me and said.

"I've just been outside to my van and your mate's there brandishing a six foot piece of scaffolding. Is he crazy or what?"

I went outside to reason with Caruzo, who was clutching the scaffolding, feathers ruffled.

"Look Caruzo the PA guy didn't know you were my friend – he's sorry," I said,

"Well tell him to come out here and tell me to my face," he replied.

This was all that was needed and the two were suddenly best of mates, and went off on a pub crawl.

There was a party back at the hotel and quite a few of the audience were invited, including a few sailors who went AWOL to come. When I got back there quite a crowd had already gathered and drinks started to flow. Several Heartbreakers and Pistols were running around drenched to the skin. They had been having a water fight upstairs. Next Caruzo pulled up outside the hotel in his newly pranged van. Out he popped with his new mate the P.A. man, who looked shaken – Caruzo had casually driven into several parked cars without even noticing.

The roadies started hatching a plan to get even with Bernie Rhodes, as he'd been bossing them around throughout the entire tour. They were somehow going to get into his room and leave a nice little surprise for him in his bed.

Everyone thought it was a good idea, especially the Clash (how wise of Malcolm to leave a day early).

Downstairs in the bar some of the 'normal' guests were viewing the frollicking with disgust and a few had complained to the manager. The manager came out and announced that the bar would be closed in 30 minutes and any more drinking would have to take place in our rooms. A big barrage of abuse went up.

Then I noticed the doors of the elevator open to reveal a chair; on it were a pair of Steve Jones' leopard skin brothel creepers. I wasn't alone in noticing this, but before anyone else's attention could be brought to it, the doors closed and the lift went back up to where it came from. A few moments later, it returned and now along with the shoes were a pair of trousers. Suddenly nearly everybody was pointing at the sight. It went off again to return with a t-shirt, next a pair of socks. We were all transfixed by the lift making its way back up to the eleventh floor – what would appear next? You've guessed it! The lift returned and this time when the doors opened there stood Steve, stripped down to his undies doing this silly dance with his hands behind his head and his donker bouncing up and down. I don't know whether it was the sheer size of it or not, but several women screamed out loud.

By the time the manager arrived, the doors had shut and Steve was away. Only hearing the screams and laughter the manager had no idea what had just happened. He stood there for a while scratching his head looking round at people pointing at the closed lift door.

"There's a naked man in there!" someone shouted. The manager wasn't convinced until it was confirmed by several other sources. The lift started to come down again – this time the manager was ready to pounce on the deviant. It came to a halt, and when the doors slid back, instead of it being Steve, it was a very upset Bernie demanding another room and complaining about there being 'some shit' on his sheets. Everyone laughed themselves silly, until the manager demanded that all of us leave the bar.

Some of the hangers-on came up to the rooms with us, especially those with drugs. And the AWOL sailors were generously offered a room for the night courtesy of EMI or whoever was picking up the tab.

In our rooms, the party continued, with the biggest congregation in John's suite. On the way up I spied the swimming pool and discovered that it hadn't actually been locked. Great, I thought, some midnight bathing is in order. I entered John's room and tried to advise everyone on the virtues of midnight swimming. No one seemed at all interested, so in a fit of frustration I upturned John's bed with its occupants and made for the door.

I just got out in time before all hell broke loose. The racket I heard inside was incredible.

I soon found Caruzo and Naomi and we went for a swim. Five minutes later we were joined by just about everyone else. My lecture on the virtues of midnight bathing must have done the trick. Rodent, the Clash's roadie was so stoned that he instantly dived fully dressed into the shallow end and had to be taken to hospital – he ended up with half a dozen stitches across his forehead and mild concussion. Sunbeds, chairs, tables and groupies ended up in the pool as we proceeded to go wild. Plymouth was a fairly rough seaport but I bet their finest hotel hadn't seen anything quite like this before.

Soon the furious manager arrived with an entourage of henchmen and we were ordered out of the pool and ejected. Caruzo, Naomi and I, however, made for the sauna and we would have gone undetected had we not switched it on. Its little red light outside gave us away. Just as Naomi was complaining to Caruzo that one of the staff had walked in on her earlier – while she was half-naked, getting dressed in the changing rooms – the door of the sauna opened and in walked the manager. Caruzo, assuming this was the culprit, leapt up stark naked and tried to land a karate blow with his foot to the manager's nose. He nearly slipped arse over tit, but the manager was impressed enough to use very polite tones as he asked us to leave. With just towels wrapped around us we were marched out carrying our clothes, only to be accosted by two policemen and a policewoman who had come to investigate Caruzo's earlier driving accident(s). Caruzo was then dragged off to the nick, his last words were;

"Don't worry, I'll be back in ten minutes," and he was as well. How does he do it?

Having been thrown out of the bar and pool, everyone was well pissed off. They took to their rooms ordering everything on the menu and then when they were bored with that, they rearranged them. How else do you get your TV in the bath and your bed on the balcony…?

You could tell which room belonged to an Anarchy tour member by the fact that it had a plate of trifle stuck to the door and there was probably smoke and water coming out from underneath it. When Caruzo and I finally had enough of the merriment, we headed back to our suite. We were asked by one of the sailors, who was speeding out of his box, if he could come too as he couldn't handle all the craziness going on right across that floor. He sat up in our room all night and minded the door while we finally got some rest.

In the morning, every hour or so the hotel manager and his heavies would knock on our door demanding to know what the hell was going on and who would pay for the damages? Our naval doorman would just tell them that we were sleeping and to come back later. Finally, about three in

122

the afternoon, he let them in. The manager was amazed to see that our room was spotless – unlike the others, which had been completely wrecked. He came in and nervously looked at Caruzo and said "None of that rough stuff, please." He must have thought Caruzo was Malcolm as he asked to see him in his office ASAP. No one was to leave until the damages had been paid for. Caruzo very casually agreed to see him shortly and he left.

"Listen Dave, I think I can sort this out pretty easily," Caruzo said with a mischievous grin.

"But you're not Malcolm," I informed him.

"Yeah, but the manager thinks I am."

Once he was dressed in a fresh bri-nylon shirt and clean stay-pressed trousers, he looked every bit 'the manager'.

"What do you reckon Dave, is a tie overdoing it?"

"Yeah, I reckon, just go casual, man," so he undid the top three buttons on his shirt to reveal his hairy chest and gold medallion.

"Listen," he said, "get everyone to the foyer and load up the bus. I'll see you there ASAP."

He picked up his chequebook and headed for the door.

"What about your pen?" asked Naomi, always keen to see her wedding present get an airing.

"Nope, won't be needing that," and he was off, leaving me with the task of rallying the troops.

"John, wake up man, we gotta get out of this place, NOW! Who's there with you?"

"Dunno, er, who's here with me?" From the amount of voices I could hear in the background it was quite a crowd.

"Right, everyone needs to pack and get down to the foyer, we've got to split in 30 minutes, the EMI staff have fucked off, Corkie and the PA guys will be back in Birmingham by now. I've just had a visit from the manager who reckons he'll call the police if we try and leave without paying for last night's damages. My mate Caruzo's gone down to try and sort it out, I'll be going back to London in his tranny with your and the Clash's backline – good tour eh? Glad to share your reality!"

(Laughs) "A milestone in history!" Click.

Unbelievably we all managed to get it together – but where was Glitterbest Ltd rep Sophie?

"Let's just do a runner." someone said, but we knew we'd soon have the police on our tail if we did.

Caruzo came out of the office smiling and miraculously, we were allowed to leave. He had craftily written out a cheque for the damages but avoided signing it by distracting the manager. The problem was EMI's again!

On our journey home, about sixty miles outside London, the van broke down. I had to hitch back to my parents' house and borrow my dad's Ford Cortina estate. I was back in no time at all. Foolishly, I towed the van back to London and although we just made it, my dad's car didn't. I'd knackered the clutch for him and didn't even offer to pay for its repair, not that I really had the money to do so. I guess the main thing was we got the bands' gear back safe and sound. Once again, my parents had supported the notorious 'ANARCHY IN THE UK TOUR'.

CHAPTER ELEVEN

JANUARY 1977

DUTCH COURAGE

We were booked to do a couple of dates in Amsterdam, supported by the Heartbreakers, at the Paradise Club and an arts centre in Rotterdam. The Heartbreakers and I had to get there overland, whilst the Pistols and Malcolm were flying. I was told to kinda look after the Heartbreakers and make sure they all returned in one piece. On the way out on the boat it occurred to me that none of them had any money. Apparently their manager, Leee, couldn't give them more than a pound a day, otherwise they would spend it on heroin. Anyway, fortunately for them I had some – money that is – and dipped into my pocket to buy some food and booze for us all. Thunders got the most drunk and I seem to remember him pouring crisps and booze over some poor girl who had become too friendly (it was all fairly mischievous and she took it well).

I was really looking forward to my return trip to 'Kool City'. Last time I was there I was playing bass guitar for New York soul divas, The Flirtations, at the Amsterdam Hilton (location of John and Yoko's famous 'Bed In'). I had stayed there along with the rest of the show, including Australian jazz trio The Peddlers and The Count Basie Big Band (minus the main man for obvious reasons). It was a splendid affair, diamonds and bubbles, killer weed and music.

This time I was heading to the famous Paradiso club – a haven of psychedelia since the mid 60s apparently. It was also the Dutch government's new legal outlet for marijuana, complete with their own quality control.

Most dealers would get their supplies from the licensed dealers who sat around playing chess, with their wares displayed next to them. You could sample a bit to make sure it was smokable and, as you can imagine, we took full advantage of this rather novel scheme. Resin this good and varied had almost disappeared from the streets of London by the mid 70s.

I knew now where all the good hash was ending up. The Heartbreakers were most impressed with the quality of the high and spent most of the evening sampling the different types until, eventually, they seemed to go into an ecstatic trance, standing at the back of the club.

I joined Thunders, who told me that he had actually been here before in the late Sixties. I thought he meant the club, but he was actually talking about the high he was getting from all the marijuana he'd been smoking. The others agreed nostalgically, "Yeah – I haven't been here for a long time but I remember it well," remarked drummer Jerry Nolan. "Mighty fine weed," Walter added in a fake southern drawl. I admit it was good but this level of admiration was maybe typical from New Yorkers, for whom I hear it's especially hard to get good smoke. Perhaps if they could, less people would be attracted to heroin – and while we're on the subject – for the record, the whole time I worked and travelled with the Heartbreakers, I never ever saw them indulge in that dastardly drug, not on the coach or in their hotel rooms or in the dressing rooms – never! They had either cleaned up or were very good at concealing their habit.

The only time I might have believed they were on it was when they were on stage. That's what a lot of punters expected and that's how they looked. But the Heartbreakers would soberly come down from the dressing room, where we had all been indulging in tea and splee and, while waiting backstage, they would mess up their hair, disarrange their clothes and hang a cigarette from the bottom lip, just to give the appearance of being out of it. They would then stagger on in a display that would reassure the audience that Johnny Thunders and his band were really living up to their lyrics.

The Pistols' performance at the Paradiso was very laid back. Lots of long-haired freaks did their usual type of dance to the band. The 'Woodstock Waltz' I called it. Malcolm sat next to me at the mixing desk and criticised the band. "They're too laid back," he kept saying, "go tell 'em to move about a bit more. Steve's been watching Thunders too much. Go tell him to liven up a bit." I couldn't imagine myself walking up to Steve in the middle of a song and telling him to liven up and stop copying Johnny Thunders, but this is what Malcolm wanted! "Can't you go and tell him, Malc? I've got a band to mix." I tried to reason but Malcolm kept on at me until eventually, when he started to stick his elbow in my ribs, I gave in, out of respect (and to get a bit of peace and quiet).Anyway it did the trick and Steve suddenly resembled a young Pete Townsend.

Eventually the audience became hip to the vibe and started gyrating more frantically. This type of music must have been new to the crowd, but they were able to accept it (watching it all and scribbling away, was the Guardian newspaper's rock critic, Robin Denslow, who's now a top reporter for BBC TV News, reporting regularly from the world's trouble-spots – something I like to think we helped him acclimatise to).

The Pistols were the first real Punk band to play in Amsterdam, and paved the way for many more to follow, but it was also to be the original line-up's last ever gig together – or at least, the last gig for the next 20 years or so. Tension had been growing between Glen and Rotten for some time.

Glen had been somewhat stigmatised for being too friendly with the hacks at EMI. When Glen tried to put his ideas forward for a piece in a song or something, Rotten often responded with a "Why don't you drop dead?" Glen felt as if he really meant it. At the Paradiso Club it came to a head and Glen walked off stage. I think, at that point, Glen had probably decided he couldn't stay in the band

In this quaint little old guest-house situated in the heart of the more beautiful part of Amsterdam's canal network, John had managed to blag the top room (the best one in my opinion). He had the finest view and maybe that's why we all congregated in his room. I had a half-decent, single lens reflex camera with me (Malcolm referred to it as a 'lens'). Stupidly, I felt I couldn't afford any film, and simply pretended I had some! I soon had the Heartbreakers posing merrily (what a dick this Goodman character can be at times!).

John's room started to become overcrowded, so he asked everyone to leave.

"Why don't you lot fuck off?" he said in his usual cheery fashion. For some reason I was the last going out and John said, "you don't have to go Dave, you can stay for a chat if you like." I told him I knew of some great night clubs we could visit, so we planned to go later that night.

We headed out on the town, Rotten, his friend Linda, and I don't remember who else. I'd lost my passport earlier in a bar, when I foolishly left my bag hanging on a chair and went to the loo. On the way to the club I was approached by some dude trying to sell me a passport. I had already reported mine stolen and certainly didn't need a false or stolen one – besides, $250 is a bit steep!

"You want English passport?" the dude kept asking.

"This one's good, looks just like you," and sure enough it did – Because It Bleeding Well Was Me! I grabbed it and thanked him for returning it to its rightful owner and before he had time to complain, disappeared into the club.

It was a really groovy disco and they openly sold speed, coke, acid and, of course, dope. The coke and speed dealers wore razor blades round their necks. John soon became pally with them. The dope dealers smoked pipes, while the acid dealers sat crossed-legged on the floor.

For the speed and coke freaks, there was non-stop disco playing fast freaky music. Lights flashed from every direction. Johnny and Linda were having a whale of a time demonstrating how to dance silly yet look really cool. I remember joining in and getting so carried away that I jumped up from the ground and smashed poor old Linda under the jaw with my head. It must have really hurt but she realised it was an accident and took it well.

For the dope heads there was a room upstairs full of cushions. They burnt joss sticks and sold groovy food. The music was very relaxing and the whole atmosphere very pleasant (for the acid freaks there was a bar on the roof from which they could leap)

The next day in the hotel, the phone never stopped ringing. Most of the calls were from EMI. They had just delivered the bombshell that they were dropping the Sex Pistols. Malcolm wasn't panicking and even seemed excited by the news. "If EMI think they can dump us that easy, then they have another think coming."

Later that day, we spent a pleasant time walking round the city with Malcolm at the helm being very boisterous. We spent some time in a café where Malcy baby was transfixed by the beauty of the waitress's golden brown skin and kept going on about it to all of us – and her! Steve and Paul had discovered the red light district and were spending everything they had there. Well – Steve was anyway. Apparently Paul used to wait for him outside. Even when it was time for them to leave, Steve was still busy at it.

"Where are those two?" said a disgruntled Malcolm, "We've got a plane to catch in an hour."

He was sitting outside the hotel in a taxi, waiting to go to the airport.

Just then Steve and Paul came running up. "Give us 50 gilders Malcolm," demanded Steve. "I've got a taxi round the corner to pay."

As soon as he had the money in his hand , he ran off for a last fuck and was back in 20 minutes. They just made the plane and arrived home a day before the rest of us sea travellers.

On the return boat journey, the Heartbreakers hatched a plan to get deported back to America, as they wanted to go home and see their wives and girlfriends. Thunders had even phoned New York to tell his lady to expect him in a day or two. You see the problem was that, when their manager, Leee Childers, first brought them over to England it was only supposed to be for a couple of weeks. They'd now been away for several months and were getting desperate to go home. The plan was to enter England in a severe state of drunken rowdiness. The way they looked they couldn't help but be searched for dope (which they had carelessly planted all over themselves). This must get them deported!

Walter seemed as if he'd taken too much acid and left the boat party to go and lay down in our little cabin. There was quite a storm brewing and you could feel the vessel shaking as it went crashing through the waves. This was all too much for Walter who reappeared white as a sheet. Our cabin was right at the front point of the ship, with only a steel hull between us and the open sea. "You should come and hear the weird noises," said Walter, "they're deafening – I know we're gonna sink!" We all ended up lying on our bunks listening to the mighty sea crashing against our bedroom wall. I must admit, tripping or not, it did sound scary.

Eventually we made dry land and when the Heartbreakers went through Customs at Dover, Thunders fell over and some dope fell out of his pocket. Walter asked one guard for a light for his joint, while Jerry knocked back neat whisky from an open bottle. I had the passports and so I was the one who spoke to the Customs officers.

"They're musicians." I offered with a smile.

"Oh! that's OK then." said the guard and waved us through. I think the band felt cheated and wanted to go through Customs again, but it was too late. They were stuck in England for a good while longer.

As the train pulled into London, I could see our welcoming committee on the platform. It consisted of punkettes Debbie and Tracie. They were more interested in Thunders than me and had bought him a snake skin tie in a jumble sale as a coming home present. Thunders and his boys didn't seem too interested in the girls and while I engaged Debs & Trace in conversation, the Heartbreakers made off across the footbridge and out of sight. I shared a cab with the girls back into town and got to keep the snake skin tie.

Thus ended the foreign leg of the infamous Anarchy tour. It was probably seen by less than five thousand people but boy did it make headlines!

Meanwhile Caruzo and I continued to develop The Label. The one advantage the majors had over indie labels like ours was 'vans on the road'. An all-important item if you aim to get your records distributed. I suppose the big labels had about thirty to forty of the things buzzing around the country selling their wares. The cost of setting up such an operation would have been prohibitive for us, so Caruzo came up with an idea. Perhaps all us independents could pool resources and help distribute one another's product. A sort of early 'cartel'.

A meeting was set up between us, Miles Copeland from Step Forward, Ted Carol from Chiswick and Jake Riviera from Stiff. The idea was that we would each invest in a van and everyone would carry everyone else's stock. Prices would be set and commission taken. Nice and simple you'd think, but doubts soon crept in when someone asked "How would we know that we'd put enough energy behind one another's stuff? Supposing one of us tried to sabotage the other's business?" Well this was one union that had to be based on trust and already that spirit had been broken. So it was every man for himself.

We were still lacking a comprehensive distribution network, but Caruzo was busy on the phone building one and eventually got many record stores, including Virgin, to stock our growing catalogue.

We then got Lightning Distribution to take us on as their first Punk item.

They were a sort of record supermarket – you wandered around with a trolley and filled it up with whatever took your fancy. To Lightning's surprise Punk started outselling their usual lines. "We want more of this Punk Junk," they said and they got it.

We also had meetings with Pinnacle, who were at that time just an electrical component distributor shifting plugs and light bulbs around. We happened to notice that a lot of electrical hardware shops stocked records too and managed to talk them into putting stock on board the Pinnacle delivery vans for a trial period. Several decades on and Pinnacle's record and CD distribution business is worth many millions of pounds. Their success is almost certainly down to the fact that we singled them out in the first place for a possible collaboration.

Our tactics for promotion were simple. We planned to throw a lot of money at advertising in the three major weekly music tabloids – Melody Maker, NME and Sounds. Caruzo went straight to the editors in question and set up meetings in the pubs of their choice – where else could such a meeting of such minds take place? The days of overt payola were supposedly dead, but there were ways around this as we soon discovered.

"Now, supposing your magazine gives our single a good review, how would the people know where to get it from?" we enquired.

"Well, you could place an ad informing them." came the editor's reply.

"Could we know in advance what kind of review, if at all, we were getting, so we could make sure we had a suitably sized advert?" we further enquired.

"Well, we can't really tell you who's gonna be reviewing it and we can't force them to like it, but I suppose you could place an ad and then pull it if you weren't happy with the review," he said casually.

"I see," we chorused – and Caruzo pushed the point, "… but what about if we booked a series of really big ads, say half a page for three weeks and we got a luke warm review?"

The Ed now smells money.

"Look, if you place a big enough ad and if you're really not happy with the review, then I suppose I could rewrite it a bit – I am the editor, after all …"

With that part of the negotiation out of the way, we set about ploughing a large portion of our capital into advertising. It worked well. We had good review after good review with many articles and features to follow. I'm not saying we wouldn't have got them otherwise, but when you're spending seven or eight grand a month on ads the music press certainly seems a lot more co-operative. As the majors have no doubt always known …

Caruzo and I used to print up posters and stick them up wherever we could. We had realised for instance, that the best target audience for Eater was school kids, so we took our product directly to them by advertising outside the school gates. During the Christmas holidays, we had identified a dozen or so of the largest comprehensive schools in London and had gone round spraying EATER! at the entrance, on the ground in massive letters.

That way everyone had to walk over it for weeks until it faded. We also put "Outside View" posters up in close proximity wherever we could. It was a very direct form of advertising but it worked a treat. It meant that at least another 20,000 school kids would become aware of Eater and that was a start.

In the music press, our first ads for 'Outside View' were half page ones and cited Virgin, Lightning, Pinnacle and all good record shops as our distributors, as well as ourselves. It was a bit cheeky, but it was more or less true. Normally the likes of Virgin and later Pinnacle, insisted on having exclusive rights to distribution, but in many cases this would prove counterproductive.

In the meantime 'Anarchy in the UK' had only reached No. 38 in the UK charts, which wasn't surprising, since only about 60,000 were pressed before EMI began to panic and withdraw it right across Europe. When we played in Holland, Malcolm had had to sell copies of it on the door as no shops were stocking it.

Eventually the band were given their contract back and kept their £40,000 advance. No one could believe their luck. Malcolm said that when he left the office at EMI with his solicitor, Stephen Fisher, they skipped all the way down the stairs clutching the cheque.

One of Malcolm's theories at the time was that someone had pointed out to EMI head Sir John Reed – who used to dine with Her Majesty the Queen – that this shocking pop group were planning to release 'God Save the Queen' as their next single. They were signed to his label. What was he going to do about it? Sir John, who probably only knew a handful of his artists, like Cliff Richard and Cilla Black, must have given the order to fire the Pistols.

One EMI insider had another theory. He seemed to think that because EMI owned shares in Thames and this was the channel that broadcast the Bill Grundy interview, the bad publicity would have been too much if anyone had got round to accusing them of staging an obscene promotional stunt on 'their' TV channel. It was all a bit hypocritical. Here was a band that was being condemned for a few swear words and EMI hadn't been too fussy until the going got rough. They came out looking pretty stupid over the whole affair, with their musical cred seriously damaged in the eyes of an entire generation – ten years later there was even an ITV documentary called 'How The Sex Pistols Destroyed EMI!' Anyway – the Pistols were £40,000 richer.

The band were now in an incredible position. They had the money to finance their own recordings and simply do a licensing deal with the next record company. They had also received more worldwide publicity than any amount of money could ever buy.

The main idea of going into Gooseberry Studios was to take everyone's mind off the EMI 'elbow'. I would arrange and produce some more tracks with them, while Malcolm went off to Paris, I assume to negotiate the Barclay Records deal. We booked ourselves into Gooseberry Studios, a neat little 16-track basement just behind Shaftesbury Avenue, a stone's throw from their Denmark Street rehearsal rooms. The lads were able to roll their amps round the corner.

The night before the studio session I was down at the Roxy Club and met an NBC film crew. They'd been sent over from America to capture the

Punk scene – especially the Sex Pistols – for a TV show that was to be broadcast all over the States. They'd been filming bands at the Roxy, including Eater.

They were now desperately trying to find out how they could contact the Pistols. They were delighted to discover that we were in the studio the very next day. I agreed that they could come in with their cameras for an hour, as long as they paid us for our time – in cash.

The band turned up at the studio. Steve and Paul had painted Union Jacks and the legend 'Guitar Hero' all over Steve's amps. John appeared to be tripping – which wasn't an unusual vibe for him to give off – but he was singing brilliantly, and his piano playing wasn't that bad either – I'd just given him my standard "learn to play the piano in two minutes" sketch (basically, just stick to the black notes, improvise, act like an avant garde musician and it will sound like music!)

The session got off to a great start with 'God Save the Queen' – which was then called 'No Future' – 'Liar', 'New York' and a brilliant new off-the-cuff song called 'EMI'. Things were going well and even Glen was in a good mood.

I hadn't told anyone that a film crew was due to arrive at 4.00pm. At the stroke of four I turned to John.

"'Ere John, what would you do if someone pointed a movie camera at you now?"

"I'd say 'Hello'!" he said.

Right on cue the doorbell rang. I opened it and in bowled the TV crew, their cameras rolling. Someone stuffed a wad of fivers in my top pocket and the next hour was documented. "Hello!" Johnny beamed into the lens. Lights went up and leads were plugged in and the band played a few songs. On the playback of 'EMI', where it gets to the big guitar solo build up, Steve and I got excited and leapt up in front of the camera, undid our flies and made like we were playing air dicks. NBC got what they came for and left as quickly as they came. "Did that really happen?" quizzed a tripped out Johnny seconds after the door shut behind them. He realized it did when we spent the money down the cafe later. There's a funny story about the fate of this film which I'll reveal later. Thinking about it, those final couple of numbers in the studio were the last ever time that the original Pistols line-up of Glen, Paul, Steve and John were to record together. At the end of this session, I stayed behind to do some rough mixes. John got all interested in the process and started asking me questions like, "How do you make things louder then?" I showed him the faders and he had a go himself. "How do I make the snare drum sound like it's in a church?" I made the reverb longer and directed him to the reverb knob. He immediately turned it up full. "So that's all there is to this mixing lark then, Dave? I reckon I could do it," he half joked. I uttered some words of encouragement and proceeded with the task in hand.

When I came to mix the Gooseberry Sessions, I booked myself into Eden Studios, Chiswick and found myself in the novel position of being completely on my own, apart from the house engineer. Once I discovered where the harmonizer/delay was, I was in my element, although I may have overused it on this version of 'Pretty Vacant'. The feedback I was getting from the engineer wasn't exactly inspiring, so I called little Helen to come down for a bit of moral support. "Oh and by the way Helen, can you bring some dope with you?"

After several joints of Helen's super hash, I was flying and the mixing desk became one giant musical instrument with infinite possibilities. Malcolm kept phoning in to see how it was going, but cancelled his planned visit when he found out that Helen was there. "I'm not sure if he likes me at the moment," commented Helen. We left it at that. I finished mixing the tracks, made an extra copy for Malcolm and delivered it to him in time for him to play it to A&M, in the hope of clinching a new deal. Tracks mixed at this session were: 'Problems', 'New York', 'No Future', 'Liar', 'EMI' and a new version of 'Pretty Vacant'.

CHAPTER TWELVE
FEBRUARY 1977

PETER COOK

My friend Rainbow George lives in Hampstead about three doors away from where Peter Cook lived. They were good friends and spent many a drunken night swapping stories. He told me of the night Malcolm and John came round to see if Peter was up for writing the script for the Sex Pistols movie that eventually became the Great Rock & Roll Swindle. He wasn't sure what to expect. He placed an upside down top hat near the entrance, full of goodies like sweets, pills and a syringe or two. When they arrived he gestured to them to take their pick. All Malcolm wanted was a cup of tea and John a pint of Guinness. Apparently Peter couldn't take on the task of scriptwriter for their movie, as he was too busy at that point. I believe he regretted this decision. Can you imagine how hilarious that melding of minds could have been?

Ironically, twenty years later in 1996 when the Sex Pistols reformed, they were asked to play at a party for the Peter Cook Appreciation Society, run by John Wallis. I'd met John in January '95, when my own band New Age Radio coincidentally played at Peter Cook's funeral party at The Everyman Cinema, Hampstead. Through me, John Wallis was able to contact the Sex Pistols. Glen told me he was really looking forward to this gig. Alas, before it could take place, John Wallis died of over-consumption at his own birthday party. When Rainbow George rang and said "John's dead!" I first thought he was referring to Mr Rotten, but soon realised it was Mr Wallis. Shame, he was a loveable eccentric with a lust for life. Very British too (whatever that means nowadays).

Anyway, it was February '77 and I bumped into John, Steve, Paul and Sid Vicious strolling down Denmark Street. They were tightly grouped and giving off this 'We're the Sex Pistols so you'd better watch out' vibe. Sid thanked me for the Eater single we'd sent him and exclaimed that he loved the bass part on "Outside View" and could now play it. John was a bit aloof. Maybe he didn't like the fact that he'd been caught out rehearsing with Sid before Glen had left. Whatever, I'm not quick to judge over these affairs. They said goodbye and scarpered into their rehearsal room.

Miles Copeland had become a familiar face on the scene. He'd keep popping up at Punk gigs and ask me all sorts of questions about record manufacture and distribution. He was a very determined man and would go directly for what he wanted. He followed Malcolm and moved into Dryden Chambers on Oxford Street, where the Glitterbest offices were. He set up on the floor below and gave Mark 'Sniffin Glue' Perry of Step Forward Records a desk. In one fell swoop he had the start of a catalogue and bought the favours of the Sniffin Glue fanzine. Clever geezer.

For prestige more than anything else I guess, he wanted to associate himself with the Sex Pistols. He offered to organise a tour of Finland for them, no doubt with some of his bands as support. The feedback that I was getting from the Glitterbest staff was that he was hard work to deal with and they'd be better off without him. Nothing came of it.

Mark Perry himself wrote in Sniffin Glue that Caruzo and I didn't know the 'first thing about Punk' and discredited Eater and our work (he omitted to mention what the 'first thing about Punk' was). Now Mark was certainly entitled to his opinion, but he'd never met us so what the fuck did he know? It was a below-the-belt attack and unnecessary in my opinion. I wondered at the time if he was influenced by Miles' determination to get ahead in the indie game. Anyway, one day as Malcolm and I were leaving the Glitterbest office, who should walk out of Miles' camp but Mister Perry himself. He took one look at me and did a 180 back into his office, slamming the door behind him as I shouted "So what is the 'first fucking thing about Punk' then Mark?" Needless to say, no reply was forthcoming.

From that point on, Caruzo and I decided to give Miles and his operation a wide berth. If this was the way I was to be repaid for all the help and advice I'd given him already, then I just didn't want to know. For those of you who've never heard Eater, you can check them out on davegoodman.co.uk. Now there's a real Punk band (over 20 years later I quizzed Mark about his article as I poured him tea in my kitchen, "Well, the thing is Dave, I didn't really know what I was saying back then," he admitted, "I don't recall an awful lot of it either ..." I left it at that).

By now, a Pistol was about to be fired. Malcolm called a meeting in the Blue Post, a little pub behind the 100 Club that the band often frequented. He had mentioned to me earlier that now was the time for Glen to either stake his claim or start walking. He invited Kim and I down for moral support, but for some reason we didn't go. The Pistols had already been rehearsing with Sid for almost a week and the outcome was a foregone conclusion, I guess. Malcolm gave Glen one last chance when he took him outside for a quick word (maybe Mal was having second thoughts about young Sidney and his closeness to Johnny Thunders?).

"Glen, I want you to go back in there right now and stand your ground."

"No, it's OK, Malcolm, I don't want to anymore – I'm off."

They then shook hands to show there were no hard feelings. A week after this meeting the press headlines read: 'Matlock Sacked From Pistols!' The main reason Malcolm gave was that the 'last straw' which led to the 'sacking', was because Glen liked the Beatles too much …

His replacement was, of course, John Simon Ritchie aka John Beverly aka Sid Vicious. Sid was raised by his mum – his father had gone off long before and for most of his school years Sid's mum had been, as she would sometimes admit, a bit of a groupie. Who also took heroin …

One day while delivering records, Caruzo spotted some reasonably priced skiing holidays on offer – if only we had some spare dosh. For some reason, at this time, all our money was tied up in our record company. We had just enough to go to the pub and share a Bloody Mary – one of the most inspiring drinks you can get, a real pick-me-up. Suddenly as the magic potion took hold, I had an idea where I could get some cash. You see, every time the Sex Pistols hired our PA we made them sign a little agreement that they would repay us for any damage they caused to our equipment. They'd just scored some advances, so now could be the perfect time to strike. I quickly made a list of damaged and lost equipment, left Caruzo in the pub licking the glass dry and scooted round to the Sex Pistols' office to confront Malcolm. It came to quite a few hundred. I was so persistent that eventually Malcolm allowed Sophie to escort me to the bank, where she drew out and handed me all of it in cash. What a day! Within an hour, I was back in the pub with Caruzo, loaded with a wad of dosh. We booked the holiday, had a few more drinks, bought some skiing clothes, had a few more drinks and then after a few more drinks, we went on a wander round the West End. Strolling down Denmark Street we bumped into Johnny Thunders and Jerry Nolan, who were going to Steve's place. We tagged along and inside we found Steve and Glen. I noticed Steve's old white Les Paul in the corner. Since he smashed it into the 100 Club sign on stage he hardly played it. It had a small crack on the neck and a Bigsby tremolo, which made it difficult to keep in tune. It had once belonged to David Johanson of the New York Dolls. Malcolm liberated it from him when he quit as their manager owing to their reluctance to conform to his visions.

"You wanna sell that old Gibo, Steve?" I asked.

"… yeah, alright, make us an offer." Steve replied. He probably needed the money.

"I'll give you seventy quid for it." I said.

"I'll give you eighty." cried Glen.

But I closed the bidding at £120. I did in fact promise Steve that he could always buy it back off me for the same price any time he liked.

This day just gets better and better I thought. We then taxied back to Caruzo's flat in Muswell Hill where I spent all night strumming the guitar. I fell asleep still clutching it and dreaming of our skiing adventure yet to come.

We were off to the Italian Alps. I'd never skied before, though Caruzo and his wife Naomi had. Dave Fowle, who shared the house with Caruzo came along too. He had also skied before, but his girlfriend Sally hadn't. "Don't worry. It's a doddle." They kept telling me.

Very early on the first morning they took me up to the highest point – the A run. "It's the best way Dave. By the time you reach the bottom you'll be able to ski – trust me." Once I got out of the final lift, it was either ski down or get back on it. Sally freaked and had to go back down. I put on a brave face and lunged forward, only to fall over. Apparently the art was being able to turn.

Naomi set off down the mountain at a very steady pace. Already high on the coke we'd snorted for breakfast, we demolished a beautiful Thai grass joint. Caruzo, showing off, told me and Dave Fowle that he would ski straight down, hit this natural ramp of snow and take off, do a double flick flack then land on one leg and carry on skiing. He took off at an almighty speed, hit the ramp, went flying in the air and came crashing down on his head. He got up, humiliated, but carried on to catch up with Naomi. Dave stayed with me for a bit to give me a few more tips. Once I thought I had it I sent Dave on his way.

Having come this far I had to go down. It didn't seem physically possible to get back up to the lift. I could go straight alright, but still couldn't turn. To avoid going off the run I had to fall over, then adjust my legs in the other direction, put the ski back on, get up and continue. People skied past me, throwing words of encouragement, "Crazy bastard Englishman!" "Idiot islander!" and so on. By now I was so wet through I had icicles hanging from me. Even children as young as seven or eight were skiing past me with ease.

I was so high up that it was impossible to see the village below. At my speed I couldn't imagine ever reaching the bottom, so I decided to ski to the next lift station which I could see in the distance. I finally got there but couldn't stop and overshot. Again, I couldn't get back, I had to keep going down. Eventually I came across a chair lift going back up to the last lift station. I managed to grab hold of one as it passed me. "Now don't cross your skis and you'll be alright." I told myself. Whoops! Try again. Double whoops! Once again I was lying in the snow, weighed down by the ever-growing ice pack that was forming on me. Now if I can just grab a chair as it comes by me – Can't Reach! – Use the ski spike! – yeah! here we go, straighten up, yeah! I'm gonna make it ... Suddenly the chair lift stopped – they didn't operate at night for safety reasons.

I noticed, with a growing feeling of dread, that there was no one else around. It was getting dark and an icy cold wind had started to whistle around my ears. This was it. I'd have to spend the rest of the night here. No. Surely when they noticed I was missing at the hotel they'd send a search party? If I was still alive by then ...

And then, thank goddess, a giant of a man came along, skiing on one leg and juggling his sticks. An expert local! "Jump on my back!" he commanded, after giving me a swig of brandy. I clambered up and he zipped down the slope in seconds flat, whistling as he went. In no time I was walking into the hotel, just in time for tea. I received a sort of heroes – well more like an idiot's – welcome.

I was the rightful producer of this band ... but what the fuck did they know, they were just kids and fast becoming a bit spoilt by all the headlines ...

CHAPTER THIRTEEN
MARCH 1977

WOT A LOAD OF BOLLOCKS!

From various comments made by the band, I would say that in general the recording of Never Mind the Bollocks was a bit laborious. I was up at Glitterbest around this time and Sophie was having to persuade Steve & Paul to get down to the studio. They seemed a bored by it all. I don't think they ever really recorded as a complete band after I finished producing them. Basically Steve and Paul laid down the guitar and drums, then Steve would add the bass. After this he'd record his usual twelve guitar overdubs a few days later, then if there was any space left, John would come in and do his vocal. They didn't really need Chris Thomas, I was the rightful producer of this band … but what the fuck did they know, they were just kids and fast becoming a bit spoilt by all the headlines …

Sid, Jah Wobble and some friends of John's visited the Speakeasy Club around this time, where they got into a serious dispute with Bob Harris of Old Grey Whistle Test fame before Sid threatened him. As it turned out, they picked a fight with the wrong crowd here. Mr Harris was accompanied by the group known as Bandit, comprised of my old drummer Graham Broad plus tough Glaswegian musicians Jimmy Litherland and Jim Diamond, along with martial arts expert Danny – who had a small sword concealed about his person. If they had wanted to they could have inflicted some serious damage, but they just bombarded them with glasses until they backed off. That was then typical behaviour from this faction of the Rotten army, Sid especially. What was he trying to prove?

At the beginning of March, after some three torrid weeks of negotiation, A&M's UK boss Derek Green offered Malcolm £150,000 to sign the Pistols. Half the cash was to be paid up front. Twenty-five thousand copies of 'God Save the Queen' were quickly pressed as the single was to be rush released for mid-March. Malcolm and the band – together with Derek Green, agreed that my July '76 take of 'No Feelings' had to be the B-side. This was a bit of an honour for me – A&M recordings were always of the highest technical quality, they were one of the first majors to spend thousands on re-mastering and they were also the first to use the better all-chrome cassettes for their albums. They wanted my £70 take of 'No Feelings' as one half of their biggest ever single, "Thank you kindly, A&M..."

A press conference was held at the record company's Chelsea offices and the band went along a teeny bit worse for drink. The whole event ended in total chaos, with Steve groping secretaries, Sid with his bleeding foot down the loo and Paul so pissed that he passed out on the floor. John contented himself with snarling insults as he drank A&M's executive bar dry. As a result of all these high jinks, the band were barred from the offices.

A few days later, the Pistols were sacked from A&M. After less than two weeks, they had been fired yet again. While Green probably did develop some genuine reservations about the group he'd just signed – for instance he wasn't told about the Sid-Glen changeover until it was too late – I also heard that many A&M artists had objected strongly to the Pistols being on their label. Malcolm reported seeing telegrams from Rick Wakeman and Steve Harley to this effect. I also heard that one major shareholder – allegedly Jackie Onassis – threatened to withdraw their investment unless this 'violent new pop group' were sacked. So Green had to give the boys half the dosh as promised (ol' Derek should have listened to Shakespeare and bewared 'the ides of March'), which turned out to be £75,000 – not bad for less than a fortnight's work. Malcolm and the Pistols couldn't believe their luck. The money just kept rolling in while the band's fame grew and grew.

A&M therefore decided to pulp the 25,000 'God Save the Queen' singles they'd pressed. If anyone could get hold of one it should have been me. After all, 'No Feelings' the B-side, was one of mine. I sent a very polite letter to MD Derek Green pleading for one, before they were all trashed, but I never even got a reply. Malcolm suggested that we drive down to the factory at night and break in and take what we could. He knew the exact whereabouts of the records and reckoned it would be a cinch, especially if we took Steve along. I should have gone for it but had cold feet. I then got a tip-off from Malcolm that a record stall in Berwick Street market had a box of ten for sale, but when I got there they had all gone – if they were ever there. My final chance of getting my mitts on one came when I was up in the Glitterbest offices, which had now moved to Shaftesbury Avenue. There was a knock at the door. It was in fact, an 18 year old Phil Strongman, editor of this book. He was selling a copy for £150. Malcolm managed to get him down to £120, but I still wasn't interested. It was a lot of money in those days for a piece of plastic. Eventually all I got was a black and white photo of it – which I then subsequently lost!

Malcolm told me a funny story just after the band's A&M sacking. He had turned up at the house of a CBS bigwig – let's call him Mickie – with one of his mates. He was becoming increasingly frustrated with Mickie's inconsistencies. "I'm gonna sign your band, Malcolm, and no one's gonna stop me," he had previously announced before disappearing out of town and refusing to return Mal's calls.

Malcolm did some research on him and found out that he'd been up in court previously on a charge of soliciting young boys. Apparently he'd been using his Rolls Royce as flesh bait around the back streets of Kings Cross station. Well, when Malcy arrived unannounced at his home he found a very nervous Mickie entertaining a young leather-clad lad. The boy was ordered into another room and Malcolm got straight down to business. "Do we have a deal or not?" was his main question. Mickie started back-pedalling and after much prodding from Malcolm admitted that he'd been overridden by asomeone who was higher up the food chain at the head office that was CBS America.

"I'm still gonna sign one punk band a week though, you watch me!" he said (he did too, for a while).

Not satisfied with seeing the big man admit to being subject to a superior's orders, Malcolm and friend set about winding him up further. They noticed that all the videos on the shelves were of CBS acts on Top of the Pops. They took over the video and played whatever they fancied, adding sarcastic narration where they pleased. A bit like Beavis & Butthead I guess. Mickie got so annoyed that his voice jumped up an octave or two and this big powerful American 'squeakily' threw them out.

Later on I produced a single with Malcolm's old art school friend Fred Vermorel and his wife Judy. The B-side was about this incident. It was called 'Cash Flow' and its opening lines were about a record company boss who had money "for knickers and honey" but actually prefers "little boys …" You have to speed up the record to hear all the lyrics properly. Anyway it was quite a hit, especially with the staff at CBS who put in an order for several boxes.

CHAPTER FOURTEEN

APRIL 1977

MORE ABOUT EATER

In the meantime Eater kept going from strength to strength and even headlined the Roxy Club with the Damned supporting. The photo on the back cover of the Damned's first album was shot at this gig. In this photo the Captain is wearing my nurse's uniform. Let me, ahem, explain that last remark …

I used to go out with a nurse, Sharon from Blackburn. She requisitioned it for me and many years later I was taking it to the Roxy with the idea of wearing it on stage as the compere. Listen – I wasn't normally cross-dressing (well, come to think of it – there was this girlfriend …). But this was the Seventies and tonight I felt dangerous. Well, as soon as Sensible spotted the dress he wanted to wear it. This saved me the embarrassment of actually donning said garment and he liked it so much he went and got his own. For the Eater set I'd also made up an EMI sign, which got burnt on stage (in memory of the Pistols' sacking). Eater got a full page article in one of the music papers and a caption read 'They think the Pistols are boring old farts!' Eater freaked when they saw it and claimed their words had been taken out of context. John took exception to this comment though, and one night when Andy Blade stayed over at Nora's – the mother of Ari Up of the Slits – John and some of his cohorts apparently terrorised him. Someone hit him over the head with a brick or something equally heavy – someone else, maybe another Eater guy, said it was boots with steel toe-caps that were thrown – and then Rotten and co burnt Andy's records in the middle of the room. To give him his due, John rang me and apologised – kind of. Anyway, the next time Eater played the Roxy, John got on stage and announced "Eater – the band who think the Sex Pistols are boring old farts and who plan to take over – I don't think!"

In general I think the Pistols camp appreciated Eater. We had made a point of giving them all promo copies of the single. Malcolm also seemed to take an interest in them and checked them out a few times at the Roxy. He thought that as they were so young it might take a little longer for them to make it. Maybe three years or so – if we could keep them together that long. He thought Dee Generate was one of their greatest assets.

We stuck Eater on the road and some very hairy situations evolved. In these early days, there weren't that many Punk venues, so you'd take what you could get. Often they'd find themselves playing to people twice their age and fights and brawls would ensue. You see the clubs would have no idea what they were getting. Imagine if you were a middle-aged man taking the missus out for a meal and a dance to the local club, and there were these loud, young upstarts on stage screaming "Why don't you get raped? Go get fucked!" People would complain to the management, who'd try to turn them down and then off – but they'd refuse to leave the stage. So bouncers would try to throw them off, then their mates would jump up and start punching the bouncers, who'd chase them round the club and eventually the band would get physically thrown out, equipment and all. Of course, they wouldn't get paid and the only way they could get home was to sell records outside the club to a few young punters who actually got off on what they did. I remember a time when Andy Blade threw a full pint of beer over the jeering front rows of hecklers. These guys looked like rugby players and soon they were storming the stage for revenge. The band always had an escape route in mind for such occasions and miraculously no one was seriously hurt. Their weird sense of humour would often get them out of trouble …

Eater were the first UK Punk band to play across Europe. Somehow we got them a gig in Belgium. They played two nights in a new club which was packed with young kids. The first night no one knew what to expect and just looked on in amazement. Eater soon showed them the ropes and, high on duty free booze, jumped and gyrated all over the place. The next night, the same crowd was back – but they'd been punked. They'd cut their hair, ripped their clothes and jumped up and down on the nice comfy seats. From their dressing room, Eater administered booze to the crowd and a wild night was had by all. When we came to get paid, we were also handed a bill for the damage to the seating!

On this trip, a young lady by the name of Ruth Lowe was travelling with us – she was my new lover. Ruth was the manageress of Riverside studios, Chiswick. This is where I first met her when I overdubbed and mixed Side A of what became the original Spunk set. Since then I'd been using the studio a lot and Eater's second single *'Thinking of the USA'* plus

'No Brains' was recorded there. After our first meeting, I next bumped into Ruth at the Roxy and we left together in a purple mini car lent to me by my ex-girlfriend Camelia (while she was away on holiday). We planned to go back to Caruzo's flat in Muswell Hill. I was looking after it for him with members of Eater, while he was on holiday. Since we had to go through Camden, Julien Temple blagged a ride with us. After we dropped Julien off, she invited me back to her flat in Holland Park instead and ,several weeks later, I was moving in, piano and all. She was a great hostess and we entertained Tony Parsons, Julie Burchill, Eater, Malcolm and many more there. Parsons and Burchill came separately, mainly to hear the Spunk tapes, although their visits overlapped by about ten minutes when they exchanged polite conversation. Did they get together over Spunk?

Parsons had his shopping bag full of sulphate with him, something you rarely saw him without in those days ...

BBC2, at this point, broadcast the strangest meeting imaginable – between plummy TV toff Derek Nimmo and the Sex Pistols. He arrived at Westwood and McLaren's 'Seditionaries' shop in the World's End, Chelsea to be casually confronted by Westwood, Sid Vicious, Johnny Rotten, Tracey O'Keefe and a brace of BBC cameras.

Transcript:
John: "Oh, hello, Mr Nimmo."
Vivienne shows DN some mohair and string jumpers.
DN: "They're cardigans you can see through are they? Or woollies?"
VW: "Erm, these restrict your arm movements somewhat."
DN: "So you're really caught right down there in bondage. Well, what actually, what's actually wrong with what I'm wearing?"
John: "They make you look so bloody boring I cannot believe it."
VW: "It's a question of how you feel. The point is to change yourself.
DN: "But why? Why does one have to change?"
VW: "'Cause then you'll feel great."
DN: "Do you think?"
VW: "Well I heard, I'd like to see."
Nimmo comes out of shop as a punk complete with one half of his mouth daubed with crude lipstick. He starts to interview people on the streets.
DN: "Are you a punk rocker, madam?"
OAP: No I'm not, I like old-time dancing.
Kid: (about ll) "Do you think I'm mad?"
DN: "Who's mad"

Kid: "You!"

DN: "Me mad?"

Kid: "Yeah! Look!" (points at DN's bondage trousers).

West Indian youth: "It's not me, but I wouldn't wear it. It's really stupid man. The music's alright."

Jack the Lad: "I think you look a bit of a poof."

Back in the TV studio Nimmo turns to Shirley Conran.

DN: "Now there, Shirley, I took your advice and became, for a few moments, a punk rocker. What are they trying to do?"

SC: "Well, they're trying to look individual and outrageous. I mean the whole thing in that particular shop is based on bondage. They're into straps and rubber goods."

Ronnie Corbett: (laughs) "I don't think the music's awfully pretty either, have you heard the music … ?"

CHAPTER FIFTEEN

JUNE 1977

GOODBYE RUTH

Life with my girlfriend Ruth started getting a bit rough. She wanted this open type relationship, but I guess I wasn't that evolved. One night I made some crass comment about the washing up and she turned nasty and threw me out. I wandered the streets and soon found myself in a phone box speaking to Lesley, an old flame from Birmingham. We arranged to meet up in London the following weekend, which was a bank holiday as well as being Jubilee week.

The problem was that, by the time she arrived, Ruth and I had kinda made up. Lesley rang me at Ruth's from Victoria coach station and I – like a geek – asked her to go back to Birmingham. "You're going to be in the way," I remember saying with all the subtlety my twentysomething self could muster. She broke down on the phone, so I had to pick her up and take her back to Ruth's. She ended up pretty cool about it and soon we were all down at the Speakeasy and getting along just fine.

The next day, Ruth went out and left us alone on purpose. She owed me one at least. As my parents were on holiday, I decided to do a runner and took Lesley there. What a cad! After a few days of nuptial bliss, we went off to a gathering at Caruzo's Stoke Newington flat. The occasion was a Japanese special day (coincidentally this flat was just a few doors down from where Phil Strongman now lives, like Caruzo, he has connections to Japan). When Lesley and I arrived, who was there but Ruth. Caruzo had thought it was a good idea and insisted she came along.

That same evening, Eater were at the Hope and Anchor and we all planned to go down. It was a bit embarrassing having two 'girlfriends' at the venue simultaneously, especially as one of them was starting to get steaming drunk. Then I got a message that there were three German girls upstairs hoping to see me. It was a 'holiday romance', Siggy, and her friends who were over for a long weekend to check out the London scene again. I bought them all pints, had a chat then sloped back to Lesley's side.

Next Glen turned up pissed and Ruth pounced on him. She was sorted for the night. Siggy's friends thought it was all a bit loud and wild, so they all left.

Eater put on a blinding show and suitably impressed the Japanese record company representative who'd come to check them out. We then decided to stage a bit of self-promotion. The Tokyo A&R guy was staying at a flash hotel near Marble Arch and we had scheduled a little trip for him through Hyde Park and on to the legendary Kings Road. We'd got our poster mafia man, Tommy the Pill, to concentrate most of the Eater posters in this area. We also conscripted certain friends and family to be present along the route, dressed in punk gear with 'Eater' painted on their backs and wearing Eater badges. We even gave a select few spray cans to graffiti Eater slogans as we passed. It was all run like a military operation, with precision timing.

'Exaggerate to get noticed!' was the rule of the day. As Mister Music-Japan left his hotel he saw an extremely young punk of 12 or so, stroll up to the wall opposite and spray 'Eater' all over it (this was Symeon, Caruzo's brother). The name Eater cropped up a hundred times more that day and the whole operation was a great success.

Leee Childers, the Heartbreakers' boss, took a special interest in Eater. He had a very flamboyant manner and they could never work out if he was gay or not. To be on the safe side, they would sleep fully clothed when they stayed at his place.

He used to design amazing one-off fliers for their gigs. When they played Dingwalls, his old mate Lou Reed who was gigging in town, came down after his show, just in time to see Eater's gig. I noticed John Peel there as well. Eater did a few songs of Lou's, including 'Sweet Jane' and 'Waiting for My Man'. They did them about three times the original speed. Leee commented that Lou liked the show so much that he stayed to the end, which was rare for him. Eater's singer Andy was over the moon and plucked up enough courage to approach the man. He gave me his camera and went up to Lou and asked for a light. Lou stood up to light Andy's cigarette – Andy didn't really smoke – and I snapped a perfect shot of the event. Andy had the photo made into a badge, which he wore with pride for months after.

The timing for the release of 'God Save the Queen' was perfect, although it was never planned that way. Apparently the song was not consciously written for Jubilee year. It should have been released around

March on A&M but because of the way things went with Virgin, it came out 2 weeks before Jubilee day. It went straight in the charts and ended up at No. 1 (except in the chart the BBC used).

It was banned by the Beeb and just about every other pseudo-respectable station. Top of the Pops and WH Smiths tried to ignore it by leaving a blank at the No. 1 spot. It was all so pathetic. The dailies were making a big thing out of the lyrics. "SEX PISTOLS CALL THE QUEEN A MORON".

The group were being snubbed by certain sections of society. They couldn't play anywhere. To celebrate Jubilee day Malcolm organised an alternative party on a boat on the Thames. The boat, by the way, was named "The Queen Elizabeth II".

Tony Parsons called me to arrange to meet in a bar near our port of departure. Although he had been officially invited, he was apprehensive, due to Glitterbest's hostility towards him. He wrote some negative article apparently – which may have been the reason he was now seeking my comradeship. He'd also brought along a huge bag full of sulphate and was soon freely passing it round.

Admittance to the party was by invitation only and many disappointed people were left on dry land. As the boat pulled out, I remember seeing certain members of The Slits leap from the quay side onto the boat. Dangerous but effective. This was going to be a special adventure. While all England celebrated 25 years of Lizzie's rule, we would be going up and down the Thames on a boat full of good booze and food. The band were going to give a rare performance later, meanwhile we set about getting into the party spirit.

Within no time nearly everyone on board seemed to be pretty out of it. A few more hours of merry-making ensued, then Sophie gave the band instructions to go and play. A stage draped in Union Jacks had been erected on deck.

Everyone became very excited and lots of people pushed to the front, obstructing the view for the others.

As we passed under Westminster Bridge and the Houses of Parliament came into view, the band struck up with 'God Save the Queen'. The boys were loud!

Everyone went wild. Then a camera came flying through the air, followed by a bloody-nosed cameraman. No one seemed to know who he was, but he must've got in someone's way. Malcolm instructed the boatman to turn around and start circling outside the Houses of

Parliament while the band played 'Anarchy' and 'God Save the Queen'. It was a marvellous moment of British history.

Malcolm kept saying to me – "Look if we pull a little closer, we could climb over the wall and we'd be inside in a flash."

"But then what are we gonna do, and what if we're arrested ?" I asked.

"Just think of the adventure, think of the publicity," was his reply.

But before he could convince me any further, a police launch pulled alongside. They were shouting through loud hailers at us but no one could hear them above the noise of the band.

A few members of the party made faces and V signs at them. Was it because we were dangerously close to the Houses of Parliament that we'd attracted this police escort? Soon another three launches were alongside and we were being ordered back to shore. The captain complied and when we arrived back at Charing Cross pier there was an army of SPG officers waiting for us.

"Come on off, the party's over!" they shouted through loud hailers. I didn't want to get off. I was having a good time and could see no reason why it had to stop.

One of the Slits got on the drums and started banging them in defiance of their orders. Jah Wobble and some others started throwing cans at the law and that was it – they stormed the boat and started dragging people off.

Wobble quickly sat down next to me and made like we were having an intense conversation until an officer came and demanded that we leave. I made some protest about having been asked onto the boat by a certain person and refusing to go unless that same person asked me to. I got a fist in my balls for my efforts.

Branson was frantically trying to calm things down on the quay side as everyone was being dragged off. I don't know what Malcolm said to the police but they suddenly had him up against the embankment wall and knocked the living daylights out of him. It was horrible to see those ten six foot bobbies senselessly attack him with such ferocity. Everyone started screaming at them to leave him alone. Ted Carroll started taking down their numbers until he was threatened with arrest.

The Pistols were advised by someone to make a getaway using the underground.

After the 'pigs' had finished laying into Malcolm, they dragged him off to a nearby van and took him down the nick. It was a really sad sight to see.

Malcolm was helpless. He had almost had the life knocked out of him and was now being dragged off for further intimidation. Sophie, Debbie,

Tracie and Jamie Reid also got themselves arrested – probably because they were showing comradeship with Malcolm. After I had cooled down a bit and finished shouting at the police, one of them pointed at me, as if to say 'shall we arrest him?' With a stomach full of booze and a pocket full of drugs, I quickly straightened up, jumped in my car, which was conveniently close and disappeared into the night.

Driving off, I noticed how the city seemed ablaze with celebrations. Did anyone really know what they were celebrating? Jubilee fever had caught hold and tonight it was at its peak. If all these painted faces around me had just seen what I had, I don't think they'd feel much like celebrating.

I pulled into the Kensington Hilton, grabbed a drink and started phoning the press. No one was interested, not one single journalist. No news staffer would even chat about the fact that Britain's biggest new rock group had had their party attacked by the police and that their manager had been brutally assaulted and arrested – suddenly the 'God Save the Queen' lyrics about a fascist regime took on a new level of meaning.

Malcolm never talked about what happened to him that night. I guess he'd rather forget …

Several weeks after this, one of the music papers ran an article on indie labels and they'd printed the phone number and address of the flat where I was now staying – on my own. One night, very late, a call came through from some very depressed stranger. They rambled on about how they felt like ending their life all the time. I listened and listened and then said something like, "Listen man, life's a fucking miracle you know. How could you think of ending it? Aren't you interested in what tomorrow brings?" At this they became very angry. "Don't call me 'maan', you fucking hippy. We're gonna get you. We know where you live. We're gonna throw acid in your face, you bastard!" Then he hung up. The worst thing was his total conviction – he sounded like he meant it. He also sounded like he might just know me. I was terrified in the flat on my own, so the next morning I invited Eater over for supper and support. That night we surrounded the house with milk bottles and slept with knives under our beds.

I had made friends with some locals in the Brownswood pub on the corner. A few started coming round and I gave some of them guitar lessons and a few Sex Pistols t-shirts. After the phone call – so that I would know it was them calling round for me, rather than the acid-wielding punk psycho – we devised a special signal. "Come on out Goodman you bastard, we're gonna kill you!" was the password (just my sick sense of humour again). When Caruzo returned from Japan I told him about the crank phone call, but forgot to tell him about my new mates from the pub and our coded call-sign.

While I was out they called round. Thump, thump on the door. "Come on out Goodman, we're gonna fucking kill you!" Obviously Caruzo thought these were the loonies who made the threatening phone call, so in his usual fearless and reckless manner, he confronted them on the doorstep. They tried to explain, but he chased them off. The matter was finally resolved when I took him down the pub to meet the lads and we all had a good laugh.

Steve and I worked out some
great guitar parts and by the
time we had six or more layers
on, it sounded very powerful.
The engineers objected to me
overloading their mixer again
to obtain that over-the-top
distortion I so liked. I
assured them that EMI
would pay for any damage
that might occur, so they
reluctantly agreed.

CHAPTER SIXTEEN

JULY 1977

THE LABEL MOVES TO DAWES ROAD, FULHAM

Our first Label single was something of a success and we soon set about recording a follow-up and looking for more bands. With the cash flowing, we bought Eater some decent equipment, a van and a PA. And we took a lease on a shop-cum-flat in Dawes Road, Fulham, yer poor man's Chelsea. I started converting the basement into a rehearsal room cum studio space and we took on a young lady called Sarah as our secretary. I think I first met her at a Pistols gig at the Nashville and she'd been a friend of Steve and Paul's for some time. She had also played bass in a band with Sid Vicious called The Flowers of Romance. They used to rehearse at his place, but I don't think they ever actually gigged or recorded.

One morning Sarah came in quite upset. The night before she'd been at Sid's and this cute little kitten – have you ever met a kitten who wasn't? – pissed in his bed, so he hung it on a hook on the back of his door, casually killing it. Impressed? I wasn't!

So, from The Label stable, Caruzo and I attempted to expand our operations. Thanks to our webweaving skills, Eater had a pretty full date sheet and the orders kept rolling in. But with every new indie release, the slice of the pie got smaller and smaller, and eaten up by more and more people. We could and did, just make more pies until one day we over-baked and they all went mouldy on the shelf – but that part of the story is yet to come.

CHAPTER SEVENTEEN

AUGUST 1977

THE TRUTH ABOUT
THE 'MOORS MURDERERS' BAND

It's Summer 1977 and Ari Up's last day at Holland Park Comprehensive School, a huge, modern, controversial, forward thinking, educational establishment, catering for the local youth aged 8 to 16. As proof of their liberal and experimental attitude, they have allowed Ari to give a performance with her new band the Slits in the main hall. All 2,000 kids have been invited.

Ari Up happens to be the daughter of Chris Spedding and Nora (subsequently Mrs 'Rotten' Lydon). Chris I'd never really met, although we'd both produced the Sex Pistols. Nora I'd met at the Roxy and Sex Pistols' rehearsal rooms in Denmark Street. A very kind woman who became a sorta 'older sister' to many wayward young Punks. I'd been booked to supply my PA system – the same one the Sex Pistols used to hire.

The party itself was a bizarre scenario with nine year olds dancing with teenagers and kids running riot, having the time of their lives. GLORIOUS SUMMER HOLIDAYS HAVE ARRIVED! It took me back to my last day at school in 1967, when my band Frinton Bassett Blues gave a concert in the main hall, which up to that point had been divided in two – girls one end, boys at t'other. The next term they were going comprehensive, and that concert was a taster of things to come …

Back to 1977 and Holland Park. There was a support band who I assumed were friends of the Slits. They had a singer dressed in black leather calling himself Steve Strange. I also remember one female musician, who turned out to be Chrissie Hynde. The other female could have been Patti Paladin. They had a certain 'first gig' quality about them, their sound being somewhat chaotic and the lyrics unintelligible.

I couldn't believe it when they announced themselves as The Moors

Murderers. That really was controversial, to put it politely. I had lived through the time of that gruesome event and could still recall the darkness it brought to my own childhood. To protect me, my mum would remove any Moors Murderers tabloid sensationalism from the papers once she'd read it herself.

After the show, Steve Strange came up to me at the mixing desk and confirmed the band's name. I'd heard right – it was as I thought. We got talking though. It turned out that they had this song called 'Free Hindley'. They'd just performed it but I hadn't noticed. He had my interest – what was the motive behind it? Steve tried to explain. He felt that it was hypocritical of the government to automatically consider other child murderers for parole after a certain length of time, while ignoring Moors Murderer Hindley.

Being a high profile case, I believe he felt they were just pandering to public demand. We also discussed change and to what level people can achieve it.

Steve wanted to record his 'Free Hindley' song with me producing. I made two suggestions:

1. To show he is not condoning murder, he should create a balance. Why not record the Ten Commandments to music, for the B-Side? You know, drop some acid in the studio, really get into it man! He liked the idea.

2. Talk to Lord Longford, he's been visiting Hindley in prison and is campaigning for her release. He liked that idea as well.

Steve wanted to rehearse in my basement in Fulham and wanted me to produce his song. I said I'd think about it.

I rang Vivienne Westwood, who knew Steve Strange and Chrissie Hynde. Vivienne suggested that the Queen was, in effect a murderer too, as she had signed death warrants. But after much soul searching I decided I didn't want to do it, and the Moors Murderers went ahead and recorded it themselves without me. They rang me from the studio and played me a very tripped-out version of the Ten Commandments. Steve also rang me later and said he'd had some very interesting conversations – and a long lunch – with Lord Longford.

The following Saturday morning, Caruzo and I had just returned from the café when our flatmate Dave Fowle announced that two journalists had been round looking for the 'Moors Murderers'. He told them that he "didn't know that they'd escaped," and suggested they come back later.

What's going on I wondered. I was sitting at my desk working, when four leather-clad beings, with pillowcases over their heads trundled down the back steps. I opened the back door. "It's me, Steve. I've got the News of the World interested in the single, they wanna do an interview and I needed somewhere to do it – so if you don't mind?" Well, it was a bit too bloody late now, so in they trundled. I believe Chrissie Hynde and Nick Holmes (Eater's roadie) were two of them. Nick apparently played drums on the 'Free Hindley' recording.

The two journalists returned and an interview took place in my office. I sat in the corner in amusement whilst the journos offered them ever increasing amounts of money to remove their hoods for a photo. It got into four figures, but the band wouldn't comply. One of the journalists turned to me, "Who are you then?" I informed him I was the Sex Pistols' producer and went on to explain my involvement – or rather lack of it – in the record.

The next day, on the front page of the News of the World there was the headline 'How Could They Be So Cruel?' and I was incorrectly named as 'the man behind the record' which was total bollocks. I should have sued them then and there for libel but I was a stoned hippy with little resources.

Months later, I spoke with some solicitors but they felt it had passed its 'sell by' date so I put it all down to experience.

I remember hearing an acetate of the two recordings 'Free Hindley' and 'The Ten Commandments', possibly played to me by Nick Holmes, the drummer. Not long after that, I heard there was an ad in the back of Melody Maker or NME for the sale of ten Moors Murderers acetates, at £10 each I believe. I seem to remember Malcolm bringing that ad to my attention. Anyway I didn't buy one, I'd heard it once and that was enough.

Years later, going into a record store in San Francisco, I saw a sign offering thousands of dollars for one. That was the only time I wished I'd grabbed one, when I had the chance.

Recently, I came across a reference to the Moors Murderers band in Steve Strange's so-called autobiography, where he claims that the original idea for the band – and the record – was mine. That is totally wrong as his publishers have since admitted (all reprints of his biography have had that inaccurate paragraph deleted).

CHAPTER EIGHTEEN

SEPTEMBER 1977

IN McLAREN'S LAIR

One Saturday, Malcolm invited me round to his flat for a 'serious chat'. I think he wanted to let me down gently over the fact that they hadn't chosen one of my productions for the B-side of "Holidays In The Sun". I felt somewhat nervous about being in such intimate confines with him, so I set up a situation whereby it was convenient to have Caruzo along with me. Basically we were on our way to check out a new mixing desk afterwards.

Malcolm greeted us with the words, "Welcome to 'Shanty Town!'" and he wasn't entirely joking. It was a 1950s built council flat just off Clapham Common. I imagined that he wasn't short of a few bob by then but you wouldn't have guessed it by his furnishings. I noticed the table in the kitchen was actually made out of piles of old books he was collecting. In the lounge you were confronted by the bare essentials – an old Dansette mono record player, on which was the Everly Brothers' rare single 'Gone Gone Gone' (I thought I'd bought the only UK copy of it way back in 1964). It then first occurred to me that he might already be researching material for a swan song recording for Sid or the Pistols ...

There were comfortably shabby armchairs and a very clean double bed and duvet. The bed was where Malcolm spent much of his time, relaxing and holding court. All the way round two walls was a work top and I could imagine eight or nine sewing machinists sitting there, knocking out clothes for the his and Vivienne's SEX shop.

The flat was on the third floor with pleasant views from the window of these big old oak trees in the rear garden. Their branches brushed the panes and I noticed many little pots of oak seedlings neatly arranged on shelves (I had a dream that night about Malcolm and Vivienne driving out to the country with a car full of baby trees – they selected a suitable spot for each one and planted it, and I thought, 'Wow, how nice of them to enhance the beauty of our countryside!') I read an article later that said you could buy a piece of land relatively cheaply without planning permission, then plant oak trees which would be worth a small fortune in 60 to 70 years' time. This is probably the sort of investment one would make with one's children's interests in mind. He also had various Japanese paintings and prints mounted on the walls, which looked somewhat out of place. He said he had a liking for them.

Malcolm's son Joe Corre came into the room. He was only about ten or eleven but had a mature persona. Joe politely said hello, then went off to make himself dinner before going out to play with his friends.

While we were there, Malcolm spent a lot of time on the phone. "Oh, it's Bingheimer calling from the States. He wants to do a feature on the Pistols," he called over from the phone, anxious not to exclude us completely from the transatlantic conversation he was enjoying. He broke out in roars of laughter several times. That was one of the marvellous things about Malcolm – he was always interesting company and could make you feel extremely good in his presence (if he chose to, that is).

One SEX customer who Malc was later to manage was Adam Ant – Adam was a client of ours at The Label too. He was sorta managed by Jordan, the SEX shop manageress (when Vivienne wasn't around). We did the PA for Adam at a gig in Barbarellas, Birmingham. He was a great hit with the girls, but I wasn't sure about Jordan coming on stage towards the end and singing.

Adam was a very well spoken lad who squatted in a lovely old alms cottage behind the Three Kings pub in Stoke Newington. He was kind enough to lend me his amp and fuzzbox for an Eater gig at the Vortex. Unfortunately, the amp got a knob broken and someone nicked the fuzzbox. I should have replaced and fixed it there and then, but I was a bit skint. I promised to sort it out but before I could, I got a phone-call from the Ants to see if they could borrow my trusty old Nichols bass amp for their gig that night at the Nashville. How could I refuse? Apparently their guitarist, Marco Pirroni needed it. I'd worked with Marco before, when he performed with Siouxsie at her first gig at the 100 Club, where Sid played drums and they did a 15 minute medley of 'The Lord's Prayer' and 'Deutschland Deutschland Uber Alles' – a sublime moment in musical history – captured on my 4 track Teac and then wiped due to tape shortage! Needless to say, my Nicols amp was never returned. Someone later claimed to have seen it in Marco's attic.

CHAPTER NINETEEN

DECEMBER 1977

EATER & PISTOLS
MEET IN HOLLAND

A van pulls up outside Label Records. We load in our gear and Eater and I get driven to Amsterdam. We're put up by this nice chap who has a warehouse full of records. We all share the attic room and have our own bar. Someone's kindly left a big piece of very strong dope on the mantelpiece. The house is amazing and was built with original 18th century tools. We're right on the canals which are frozen solid. Every other day or so we take the van and navigate to some gig or other. Most are youth clubs and they are very cool.

They pay handsomely and they look after you well. At one we meet a DJ who informs us that the Pistols are playing 200 kilometres down the road tomorrow. We all go apart from Ian 'Wally' Woodcock (Eater's bass player).

This Pistols' gig is in a huge aircraft hanger and over 2,000 people have turned up. There seem to be a lot of interested, English-speaking people, probably workers abroad. We look for the band but there's no sign of them. The support band comes on stage. They're punky – and Dutch – and have a girl singer. They can't get started until someone switches their mics on. After ten minutes it seems obvious to me that no one's there to do it, so I climb up the PA tower and appoint myself in charge of the mixer. After a few songs I thought I had them sounding pretty good. Half way through their set Boogie arrives and taps me on the shoulder.

"What! Did Malcolm send for ya?" Boogie asks in mildly outraged tones (he was the Pistols' new sound man).

"No" I said, "I'm just helping out – you're late."

"Ah – that was Malcolm's idea, but looks like you've fucked that up."

I left the mixer and Boogie to it.

Backstage the Pistols had just arrived. It was a different vibe now Sid was in the band. Sid immediately ripped me off over a dodgy currency deal and then started laying into me for 'bootlegging' tapes of 'his' band. As if he was even in the band then. Sid claimed Malcolm had started this rumour, but I know he knew better. Malcolm looked a little nervous and changed the subject. I wasn't made to feel terribly welcome. You'd think that seeing an old buddy this far from home they'd be overjoyed, but this wasn't the case.

Malcolm was evasive and told me to leave him alone, he wanted to watch the band in peace. The band didn't seem too keen to go on stage though.

Apparently they hadn't sound-checked and it sounded like they hadn't tuned up either. This was the first time I really had a good chance to observe the band with Sid. They sounded less proficient to me. They had lost the tightness they had with Glen and the live tapes show it. Sid looked great though and he still had time to improve. Steve had all these new amps but it didn't sound as good to me as his trusty old Fender Twin Reverb.

The guys in Eater and I made our way to the side of the stage to get a close up view of the show. We were right next to Sid who seemed delighted to perform to us. The crowd were motionless. They'd yet to discover the Pogo.

The 'Pogo' – as all of you who've danced it will know – is great fun and good exercise for ageing limbs. It promotes physical contact and self-expression. The story goes that one Harley Street quack once prescribed the Pogo for his patients' depression. It worked a treat!

I went out in the hall and made my way to the front of the stage. I wanted to gee the band up. I felt a sudden urge to go mad. I had just looked round at all the zombies behind me. Imagine 2,000 people all facing the same direction, absolutely motionless, with about two feet distance between them.

John and I glanced at each other. We had been in this situation before. I was the spark that could light the fire. In a fit of gay abandon I leaped right in the air, I bumped into someone and they too started dancing. Soon there were about 10 of us at the front leaping up and down. The guys in Eater could see what was happening and came racing down to join us. I went running through the crowd grabbing people's ties as I went. This was all they needed to spark them off. Suddenly the whole crowd was ablaze with pogo fever. I fanned the fire for a while to make sure it wouldn't die down, then took a well-needed drink at the bar whilst viewing the spectacle I'd been instrumental in instigating. The band was playing better now and moving about a lot more.

162

They did a surprisingly short set and no encores. Before we had another chance to chat with them they were ordered out the back door to a waiting coach. Malcolm explained that all the time the band were in the hall his insurance was liable for any damages. Malcolm made a comical sight poking his head round the exit doors for a last look before closing them behind him.

We stayed with our DJ friend for the night and sat up late listening to a three hour long interview Rotten did for radio. He sounded very out of it.

He talked endlessly about religion, politics etc … In my drugooned state he sounded very prophetic. I wish I had a copy of it to listen to again.

Apparently on the way back Sid was strip-searched at Dover. When they shone a torch up his arse, out gushed a stream of diarrhoea. "Sorry," he said, "must have been something I ate …"

The Pistols were going to play Brunel University back in London I was told in confidence some weeks later. It was to be the start of their first and last UK tour with Sid. A secret tour. So I went along to see them – en route I drove past Jaf vans where the 'Sex Pistols Saga' had started for me some 18 intense months before. The main Brunel bouncer was the stepfather of Eater's Dee Generate and he squeezed me in along with a few other ticket-less punters. The gig itself was awful, though. The band sounded rough, Sid went out of tune, while the pogoing in front of the stage had mutated into 'moshing', a more aggressive type of pushing, grabbing, kicking and punching. Several six foot bullyboys armed with flagons of cider kept leaping into the mosh-pit and dishing out some seriously nasty punches to the innocents around them. Noses were getting broken and eyes blackened left, right and centre.

Two of the vans selling t-shirts outside had their lights smashed that night. They were nearly turned over later when the atmosphere turned even darker. I'd been up and awake for almost three days, taking blues – a chalky type of speed pill – and I was really freaked out by the menace of it all. During this concert, I felt I'd lost the thread of life and then found it again, albeit now a different colour. That was the last time I saw them play – for almost twenty years.

THE ROCK 'N' ROLL SWINDLE SOUNDTRACK LP

As I've already mentioned, I managed to record all of the Swindle's 1976 songs at the EMI Anarchy Sessions and no one outside the band really knew about them at the time. As the Pistols had more or less disbanded, I thought it was time to break news of their existence to Malcy who was trying to find more music for the Swindle. He seemed delighted and rushed off to the studio to check them out.

In the can was 'Doncha Gimme No Lip Child', '(I'm Not Your) Stepping Stone', 'Whatcha Gonna Do About It', 'Road Runner', 'Johnny B. Goode', 'Substitute' plus a half-hearted stab at the Creation's 'Through My Eyes'.

Also there were about a dozen versions of 'Anarchy' along with many other takes of their own songs that had already been re-recorded for Bollocks.

Mind you, when I heard them again they sounded fresh and ballsy – I'm not sure what happened to these multitrack tapes after I finished work on them. I know they went back to London with Steve and Paul and I presume they were returned to Malcolm at some point. It would be great to get my hands on them again someday, just to spend some time on them and at least get them mixed so they can be heard.

The tracks that were selected for the Swindle album needed working on and knocking into shape. Steve, Paul and I had the task of doing it, which is how we ended up in Rockfield Studios in the Wye Valley.

I already had a Rockfield connection. You see, by then I'd built up quite a collection of productions, the Pistols, Eater, Front, The Maniacs, The Users... this portfolio was impressive enough to attract a contract to produce Swiss experimental punk band Expo for CBS – sort of Talking Heads meet the Clash. I had produced their album down at Rockfield Studio. It was cut in a week and I got paid £1,000 plus expenses, plus a royalty – which wasn't bad going for 1978. We took down sound engineer Glyn Mathias who worked at Berwick Street Studios and a spiffing, spliffing time was had by all. When we finished mixing it, the band wrote on the studio wall; "Dave Goodman is a great big harmonised phenomena". How cute.

Anyway, to celebrate the completion of the Expo album, I attempted to organise a big weekend party at the studio as a promo for the band – at CBS's expense. I invited lots of mates down, including the Banshees and Eater, but Expo's CBS representative got cold feet and fucked off back to London leaving me to sort out the mess and cancel the invitees (Expo felt annoyed about their label's lack of bottle and later abused Swiss CBS mightily, launching a 'No CBS' campaign complete with t-shirts and badges – the CBS staff retaliated with a 'No Expo' campaign, firing the band – and as CBS were the only Swiss label then, I've not heard of the band since. Pity, cos they were fucking brilliant).

After many frantic phone calls to the beautiful Sophie, I managed to narrow the new party guest list down to just Steve and Paul. As I still had the studio booked for a few more days, it was decided that we would work on tarting up the 'Wessex Out-takes' as mentioned above. Malcolm also wanted me to help them finish off these new songs they'd been working on, entitled 'Silly Thing' and 'Here We Go Again'. He kept singing the chorus to me over the phone adding this "Now-e-ow-e-owo-e-ow" line on the end.

"It's a hook Dave, a solid gold hook ... make it so."

"I've got it Malcolm, consider it done."

The boys arrived in Steve's newly acquired, untaxed and uninsured BMW which he'd just prised out of Malcolm. Armed with reels of tape, we sat up all night in the studio listening to what we had. As John had refused to record again for Malcolm or the band, his vocal was about the only thing we had to keep. On quite a few of the songs, we completely re-recorded the drums, bass and guitars.

When we set up 'Silly Thing' and 'Here We Go Again' they wanted to know why they hadn't been able to get a decent guitar sound down at Regent Sound, where they'd been recording. I reminded them of my old 'close mic on the amp and mic facing the flight case' trick that we'd used when I recorded them in Denmark Street. I demonstrated it again for Steve and Paul and they sat back in amazement at the sound we got.

We were pretty impressed with the Rockfield drum sound. We did the normal close miking then put a mic out in the corridor and left the door open. The toms sounded big, like atom bombs. With everything tuned and amplified we were ready to roll. It was an extremely tense moment replacing the drums on the first track as, to record them, we had to rub out the old ones. If Paul didn't get it right, then the whole track could be ruined. There was no 'undo button' in those pre-digital days! My hat off to the man – he did an excellent job.

While I had the dynamic duo there, I talked them into giving me a hand to record 'Justifiable Homicide', a song I had in mind which questioned whether the police were responsible for murdering a chap named Liddle Towers. I spent only about 10 or 15 minutes explaining the song to them back in one of the chalets we were staying in. Steve worked out the right chords for the intro whilst Paul pounded out a rhythm on the arm of a chair. I was amazed at how quickly they picked it up – real professionals.

We went over to the studio across the courtyard – we were on a farm you know – and on the way we passed The Boomtown Rats, their producer, engineers and roadies playing football in the adjacent field. They attempted to get us involved but we made our excuses "far too busy mate, maybe later". We spent the next hour or so setting up, then I got on the bass and we started jamming. Steve showed me a big brown heroin crystal that Johnny Thunders had given him … it didn't shine in my eyes. We ran over 'Justifiable Homicide' a few times while the engineer made some adjustments in the never-ending quest for absolute perfection. With everything set, we were about to start recording when a few of the Boomtown Rats ambled in (including Sir Bob Geldof).

"Right! Justifiable Homicide, take one!" And I couldn`t believe it. This was the first time we had ever played the song together but it sounded like we'd been doing it for ages. We started leaping around and the adrenaline really flowed. We could see the smiles on the faces of the Rats, who were also jumping about in the control room. We put down three or four takes just for good measure.

It was a real pleasure to play with Steve and Paul. They put so much energy into their playing. We went and listened to the playback. The first version sounded so good we didn't bother listening to the rest. The Rats patted us on the back then went off to their own session leaving us to ours. I worked right through the night until about 10 a.m. when we had all the tracks finished. We said our goodbyes and raced back to London in Steve's black BMW.

Steve and Paul were in a hurry to get to Tracie O'Keefe's funeral – she had tragically died of leukaemia. They dropped me off at The Label headquarters in Fulham and borrowed some dark clothing from me. They seemed apprehensive about the possibility of meeting John at Tracie's wake. They tried to talk me into coming along but I declined and went off to deliver the mixes to Malcolm. On hearing the results, he complimented me on the job I'd done.

His ultimate quality test at this time was to play them on his trusty hand held mono cassette recorder, if they sounded "good on this then they sound good anywhere" and fortunately for me he was right. Having these extra tracks meant that the Rock & Roll Swindle LP had mushroomed from a short single album to a complete double.

I decided to take a copy of these tapes round to John so he could be aware of what we were up to. He only lived about two miles from me and I wanted to see his reaction to them. I was proud of my work and I guess it gave me a good reason to visit him. Since the breakdown of communication between Malcolm and himself, it made it a bit difficult for the likes of me, who sort of had their feet in both camps. I found him in on his own and he seemed genuinely pleased to see me. He kept asking if Malcolm had sent me round. It seemed important to him so I kinda went along with it.

He had been given these big Tannoy speakers, along with a large collection of reggae and dub records. When he put on the Pistols tape, he switched to headphones and sat there in silence listening intently. He never said that he didn't like it, so I took this as positive. He thanked me for bringing round the tape and asked if he could have a badge that I was wearing. It was one of my home made items and said "PURE PAP FOR NON PEOPLE" (it was my reaction to Nick Lowe's 'Pure Pop for Now People' LP title). Anyway, I gladly pinned it on him as I said my farewells and headed back to the Label HQ, while he went off to do some interviews. I came across one of them later and there's John proudly wearing my badge.

After my successful endeavours reworking the Wessex out-takes i.e. 'No Lip', 'Steppin' Stone' etc, I was given the chance to tart up 'My Way'.

Malcolm was worried that the original mix was lacking in something. I took the tapes into Berwick Street Studios where I'd worked previously, overdubbed a few instruments – crash cymbals mainly – and re-mixed it. I spent all day getting to know the track while building it up in stages. The string parts alone are classic and they attracted many compliments from the office staff. They were scored by the chap in Penguin Café Orchestra.

Malcolm had left me some notes on a fairly complicated edit where I had to mix one verse twice, each time with a different lead vocal, then splice it in place. After a few abortive attempts I managed to pull it off. Hey! I was already getting the nick-name Mr Scissors. To me it now sounded magnificent.

I called Malcolm who came down with Steve and Paul to give it a lug. With a bit of time left, I felt in the mood for attempting a lead vocal on 'Justifiable Homicide'. I guess this would have been the first time Malcolm and the boys would have really heard me sing. I put everything into it and on the second run-through, I became possessed by some punkoid spirit that took over my body and delivered what was, to me, a spine-chilling performance. I was worried that it was too OTT, but Glyn the engineer and Malcolm gave it the thumbs up.

Malcolm started getting all enthusiastic, so I hatched the idea of getting him to sing or speak something over the end. I'd never heard him sing before, but he had recently announced to me his intention of recording a few tracks for the Swindle LP so I thought, let's check him out. He was well up for it, but I soon abandoned the idea when I saw that his lack of experience might be a bit time-consuming. I regret this decision and wish that I had made more of an effort. This would have been his debut recording and I didn't even give him the chance to warm up.

Also at these sessions, I re-did Glen Matlock's bass on 'Substitute'. It had been annoying me that the original bass was a bit out of tune so I rehearsed the part and confidently recorded it in front of Steve, Paul and Malc. I'm not saying it was any better than Glen's, just a bit more in tune. The sound of it could have been a lot better if I'd taken the time to record it through an amp, but I just wanted to get it down while I had the chance.

The studio wouldn't release the tape of 'My Way' until the bill had been settled, so unfortunately the tape was delivered to Virgin too late to replace the earlier mix and, as I never got a copy, I only have the memory of how it sounded. It's lost in the EMI-Virgin vaults somewhere, like many other great recordings …

It was while Malcolm was leaving these studios that, being the inquisitive gent he is, he ventured upstairs and discovered a small indie film distributor with whom he eventually did some deal on The Great Rock 'n' Roll Swindle movie. I think Don Boyd, the guy he dealt with, was an old college mate of Glyn's – our friendly engineer in the studio below.

CHAPTER TWENTY ONE

D.G. BECOMES A PISTOL FOR A DAY AT RAMPORT STUDIOS

The next studio I shared with Sex Pistols Steve and Paul was Ramport, just south of the Thames. It belonged to the Who and had one of the loudest playback systems in the world – 12 giant JBL speakers. On the way there we stopped off in Chelsea for some charlie and blow. The task in hand was to record backing tracks to Rock Around the Clock and The Great Rock 'n' Roll Swindle. I was on bass once again.

After only a few hours in the studio we had to head back to Chelsea for more supplies. Mickey, the chap we scored from had been dealing to the stars for years. Although he couldn't play, he had an incredible guitar collection, mostly taken in hock against some rock stars' rocketing coke tab. There were a few of Keith Richards' old strats and a few Clapo axes I believe.

It was always fun to visit Mickey and his guitars, not to mention his incredible record collection. He loved the Pistols and had already invested in a dozen Spunk albums which he acquired from who knows where, but he gave me the only copy I have. We hung around long enough to get an earful of some new demo he'd been given by Muff Winwood. "What do you think of this guitar sound, guys?" Mickey asked as he played the demo of 'Sultans of Swing' for the umpteenth time. "No, never catch on, too old-fashioned," was our considered opinion – but what the fuck did we know? We got up to leave and discovered we'd nearly done all the drugs we came to buy, so Steve dipped in his pocket again and armed with a few packets of white powder and brown resin, we headed back to the studio.

Boogie had turned up with a few of Steve's amps. In no time at all, Paul and Steve were playing practical jokes on him, culminating in Paul kneeling down behind him while Steve engaged him in conversation and when he least expected it, Steve pushed him backwards over Paul. He took it well but I felt embarrassed for his humiliation and relieved that this type of relationship hadn't developed between me and the band.

After we had the backing tracks down, Steve insisted on recording guitar after guitar until he had about ten layers. They all seemed to merge into one. It sounded OK on all these monitors at mega volume but not so good on the grot boxes. Malcolm also expressed his disenchantment with Steve's overly over-layered guitar sound. He said it just didn't sound real.

SID & NANCY

Sid and Nancy were staying at the Chelsea in New York. Nancy is found dead and Sid, who is with her, is arrested on suspicion of murder. The night before Nancy was stabbed, Sid gave his most cherished leather jacket to Joe Stevens, a music journalist friend. This gave rise to the theory that the couple had made a suicide pact and that Sid wasn't able to go through with it. Another theory was that Sid may have woken up to find that Nancy had taken his share of the drugs and in a rage of uncontrollable temper, stabbed her without realising what he was doing. At one point, Sid claimed he knew nothing about it and someone must have broken into his room in the night while he was asleep and committed the gruesome act. The CIA perhaps?

Maybe not …

Sid was arrested and placed behind bars pending trial. He was put into a padded detoxification cell, which must have been hell. I remember Malcolm and the others being very concerned about him and spending hours on the phone to his lawyers in New York trying to find out what was happening. He was granted bail and Virgin promised to send the money out within a few days.

Sid was released on bail but, shortly after, he attempted suicide and was put in the psychiatric ward of Bellevue Hospital. He came out and a month later attended a further hearing where his bail was allowed to continue as long as he abided by certain conditions. He subsequently got into a fight, hurt someone and was sent back to Rikers Island prison, where he was to remain for the next couple of months.

Malcolm planned to take Steve, Paul and possibly myself out to meet him on his release. The idea was to get him in a recording studio and take his mind off things. A new Sex Pistols album of covers maybe, 'Mack the Knife', 'Mean Streets', 'I Get A Kick Out of You' – those were some of the titles on the table.

Unfortunately, he was released early and before we could get there, he was out. His mum was waiting for him and laid on a party at his new girl friend's place. At the party, his mum gave him some smack and he must have fixed up an ultra-pure, ultra strong 'hot shot' (he had previously tried to slash his wrists with a light bulb when he was in prison, but it hadn't worked). The next morning his girlfriend found him dead in bed beside her.

Malcolm later described it as "an act of God."

During this seminal year, there was still a lot of work to be done – and fun to be had. The Banshees started rehearsing in The Label basement studio and auditioned guitarist John McKay there. I think Malcolm put them onto us.

It felt good having them in the place.

I got to know an A&R man at Polydor and he came round to the studio while Siouxsie was rehearsing. Amazingly, The Banshees still hadn't been signed by anyone yet. I took him upstairs, where I had a mixer and 4 track tape machine connected to the studio two floors below. I was able to treat him to a sneak preview as they played 'Hong Kong Garden' live in the studio. It sounded great. I advised him to sign the band immediately. Within a few weeks he did and 'Hong Kong Garden' was their first single – and their first hit.

The Banshees also used our PA and van for a gig. Unfortunately, my assistant, Tommy Gargol, brought along some opium on the first night they booked us. Big mistake – we both got out of it to a frightening degree.

Things just didn't work too well and to cap it all, we ran out of petrol on the way home. We had to draw straws to decide whose task it was to find some petrol. I can't remember who drew the short straw, but it definitely wasn't me.

It was getting cold as we all huddled in the van. I remember floating off into some magical land as I fell asleep on the floor next to Siouxsie, engulfed in her sensuous aroma. I had the most vivid dreams that night, all stuff about being heroic while on some Arthurian type adventure. But we got back to London incredibly late and, understandably, the Banshees never used us again.

To be honest, I was hankering to come off the road even before the opium disaster. I'd just spent most of the last 11 years gigging and I was looking forward to a break. I needed to concentrate on some composing and recording of my own. And our rehearsal base did take a bit of maintenance.

The Members were one band who used our rehearsal facilities. I remember the first time I met them, I was in one of my mischievous moods. I walked straight in on their rehearsal and announced myself as Zeno Wagmaster, their new manager. I fired a string of commands at them, then gave them oodles of advice. I guess I was improvising in a McLarenish style.

"From now on it's us versus the world. I want you to go home and write the most controversial song ever. Take on the government, attack formalised religion – and I want you to build your own new instruments that look and sound like nothing before – and we'll all be wearing period attire from now on!"

They all stood there listening, seemingly taking it all in. When I finally couldn't keep a straight face any longer and owned up, they seemed disappointed to say the least. All you need is front – blah blah blah.

Talking of Front, they were our other Punk band on The Label. They were formed by Andrew 'Drew Blood' Lipscom, who I first met in 1974 when he was driving 'soul divas', The Flirtations, for a short spell. Well, I bumped into him somewhere and happened to mention this great new scene happening down the Roxy Club. He came, saw and was converted. He wanted to start his own Punk band and begged me to help.

He became friendly with Don Letts and shared a flat with him in Forest Hill. Now a punk, he got himself a guitar and a few musicians. He had Ben Brierly aka.Tommy Trouble on bass (who used to play in the Mancunian glam band The Arrows). Then he added John Porter – who played in Clapton's band and later produced the Smiths – and my old drummer Graham Broad.

We went down to Matrix studio to cut their debut single 'Queen's Mafia' with engineer/guitarist Andy Dalby (ex-Arthur Brown's Kingdom Come and Camel). A grand session, but subsequent press reviews thought it was all a bit too musical.

Another 'overly musical' act who supported Eater were Squeeze (who were managed by Miles Copeland in those days). This came about because both bands were booked on the same bill in some new college building near the Tower of London. When Eater and I arrived, they had already set up and sound-checked. They assumed Eater were supporting them, so I had to point out that it was the other way round. Eater were the headliners – they had more records out and were better known due to the amount of press they had received. Much heated debate ensued, until their keyboardist, one Jools Holland, agreed with our argument – and the bands played on.

One day, back at The Label, Rasta musicians Skito and Pageat walked in and told Caruzo they wanted to start their own band. They'd previously been playing as session musicians for reggae stars like Dennis Brown. Caruzo offered to lend them our studio to rehearse for a while and see what they could come up with. In no time at all, they had recruited another six musicians and the all-rasta band Tribesman was born. With the help of my trusty old 4-track Teac, we soon had an album's worth of demos, which we pressed up as a white label album.

It was at this time that the Banshees were going round places like Camden Market and the Kings Road with Nils Stephenson and their lawyer, to sniff out Banshee bootlegs and issue writs to stop them. This was a unique exercise for a Punk band, let me tell you! Anyway, previously I'd been recording bits of their rehearsals and with the help of Andy Blade, I mischievously started a rumour that I was gonna bootleg them. Nils must have taken it seriously, since I already had the reputation of a pirate due to the Pistols Spunk bootleg – but I didn't do it – honest! I wish I had . Anyway Nils came over to The Label to confront me about the supposed Banshees bootleg, only to find we're all out. However, he spots a stack of white label albums in the office. Convinced these are the bootlegs of his band he returns on Monday morning, lawyer and police in tow, writ in hand.

They burst in, slam the writ on the table and pick up one of the records.

Once they had taken it out of the sleeve they realised it was the Tribesman's demo album. We had to laugh. I think they were genuinely disappointed that we hadn't bootlegged them, but that wasn't our style.

By the end of 1978, The Label had firmly established itself among the itinerants and misfits of the tribe calling itself the Music Industry (well, the London chapter at least). Caruzo and I had been cordially invited to just about every music rag's festive celebrations. You'd find us hanging out in the punk corner next to the free drinks bar. We would devise ways to liberate any surplus complimentary refreshments from the likes of Melody Maker or NME (well, we were paying them a small fortune to advertise our products).

Although we had quite a big turnover for a little indie, we never got to see much profit. It felt like we were forever treading water just to keep afloat and cover the endless overheads. 1979 was probably our best year financially. I remember driving in our old van to the pressing plant one day and collecting over 60,000 records. I guess they were Eater singles and 12 inchers, plus Tribesman LPs, Front singles and a few other releases. From the pressing plant I took them directly to certain distribution points: Lightning, Caroline Exports, Virgin, Pinnacle and Red Star Parcel Express. By the end of a very long day, there were only a few hundred records left on board. We had managed to shift over £100,000 of vinyl in a single day. But getting paid for them was another story, which was just about to unfold.

By now there were hundreds of Punk/New Wave bands popping up throughout western uncivilisation, spewing out an endless stream of multicoloured vinyl. The kids had reclaimed music and made the major record companies somewhat redundant. For about £500 a band could sweat their hearts out for a day in some smoky little studio, then have the results pressed onto shiny coloured bits of plastic wrapped in nihilistic graffiti. These would be sold to their fans, the growing number of punkoids who were constantly demanding more 'punk junk' from their local record stores. Some of those early indie records like Stiff's 'New Rose' by the Damned, 'Spiral Scratch' by The Buzzcocks and Eater's 'Outside View' sold in their tens of thousands within weeks of their release ...

But it had, ultimately, all started with the Sex Pistols and I believe I helped the Pistols develop their sound. What I got out of it was great memories, some good friends, lots of recording experience and some dynamite tracks – a few dozen in all (not to mention all the out-takes, rough mixes, live recordings and remixes). What I didn`t get was all my royalties. You see, originally my contract was with EMI. The band got sacked and I was just about to sign with A&M when that label fired them too. So I ended up signing with the Sex Pistols' management company, Glitterbest. It was in fact my original idea. I felt I could trust Malcolm and hence Glitterbest.

Had my producer's contract been with Virgin, I would theoretically have been paid direct. Instead it all went to the Court Receivers, who were left in charge of the Glitterbest/Matrixbest accounts after the initial court case brought about by Rotten. I now became just one of the many creditors. You wouldn't believe it, the receivers are supposed to act in the interests of the creditors. That's what they`re paid for. In reality it was, I believe, a different story. They made sure the tax man got paid all right, and themselves (£5,000 a month I heard). If you happened to be one of the blokes who helped make the actual recordings you were put at the bottom of the creditors' list. Virgin, record distributors, wholesalers and shops were all making good money out of our product. They were deducting their cut at source. It doesn't seem right that I've been waiting this long to collect my producer's copyright royalties. The records have been sold so why aren't I getting paid?

CAUGHT IN COURT

Malcolm was unable to pay John his share of the record royalties since he had invested them in the film he was working on, starring the Pistols. Unfortunately John had not wanted to play ball on this project. He fell out with Russ Meyer, the director Malcolm had chosen and removed himself from the proceedings.

One day I received a call from Sophie, Malcolm's secretary, asking me to sign a sworn statement supporting Malcolm. I foolishly declined, mostly out of fear of reprisals I might attract from the 'Rotten Mafia'. If Malcolm had called me himself things might have been different. He must have felt gutted about the whole affair, although he put on a brave face. Steve and Paul, who had initially rallied round him, deserted the sinking ship and swam to the Rotten camp.

John probably relished the chance to hold Malcolm accountable and soon they were facing each other in the High Court. He admits now that he was worried that he might not have a strong case – but luckily for him, after a few days Malcolm decided to 'throw in the towel'. Malcolm felt that due to the number of witnesses and statements John had lined up, the case would go on for so long that the lawyers would end up with all the money. After the trial he said to me, "If John wants the money that badly, let him have it." With that he took off to Paris and a new scene.

John was overjoyed – and probably very relieved – that Malcolm had given in fairly easily. He appeared on the evening news that day and boasted "I've won on everybody's behalf." But it wasn't that simple.

Glitterbest's fate was now sealed though and all the company assets had to be handed over to the Court – cheque books, keys, master tapes etc. The Court had appointed Official Receivers to collect any monies due – bearing in mind that Virgin took their share at source – and to administer appropriately. The result was that the only people to receive any real money for the next few years were the tax man, banks, lawyers, courts and not forgetting the Official Receivers who paid themselves a pretty handsome fee.

The band, their producers (including myself) and the management didn't get a bean during this time. Interestingly enough, I read in the papers a while later that this Official Receiver had apparently been prosecuted for "misappropriation of funds in receivership"! All seems like some sort of legal loophole if you ask me.

Anyway, Tricky Dicky Branson took control. Virgin sold millions of Sex Pistols records worldwide without having to invest heavily in production and promotion. Thanks largely to Malcolm's skill, the band were an international phenomenon and there were Punks all over the world just waiting to get hold of the next Sex Pistols offering. And the bootlegs!

The record pirates were having a heyday pressing up re-packaged versions of Spunk or Indecent Exposure – the sound quality deteriorating with every re-pressing.

I decided something had to be done about the bootlegs and went to the Receivers to suggest that I could work on some of the official, unreleased tapes I had in my possession. There were a good three or four albums worth of some of the Pistols' finest performances (in my opinion).

The Receivers had to back me on this one, after all, they were being paid to look after the creditors' interests (including mine). I already had written proposals from various record companies interested in releasing the material. They were prepared to pay a decent advance and a damn sight better royalty than Virgin were paying. What did we have to lose?

All the Receivers could say was, "Go and talk to Virgin." Which I did – and all they said was, "Well, maybe in a few years, or when we reach the tenth anniversary."

Well, that was crap – I needed my money now. Steve, Paul and Glen were also financially destitute. They hadn't received anything from their record sales either. Glen was on the dole, Steve fucked off to the States and left a load of bills behind for Paul to sort out. Paul had just fathered a daughter and was in fear of having his phone, gas, water and electricity cut off.

Since we all needed some money now, I decided to do some short-term licensing deals on the tapes and see how it went. After all, these tapes of my productions were recorded on my equipment, well before the band had signed any management or record contract. As long as I made sure the band received their fair share there was nothing illegal about it (your honour!).

First I licensed a live album into Japan and they sub-licensed into America etc etc. For a long time, things went smoothly and we all made a bit of dosh. Then some lawyers – purportedly representing the band – threw spanners in the works and hundreds of thousands of dollars which should have come our way disappeared, apparently into some escrow black hole.

What a mess! And the bootlegs kept coming out and certain people conveniently pointed their grubby fingers at me. If I had had the balls, I could have made an absolute fortune bootlegging the Pistols – but, alas, me hearties – a pirate I am not!

I used to meet up regularly with Glen and Paul – usually when I had some royalties come in for them. We'd either meet in a pub, or go to one of our gaffs. We would listen and give feedback on one another's latest recordings.

When it came to recording at the end of the Seventies, I was one of the early pioneers of music sequencing – I'm talking pre-midi here. I had the opportunity to play around with Abba's custom-made music sequencer when it was stored at a friends' place, during a break in between concerts. It was a pretty Heath-Robinson type affair, with hundreds of switches and flashing lights, but I realised then the potential for programming your own music in almost perfect timing. I was hooked and immediately began building my own computer. Okay, it was only a Sinclair ZX81 kit for £50 – but it worked and I added a self-built 3 track sequencer.

I signed up for an Advanced Music Projects course at Goldsmiths College. As part of a team of 'boffins', I helped design a more advanced computer sequencer based on the BBC micro. We had almost completed it, software and all, when Yamaha released their 8 track dedicated computer sequencer. If we hadn't spent so much time down the pub discussing the thing, we could have beaten them to it!

Anyway – Yamaha had done it and the computer music revolution had started. Come to think of it, a couple of clever guys from New Zealand had already invented the Fairlight music workstation, but they cost about £50,000 and Yamaha had made it affordable at around £500. I went straight out and bought one and never looked back. As the technology developed, so did my love and appreciation of it.

Glen spent a week in my studio demo-ing some of his songs and he must have been impressed with the set up, because he went out and got himself a similar one. I spent some time over at his pad helping him get it together and soon he was knocking out his own recordings.

The great thing about midi-sequencing is that you get hundreds of sounds plus drum kits, all in one box. If you want a Hammond organ on a song for instance, you just turn the dial to 'Hammond organ' – you don't have to go out and hire one, drag it up the stairs and set it up, just to see if it suits the piece – like you did in the old days. I suppose the disadvantage of all this modern technology was that it gave you too many options and you could waste a lot of time going round in circles trying things out.

On one occasion Paul played me some of the recordings by his Chief of Reliefs band and asked my opinion. He admitted that the drums had been sequenced – "they used a drum machine". I couldn't believe a band with such a brilliant live drummer hadn't made the most of him. Paul said, "it saved time in the studio," but I have rarely found this to be the case.

When it came to Paul and Glen, I used to encourage them to re-form the Sex Pistols as a sure-fire way to make some money. They were kind of up for it, but felt John wouldn't be interested. John had apparently announced publicly that he would never re-form the Sex Pistols. "Get another singer then!" I'd say. I spoke to various agents and promoters and there was an offer of at least $1,000,000 if they re-formed and went on a world tour, with a televised concert from Madison Square Gardens. I was also up for helping them get a new album together. But nothing came of it.

I felt it really needed the original four members to create the sound I loved so much. By not going for it they were letting a massive opportunity slip by. It wasn't that any of them had found much success individually at that point – even Rotten's Public Image Limited were struggling financially.

After a short career with the Rich Kids, which wasn't that successful moneywise, Glen formed a whole series of bands. It was hard to keep up with the latest Matlock creation! The Philistines, The Hot Club and eventually, Concrete Bullet-proof and Indestructible or CBI for short. They featured Jackie from Doll by Doll on vocals and various drinking pals of Glen's.

On top of all this, Glen's wife Cecilia walked out on him – taking all his Sex Pistols memorabilia with her – and headed back to Oz. So Glen started to hit the bottle. You'd find him almost every night at his local.

The landlord would let him work behind the bar at lunchtime to pay off his tab from the night before. He was a loveable, cheeky drunk and only became insulting at closing times, before he passed out. Friends would carry him home and get him to bed.

Despite this there was still a window of opportunity each day, when

Glen was capable of doing some decent work in the studio. Usually between 1.00pm and 7.00pm, when he had sobered up from the previous night and not started drinking again. He got me in to produce CBI and together we cut a 12" single, *'Big Tears'* and *'Braid'* were the main tracks on it. It sounded mega and sold quite well I hear, although someone ran off with the royalties.

Shortly after this, Glen hit rock bottom financially. He wasn't receiving any Sex Pistols royalties, publishing royalties were spent, he owed the tax man and mortgage interest rates were rocketing. He had also become an alcoholic – but not for long!

Glen cleaned up his act and was soon on twelve pints of tea a day. He got busy composing and recording demos in his home studio. He soon had an album's worth of material and attracted interest from several companies. He signed a deal with Creation Records who released his first solo album, *'Who does he think he is when he's at home then?'* It was great that Glen had found his feet again – both in terms of drink, song-writing and recording.

It was during this period of Glen's recovery that I met 'Mr Charisma', Darryl Read. I think it was at Rainbow George's in Hampstead (we were celebrating John Lennon's birthday). Darryl had been an actor since his youth – in the Famous Five, Sands of the Sahara and various other children's films – and was also a drummer in a proto-punk band Crushed Butler in 1969.

He went on to help start other proto-punk groups Third World War and the Hammersmith Gorillas.

Darryl looked like a mature Bolan or Syd Barrett and was full of ideas for movie scripts. He was planning to make a film about Syd Barrett's twilight time, after he'd over-dosed on acid and been dumped by Pink Floyd.

Apparently he was kidnapped for a long weekend by an especially manic fan and locked in a studio, in the hope that he might come up with something reminiscent of his former genius.

I told Darryl the story Malcolm had told me about the time he visited Syd in his hotel and attempted to persuade him to produce the Sex Pistols (before my time). Anyway, Syd had seemed too out of it to even remember what Malcolm was doing there. Darryl lapped it up and before long, production of the film – Remember a Day – began in earnest, using my studio and home as the set for the kidnap sequences etc. He even wrote in the Malcolm scene and got Charlie Harper of the UK Subs to represent Malcolm.

During the shooting of the film, one of the crew managed to obtain an early preview tape of the Sex Pistols' upcoming feature length documentary movie, The Filth and the Fury. He gave it to me and I sat down, watched it and made a list of my productions which were included in it. It turned out to be quite a few in fact, so when the end titles rolled and I wasn't credited anywhere I was both confused and saddened (by contrast, fellow producer Chris Thomas got a nice big thank you). I immediately informed my lawyers and asked them to let the Pistols' solicitors know about the omission and ask them to rectify matters – but nothing was done. Were the band now trying to write me out of their history so they didn't have to pay me?

The twenty-five year anniversary of Punk was drawing ever closer and certain people's interest in the phenomenon were being rekindled. Articles on the Sex Pistols and Punk started to appear in the music press, giving a bit of colour and life to the mediocre norm (though I couldn't help noticing that the few pieces that talked about production either credited the band – or Chris Thomas again).

The Sex Pistols themselves started to receive all kinds of accolades, like Best Single of The Last Century – 'God Save the Queen' and best album Never Mind the Bollocks. Soon documentaries were appearing on TV, like 'Top Ten Punk Bands' and TV networks were devoting whole weekends to Punk.

Then one day – September 11th 2001, to be precise – I did a rare thing and took the radio with me to the tea house I'd built at the end of my garden. I wanted to escape from the recording session that was happening in my studio and have a quiet tea and splee with the missus. The moment I turned the radio on the devastating news came through live from New York – the Twin Towers – the first plane had struck about six minutes earlier. We sat transfixed following the news – then the second plane and finally the collapse. I spoke out loud to some higher force and begged it not to allow this event to develop into a world war. I couldn't believe it could happen and I still don't somehow. My cynical mind posited the idea that it could have been an 'inside' job. A distraction from the Enron scandal and a trigger for war. I became very frightened. I decided not to tell the musicians recording in the studio until later that day, so they could carry on working.

That night over dinner, we discussed my feelings that 'all may not be what it seems', but I think people found it too unbelievable for words.

Nevertheless, slowly, similar conspiracy theories started to come out in the alternative media as certain inconsistencies emerged.

Finally, the BBC broadcast a programme attempting to prove that it might have been an 'inside job'. But it was already too late. America and her ally, Tony Blair, were waging a war against terrorism and the first casualties were the Taliban and Afghanistan. Massive great arial bombardments against rifles. Villages were set ablaze and thousands disappeared. Innocent women and children were slaughtered through ignorance, greed and neglect. Yet the Bush-Blair regime rejoiced in their ever-increasing arrogance. An alternative profile started to emerge on George W. His family had apparently had ties with Nazi Germany, supplying them with raw materials prior to WW2 and they also had business links with the Bin Laden family. The Bush family made a great deal from oil ... I really didn't like the sound of it. It still wasn't clear if he really did win the election. Here was this arrogant Texan taking us to war over matters that to my mind, had not been sufficiently proven. Lecturing countries on democracy when he hadn't even won an election himself (well, not fairly anyway).

Once the Taliban were crushed and Bin Laden couldn't be found, interest in the Afghan war started to wane. Then Osama was apparently spotted at a wedding in the nether regions of Afghanistan and Bush was on his tail again. Shortly after that, I opened the Sunday paper and read an article entitled "Afghan Wedding Fiasco".

It described how a wedding celebration was bombed by an American plane, leaving many dead and wounded. In addition 1,000 British troops were called in and found the village in shock. Apparently it is a custom for wedding guests to fire rifles in the air in a form of offering to God at the end of a wedding. The American war plane took this as a hostile act and fired a missile into the celebration.

When I read the article I was so angered I decided to channel this energy into a song. I asked the angels for guidance and had a flash of inspiration on that Sunday morning, on the sacred spot on the Isle of Dogs, situated on a powerful ley line, in line with Greenwich Observatory and the Meridian line, where time itself starts. The spot where friends and I had danced in our raggle taggle rainbow clothes during planetary alignments. Where we had lit fires and joints on full moons, planted saplings and buried crystals during eclipses. The same spot where the British National Party were said to have held a ritual to conjure up the energy to gain them a political victory for this area (which they later lost after – I'd heard – some 'geomantic' activists had taken against them but that's another story).

The same spot where it was said Queen Elizabeth I 's magician, Johnny

Dee, held a sacrificial ceremony and made a pact – with some dark forces, no doubt – to give the British monarchy protection and enable them to go out and build their empire.

I had about three quarters of an hour to write the song, before I'd arranged to go back across the river and meet my family. Words started coming to me and when I sat down on that ancient circle they flowed.

'Wedding Day' to the chords of 'Anarchy in the UK'.

I got out my guitar and started singing them to the 'Anarchy' tune.

Perfect. I wandered down the ridge into the natural horseshoe shaped grass amphitheatre below. There were three cows in it and a lone girl. I asked if she minded me disturbing her peace? "No – go ahead," she said. I stood on the spot where I believed many a minstrel, seer, sage, poet and prophet had stood and gave a heartfelt debut rendition. At the end the girl clapped, the cows mooed and I went off to meet my destiny.

When I got home I recorded the song. The very next day shiny CD copies were sent by registered mail to the Queen, Prince Charles, Princess Anne, Princes William and Harry, Prince Edward, Tony Blair, the BBC, the Press Association, Roy Carr of IPC magazines, John Peel and various others who I thought might be interested.

The idea was for the record to raise money to build a sustainable, futuristic temple on the site of the massacre, in honour of the victims. I sat back and waited for some feedback, but instead there was stony silence.

Then things started to become a bit weird. I got a series of intimidating emails like 'cell padding', 'we want to ask you questions in a box' and 'i have some new tools that I'd like to use on you' etc ... I traced them to various anonymous addresses in Europe. I was also offered a lot of child porn and secret information on people via the internet – all of which I immediately deleted. Next, after a blizzard of clicks and buzzes, it appeared my phone was being tapped and other people who I was phoning got the same feeling. My partner Kathy got a call from America asking if she was Mrs Goodman, and when she said yes, they hung up. Do I sound paranoid?

You bet I was. I'd named the song 'Wedding Day', which I then discovered was a key code word used by Muslim terrorists. As in, the final act of a suicide terrorist – getting wed to God.

I guess I also had a bit of a reputation as a controversial record producer, producing and in some cases, writing such records as 'Anarchy in the UK' (anti-establishment), 'God Save the Queen' (anti-monarchy), 'Justifiable Homicide' (anti-police), 'Fascist Regime' (anti-apartheid),

'Land of Hope and Glory' (anti-imperialism), 'Legalise Cannabis Campaign' (anti-dope controls), 'Crying in the Desert' (anti-war), 'CND or END' (anti-nuclear weapons), 'Burning the Books' (anti-fundamentalism), 'Are You Going to Stonehenge?' (pro-New Age travellers)and 'Last Vestiges of our Autonomy' (anti-Criminal Justice Bill).

I imagine that someone in authority might have noticed my anarchist leanings before now. Quite a few of the above records had already been banned from the radio and now it was happening again. 'Wedding Day' by the Sad Pistoils (sic) seemed to have been stamped with a D Notice by the MoD.

As far as the media were concerned, they had to make out that it didn't exist in the interest of national security. My emails to the press were being diverted through some kind of black box and censored. For a few days, all emails to the music press were being held up for over five hours and vetted. I received written notification of this from my Internet Service Provider to prove it.

I'd sent a copy of 'Wedding Day' to EMI-Virgin and went to visit them the day they would have received it. I got Kathy to dress like a female lawyer in neat skirt suit, leather attache case and all, and I dressed in jolly rainbow coloured clothes, bandanna etc (more for protection than anything else really).

We arrived and just as we were about to enter the building four big, smartly dressed heavies came out and gave me the 'who the fuck are you?' look. I asked them if they worked for Virgin.

One of them said "So what if we do?"

"Well I'm from Vagina Records," I said, pushing a copy of 'Wedding Day' into his hand, "and this is going to be paying your wages."

In my rainbow colours, with an ice cream in one hand, they must simply have taken me for some flamboyant plugger who was working for the company. I gave them some stickers and a few fliers, including the one which read – "I woke up this morning and discovered which side of the bed I was dying in ..." (a parody of the 1975 Bernie Rhodes / Malcolm McLaren t-shirt).

When I set eyes on these hulks barging out of EMI, I had the strong feeling that they were ex-public school, 'rugger buggers' – MI5 goons. It occurred to me they might even have been sent round by Blair's regime to warn EMI against having anything to do with the Sad Pistoils' 'Wedding Day' single. Probably paranoia again but it felt a real possibility at the time – I kept my distance from them and didn't turn my back once. They went through a side door, into what I thought might be a mail room.

I proceeded to reception, where I encountered another heavy-looking security guard. The receptionist seemed nervous.

"We've come to see …" I named the A&R in question.

"Okay, sign in," she said "then take the lift to – what time is your appointment?"

"I don't have one," I admitted "but call him up and tell him I have the Sex Pistols' master tapes here and tell him he has just seven minutes to come down and collect them."

While she was getting him on the phone, I started leaving fliers around the reception area. Mr Heavy Security picked one up and gave it a long, hard stare. The receptionist said, "He says, 'Can you leave them here?' He's a bit busy."

"No!" I said, "he's got five minutes, then me and the tapes are off!" She spoke to him again on the phone.

"He says could you go to the mail room and he'll send someone down to collect them?"

Not bloody likely! Not with those four goons still lurking in there. No, this sounded like some kind of a trap to me. I told her, "He has to sign for them in person. He has three minutes left." I got on my mobile and made as if I was talking to someone important. "Yes, Richard, I did what you said, but they seem scared for some reason. What's that … Harvey and the boys are picking us up outside – lunch with Clifford – okay. Just a couple of minutes and we're out of here …"

The security guard kept following me around the room, but I managed to stay at arms length. With ten seconds left, Kath picked up the leather case – supposedly containing the master tapes – and we made for the door. I dropped an envelope onto the counter on the way out, addressed to (name deleted) containing three words, which I'll leave to your imagination.

As we exited I noticed a security camera scanning the street outside. I had one more thing to do. I couldn't resist – I just had to put a 'Wedding Day' sticker on the giant EMI window, next to their logo (these stickers were the size of a 10p piece and no threat to anyone). Just as I was about to stick it up, a hand came out of nowhere and snatched it from me. It was the security geezer from reception, who must have been watching me on the CCTV. "No, you fucking don't!" he sneered. I just laughed and said, "Call this a record company?" and walked off.

I thought EMI – like most record labels – had been illegally sticking up their posters and stickers all over the streets for years? As we were walking away, three of the original goons came out of the mail room and one of them began following us. I told Kath to run to the van, drive it round the corner and I'd meet her there. I quickly crossed the road, ducked down behind some parked cars, put my colourful jacket in my bag, changed my pink sunglasses for reading ones, swapped my bandanna for my Dad's flat cap and calmly walked into the nearby kids' playground. I continued to the end of the street, round the corner to where Kath and the space bus were waiting – its shiny bumper sticker "Magic Happens!" glinting rainbow-like in the sunshine.

Kath chuckled as I climbed aboard in my disguise – "You're getting a bit too good at this clandestine lark," she said, "they'll have you working for MI5 soon."

"No," I replied, "I wanna work for MI-1 or at least MI-2. Come on – let's go visit Glen, I haven't annoyed him lately."

The short distance by road from Hammersmith to Maida Vale can take anything from 20 minutes to several hours, even if you take the same route at the same time on the same day of the week. It's what taxi drivers affectionately refer to as the 'Cabbies' Chaos Syndrome'. A bit like the butterfly effect, but even more random. For instance, the London road network can be brought to a standstill if a bus driver even dreams of a butterfly flapping its wings in Tokyo. This is why you'll never get a cabbie to commit himself on how long a journey will take. "Well," he'll say, "the last time I went there it took me less than an hour." Or "How long do you want it to take?" Any correct prediction would be down to luck.

On this day, the short hop under the Westway to Glen's was a breeze. En route we were passing Abstract Records – the boss, Edward Christie was an old acquaintance of mine. I produced the laudable 'Punks on 45' single for him, way back in the heyday of medleys i.e. 1980-1983.

I happened to have a spare, early copy of this book with me and I thought I would get him to have a look at it since he also now published books too.

I buzzed on the doorbell. "Delivery for Mr Christie," I bellowed into the squawking box. "Come on up," a voice replied. The door opened and at the top of the stairs I spotted an old familiar face. I approached it and thrust a copy of the then-titled 'Dave Goodman Story Part II' in front of it. It glanced at an early, punky picture of me on the front cover, then peered round the manuscript to give me closer inspection – who was this messenger boy?

Of course – I was still 'in disguise'. He looked past the peaked cap and glasses and finally it clicked.

"Dave – what a surprise – to what do we owe this honour?"

"Well, it's me book, really, Edward – you're in the publishing game aren't you?"

"I sure am," he replied. He crossed to a shelf and picked up a copy of the Alan Parker/Paul Burgess tome *Satellite* and showed me.

"We put this out," he said proudly (I had a copy myself, and although it is excellently done, it's really only about T-shirts, posters, badges and bootlegs)

"How many have you sold?" I asked him. I'd put him on the spot and he blurted out 'about 5,000,' which I took to be the true figure.

"Not a lot really for a book about the most controversial band in history!" I exclaimed.

"Well Dave, people just aren't buying books like they used to," he started to explain – but I was already heading for the door.

"Gotta go, Edward, I've a lot to do. Take a look at me book and just remember you can't compare it to anything else – it's the inside story – a story only I can tell. It's outrageous, humorous and profound. Handled right it could sell in its millions." With which I left him to ponder.

Off we went to Glen's – a real parking nightmare – pounds an hour on a meter, and that's if you can find one! He wasn't in, so I put a few tapes through his door.

Boogie lived about a mile away, so I called him and we met up for a chat and a jar. After much discourse about those 'little shits' the loveable Sex Pistols, I plucked up the courage to head back to my castle and its possible stake-out. I got Boogie to call my ansaphone on his mobile, leaving a message that he would meet me in Glastonbury that evening. If anyone was listening in that should confuse them.

I arrived home and all was normal. No one had broken in – as I often pointed out to some of the kids on the street, "I can't understand those idiots who break into people's houses – I mean, don't they realise that they'll spend the rest of their lives worrying that someone will break into theirs?"

I know some of them get my point, because I've heard them repeat it to one another, but you always get some clever dick who says that if anyone tried to break into his house he'd shoot them and feed them to the dogs. Well – there's another good reason not to break into people's houses then!

I once went through a period of nicking things myself, in my early twenties. Things like old microphones I might find laying around in the back rooms of clubs, or abandoned amplifiers covered in decades of dust.

I felt I was just putting them to good use. It got out of hand though, when one day I found myself unscrewing a pick-up from a fellow bass player's guitar – but when I realised what I was doing I screwed it straight back on and vowed to go straight – which I pretty much have (apart from that bank job in Monte Carlo, of course – just kidding, officer …).

Now, if anything is stolen from me – and plenty has been – my precious 1961 Fender Precision guitar, a few amps and microphones (not to mention a small fortune in royalties!) … well, what can I say? It's like I'm still being taught a lesson. You can't go back and change the past – not yet anyway – so I guess I'll just have to live with it. These days, if a shopkeeper gives me too much change and I discover it halfway down the road, I'll more than likely go back and return it. Am I over-compensating?

Anyway, back home to relative normality – to relax, we loaded a pipe with some very strong home-grown weed. This turned out to be a bit of a mistake, as a sudden cloud of deeper paranoia descended on me. I kept thinking of the weird emails, including the offers of CDs of personal information on people and CDs about how to change one's identity, disappear and escape detection. I didn't know what was going on or who was sending me the stuff. They were coming from names like 'Prod', 'In Timy Dating' and 'MIA'. My imagination was working overtime. I'd read enough conspiracy theories to understand what can happen to you if you get on the wrong side of the UK/USA security forces, not to mention the Illuminati! The worst I could imagine was disappearing in the night and ending up locked inside a small padded box till I suffocated in my own body waste.

As chance would have it, the very brilliant anarchist comedian Mark Thomas dedicated a whole TV show to state censorship at this time and explained in great detail the D Notice and MI5's black box – a real eye opener. So much for 'freedom of speech'. And then it hit me – what were all those brand new, shiny silver Mercedes doing in my street? I planned an escape and slipped out under the cover of darkness, in disguise. As me and my gal got into our space bus, I noticed a black van with blacked out windows parked down the road. Before we pulled away I checked there were no bombs under our vehicle (listen, if you're gonna be paranoid, there's no point in being half-hearted about it).

Off we went, mobile phone in one hand, just in case. We turned the corner at the end of the road, and would you believe it, another brand new silver Merc was coming up the side street towards us. I was taking no chances so I hit the gas and at the next junction turned right, back into the estate. It was on my tail. Of course, this might just have been coincidence, but my heightened sense of survival wouldn't allow me to take any chances, and soon I was swerving down some back alley into the shadows of darkness, with my lights off – we were free again.

I decided to head for Primrose Hill – a sacred spot, if ever there was one. I needed some good energy and people around me. I called up Boogie and arranged to meet him that night. We checked into a hotel and took a walk down Camden High Street to get some spare clothes, toothpaste etc ...

On passing Virgin Megastore, I couldn't resist the temptation to go in and plaster a few stickers of the banned single around. They said "... 'Wedding Day' by Sad Pistoils – Get it before they get you – limited edition no 999,977 ..." or whatever number it was. I was printing the numbers backwards from 1,000,001, so really it was only number 34.

We carried on down the road and stopped to buy some socks from a street vendor, when three dudes came up and thrust a watch into the vendor's hand. They proceeded to accuse him of selling it to them – it was a dud and they wanted their money back. Poor old sod, he could hardly speak English and these three hoods were giving him a hard time. I could tell that it was a set up and that things could turn really nasty. It was almost as if they were trying to draw me into the argument. I managed to keep my distance and alerted the staff of a nearby shop. In my paranoid state, the thought crossed my mind that maybe the powers-that-be had traced me to Camden and enlisted these dudes to cause a scene and bump me off in the process. It's amazing what your mind can come up with when you're paranoid.

I made a quick exit into the market, tied my hair back, changed my hat, put on some glasses, removed my jacket and lost us amongst the crowd. I wasn't taking any chances.

We spent that evening in various wining and dining establishments with Boogie. Amongst other things, we discussed various conspiracy theories and Boogie pointed out that 'Taliban' apparently translates as 'student'. We criticised Virgin-EMI for not understanding the original message behind the Sex Pistols. We reminisced about the good old days when the Pistols were still on their way up and anything and everything seemed possible. He then generously allowed us to treat him to a meal, and shuffled off into the night. I had hoped he might have offered us his floor to sleep on, and I'd dropped some pretty big hints, but anyway no offer was forthcoming.

Kath and I headed back to the hotel, where I must confess, I didn't feel a hundred percent safe. When we'd checked in I thought the receptionist might have picked up on my paranoid vibe – after September 11th hotel staff were told to look out for anything suspicious (I suppose colourful clothes and a bandanna might be mistaken for Middle Eastern attire – added to which I had torn up the first registration form Kath had filled in, as she had foolishly put my name). Anyway, when we returned it felt quite calm, so we sat in the lounge and sank a few nightcaps, while reading in the paper about the ever-increasing number of arrests of suspected terrorists. An immense tiredness came upon me and we retired.

Bright and early next morning, I decided to head for home, pack up all my valuables and remove them from the house for safe keeping. We got back at about 7.30 am and, as we turned into the road, there was a woman standing there in Arab attire, with only her eyes revealed. It felt like she had been looking out for us and when we came round the corner she started to walk down the road, arriving outside our place as we got out of the van. We appeared to be keeping our eyes on each other – and I feared I might be about to be assassinated, but thank God, she continued walking along the road.

Straight away I started packing my trunk. Passport, birth certificate, master tapes, the book I'd been writing, valuable photos, recordings of phone conversations, records I'd produced – it was like viewing my life's work in the space of half an hour. All the time I was half expecting the front door to be kicked down – boy, was I scared!

We threw some clothes in a case and loaded it, with the trunk, into the bus and high-tailed it out, to visit some friends. I dropped the trunk off at Dave and Jane's, my friends in Brockley and went on to pay a surprise visit to Ray and Karen in Stanford le Hope. They had organised a protest gig against the giant London Gateway development for the next evening. Shell and P & O were planning to devour their village and surrounding countryside by building a massive container port on the farmland down on the estuary. Funnily enough the site where they're intending to build is at the end of Rainbow Lane. If they get away with it, it will mean an endless convoy of container lorries crashing back and forth through their peaceful village. The developers say they will create more jobs but, in fact, there is virtually zero unemployment in the area.

Meanwhile the Sex Pistols were rehearsing for their up-coming reunion gigs and I thought it would be a brilliant idea for them to play at the protest gig. I could have arranged to erect a 'free energy' stage run on solar, wind and bicycle power. We could have filmed it and broadcast it on pirate radio too. It could have attracted a lot of crusty, new age travelling, zippy, fluffy, eco, rainbow warriors. The site was perfect – acres of disused, arable farmland right next to sandy beaches. Loads of disused buildings too. The event wouldn't have disturbed anyone – except of course the developers and their cronies.

I proposed the idea to Glen – who dismissed it pretty much out of hand.

"We're too busy rehearsing, Dave you'll have to do it on your own." he said. Enter the 'Sad Pistoils' – "I Wanna be Apathy" – don't bother me. I wondered if they've made some pact with the powers-that-be to be good boys now. Only regurgitating their past, never adding anything new. Why hadn't they written any new songs? What about all that bitchy rhetoric? Maybe someone took them aside and ordered – or hypnotised – them to play ball.

Anyway, I live in hope again now and have these positive dreams about the band doing great forward-looking gestures ...

Having been so frightened by the intimidating emails and my suspicions about what had happened to other people in similar situations – the suspicious death of John Lennon, the shooting of Bob Marley etc – I decided not to push the record any further. After all, I was proclaiming the leaders of America and Great Britain guilty of crimes against humanity, with a Sex Pistols rhythm section to back me up. Boy band pop it wasn't!

I announced to the world on my tapped phone, that I was burying the 'Wedding Day' song and not pushing it any further. "The US bombing of the wedding party was just one of those unfortunate things that happen in a war – an accident. I've made my point, I'll leave it at that." I thought I'd start ringing some people I'd sent it to and persuade them not to push it any further. I called Phil Strongman, co-editor of this book.

"Phil – hold back on reviewing the record, I feel like my life's in danger."

"It's only a song," said Phil, "you've been involved with lotsa outrageous records, you've never seemed worried before."

"Look Phil – I'm accusing the US President and our Prime Minister of being murderers. This record has the potential to bring down – or at least embarrass – the governments of the two most powerful nations in the West.

There are a lot of people who'd like to see that happen and I've just created their anthem."

"I think I know what you're saying, Dave," replied Phil, "I've just been to see Roy Carr and he was acting a bit strange." Roy was – and still is – a dear old friend, one of the very few I had at IPC magazines – NME, Vox, Loaded, Uncut etc.

"So what did Roy say?" I asked Phil.

"He said it was down to the editors whether they covered it. He's just had a heart bypass and is taking it easy. He sends his regards. And he says 'be careful'."

Funnily enough I'd just read somewhere that IPC magazines had been taken over by AOL/TimeWarner, who had also taken over EMI-Virgin. It seemed like the Americans were devouring the British music industry. Did they feel a need to control it and castrate the next musical protest movement, before it had the chance to 'corrupt' the youth of the country, as it has so often in the past?

I bet the American establishment still felt that the war in Vietnam failed largely due to the peace movement, who were no doubt inspired by the psychedelic and protest music of the 60s. British artists like Pink Floyd, Donovan, Yes, The Beatles, The Who, Incredible String Band -they all took people on a journey with their music – away from war. Just when the music industry thought it had everything under control, under a blanket of blandness, Punk Rock suddenly raised its spiky head. The DIY nature of the scene made it more difficult to control and before anyone could say "gabba gabba hey", the kids were running wild, questioning their elders and redefining 'yoof culture' once again!

"So Roy – how are you? I heard you've had a heart operation. My dad had a pace-maker fitted – it put years on his life. Did you get the single?"

"Uh huh."

"This is terrible shit that's been going down in the name of democracy. Just imagine it, it's your wedding day, you make your vows to God, start to celebrate, someone lets off a few fireworks and the next thing you know, hellfire rains down from above and the whole congregation are blasted out of existence. Over sixty lives those trigger-happy Yanks wasted."

"Yeah –"

"Okay – I can accept that it may have been a terrible mistake, Roy. So why can't they acknowledge it and allow the record to raise money to build a One World Earth Temple on the bomb site – as a small tribute to those who lost their lives? I mean – Bush and Blair shouldn't be allowed to get away with this blatant rhetoric that they are the good guys fighting evil. There's nothing good about massacring innocent people. This record could be a turning point in the history of warfare. Let's show some direct action and more compassion for the innocent victims."

"… hmm …"

"Anyway – the government's slapped a D notice on it, so your media empire can't write about it, even if it wants to."

"It's not an empire," protested Roy.

"I also feel like my life's in danger," I continued, "I either need this thing to go public in a big way, or I'd better bury it."

Roy thought for a while. "Erm … you should be talking to Max Clifford, he'll tell you if you've got a story. Max Clifford is an independent press agent extraordinaire."

"Yeah," I say, "I have been thinking of calling him. Did you know I'm actually related to the Queen, Roy?" I said proudly.

"Yeah Dave, I'm sure we're all related somewhere along the line."

"No, Roy – listen – my great grandmother is the half-sister of the Queen Mother. They have the same father. They even looked alike. My cousin's been researching it. She says she can prove it. What a turn up for the books eh?"

Roy laughs – "Well you'd better get on to Max then – by Royal Appointment!"

"Listen, Roy – thanks for your time. I hope you make a quick recovery. If you get time give me book a look over. Have you got Max's number there?"

"He's in Brook Street – Max Clifford Associates – you can get him from the directory."

"Okay thanks – I'll call him now. See you." I hung up and rang Clifford a few moments later.

"Max Clifford Associates, can I help you?" his friendly-sounding secretary answered.

"I need to talk to Max," I said, "it's highly confidential."

"Max is busy right now," she says, "you'll have to deal with me."

"Alright then. It's a story about a record that involves Tony Blair and George Bush, the Royal family, a massacre in Afghanistan, the Sex Pistols and MI5 … I could carry on."

"No, no – I get the picture, can you fax the story to me?"

Now I can't believe the great Max Clifford doesn't have email, but luckily I had a fax. "Send it over and we'll get back to you if we're interested."

Blimey, I thought – what does it take to get their interest?

So the fax went off … no reply. The next day I called. "I'm sorry, Max has gone on holiday for two weeks. He'll be back on the 23rd."

"That's strange – I just got an email saying the exact same thing about the editor of The Face after I sent him the story!"

I rang the Press Association – I'd biked a package over to them the day before. I spoke to a chap who said. "Look Dave – we don't think they'll be interested in this one.

"What do you mean?" I barked, "I read your papers and I would definitely be interested. This is a cover-up. I want to speak to your editor – now!"

"I'm afraid that won't be possible," he said limply.

"So much for freedom of speech and democracy!" I responded and put the phone down.

D notice, national security, MI5, CIA, Government whitewash, media cover up, arrogance, deceit, fear …

On the other hand – I felt my gesture was loving, understanding, brave, futuristic, honest, sympathetic. But what were my real motives?

Things seemed to calm down a bit. Although occasionally as I left the house I would still see a shiny, new, silver Mercedes parked up the road with a suited gent in shades leaning on it, watching me and talking into a mobile. Nowadays I'd wave to them and carry on about my business. As I had sent the record to the British Library, along with certain taped phone conversations about it, I figured if anything happened to me it would just draw attention to the record and the incident to which it referred …

As the Pistols' gig was coming up and Virgin-EMI were planning to release a box set, there was some movement on my legal case. I figured they would want to lay their hands on the master tapes I had. If they were putting out any of my productions, I certainly wanted them to take them from my original masters – not from some scratchy old bootlegs like they seemed to have done in the past! Since EMI were ultimately releasing it, I appealed to them, but they said they just accepted whatever the Sex Pistols handed over. I spoke to Scott Murphy, the chap who was putting the box set together and he told me he had very few master tapes to hand, so I sent him and EMI cut-down versions of the re-mastered original recordings, but no one would deal with me, although they told me how good they sounded.

I really had to nag EMI to make sure my previous credits were on the Pistols' three CD box set – which had been given the imaginative title 'Box Set' … They were as bad as me and my 'Label' some 25 years before …

Despite some umming and aahing, in the end EMI did finally restore my production credits – for that release at least. The first two CDs consisted of *Bollocks, Spunk and Swindle* – the third was taken from a Japanese bootleg of the first Screen on the Green gig, where I was their live sound engineer. I didn't get any credit for that one, although it was a great reminder to me just how good and original I helped them sound. Oh well – I guess the original owner can't really complain as he has probably been exploiting it illegally ever since the gig.

I got the feeling EMI-Virgin were expecting to sell shitloads of these items, but despite all the advertising and rekindled Pistol mania, it apparently struggled to sell. Mind you, it wasn't cheap and most of the stuff on it the Pistols fans already had.

Earlier that year – on 2nd February, 02.02.02, in fact – I had sent a long letter to John Lydon, via his solicitor, who had once informed me at a meeting that I could send anything to John through him. Anyway, it had been many months and I still hadn't heard anything back.

I finally discovered John refused to receive it. I had included some CDs in the package, which I thought he might have found interesting. I was flabbergasted. I felt that since I had gone to the trouble of soul-searching and putting my thoughts and ideas down, John might at least have had the decency to have a look at them. What was he afraid of? It was a genuine attempt on my part to clear up misunderstandings and resolve matters for the future in a way that would benefit us all. Alas dear reader – it fell on deaf ears.

The whole atmosphere surrounding the Pistols felt very negative to me. So much denial, so much back-biting. It seemed as if there was little respect for what Malcolm or I had done for the band. No new ideas or music were emerging. In true situationist style I wanted to help transform this whole negative scenario into something really positive.

I had been spending a lot of time in the studio remixing and remastering some rare vintage Pistols' recordings. I took it on myself to compile two new albums. One I called X-Spunk, which was made up of entirely unreleased out-takes, monitor mixes and backing tracks, plus various quotes and soundbites from the band. The quality was far superior to anything Virgin had previously 'bootlegged' from these sessions. I made up some sample copies giving a minute of each track – you can't be too careful – and sent one to EMI. They agreed it sounded great, but they had to release what the Sex Pistols gave them. They said that maybe in the future they could do a deal.

Another idea I had for a new Pistols album was the 'Sex Pistols Rainbowland Project'. It consisted of a lot of unreleased alternative mixes etc with various quotes and statements from the band in between. I even had one from John where he says "the rainbow – I'm promoting the rainbow myself."

Actually he was referring to the 1978 PiL gig at the Rainbow in Finsbury Park – but to me it really fitted.

My idea was to bring the band up to date and connect them with the eco-rainbow warriors out there in abundance, struggling to save the planet whilst having a good time dancing on mother earth, jiving round campfires at full moon on sacred sites. I'd been involved with this scene since the mid Eighties. Many of these folk had been inspired by the Sex Pistols and their ability to challenge and change the status quo. I wanted to reconnect them.

The Sex Pistols Rainbowland Project was to be a limited edition of 1,000,001 copies, individually numbered backwards (again). Once they had all been sold that was it – the record would be deleted. Okay, I know a million and one is a lot to sell, especially when it's an ageing punk band, who hadn't done anything new or exciting for years, but there was an added incentive for buyers. Each CD would also be a share in a piece of land to be called 'Sex Pistols Rainbowland'. The purchaser could register his unique number by post or internet and get a certificate with co-ordinates of his own piece of land which he would own forever. Okay, he couldn't build on it, but he could visit it occasionally and I figured it should be about 16 square metres, big enough to put a tent on. There would be a monument built in honour of the Sex Pistols for future generations to marvel at. I thought this was a splendid idea, but many people I spoke to about it thought I was mad. I also wanted there to be a low impact, self-sustainable music complex on the land – run on solar and wind energy, complete with its own organic, permaculture food garden. A web site hub could be developed around the project, encouraging others to create their own rainbowland, sharing information and networking events. I haven't given up hope entirely – watch this space!

I needed to have a break after all this 21st Century craziness and so, in late February 2002, I booked a holiday to Malta. I wanted to put in some uninterrupted time on finishing this book and get away from the mayhem of city life for a while. Malta wasn't our first choice, it just came up on the computer at the right price.

Yet from the moment I stepped off the plane I felt at home. Driving to our hotel, the myriad of flat roofed dwellings gave me the impression of a middle eastern type of land, though it's very much a Catholic stronghold.

The people were friendly and spoke English, the atmosphere was relaxed, the weather pleasant.

This was my first visit to Malta, but within three days I found myself sitting in a notary's office, handing over a small deposit and signing documents for the purchase of a lovely 'house of character' at an affordable price. I had six months to return home, sell up, pay the remainder and move to our new dream home in paradise! What an adventure!

As I write this I am sitting on our roof terrace gazing out across the Mediterranean at the islands of Comino and Gozo – where, respectively, the herb Cumin originated and the Med's first beatnik 'circuit' started. The weather is hot with a slight breeze and Kathy and I have just polished off a bottle of local Special Reserve red wine (at less than £1 a bottle, if you please!).

In an hour or so, the son of our local doctor will come round for a guitar lesson and, in return, he will teach me some more Malti words. Since arriving seven months ago, I have done eight gigs, built a new studio, recorded three albums, produced a local band and made a dozen radio shows!

Still very busy – but this time with fun things!

I suppose the main reason I really moved was that I couldn't afford to live well in London any longer. Whilst there I earned a fair bit from the studio, but it never was enough by the time you'd paid the mortgage, insurance, council tax and services, studio and office supplies. Not to mention feeding and watering yourselves and our many visitors. In Malta, Kathy and I can live on about a third of the amount we spent in London – and enjoy glorious views and beautiful warm weather.

Ideally, one day I'd like to buy a bit of land back in old England and build my 'eco-pod'. I could spend time in both countries – but for now I'll be very happy here.

AFTERWORD BY THE EDITOR

Dave Goodman passed on a few days after completing the notes for this book, killed by a massive heart attack. The various obituaries that followed filled pages in Mojo, Record Collector, Uncut, Songlinks, The Independent newspaper etc .

The media attention he was increasingly denied in the last two decades of his life was finally granted after his death – as is typical, I suppose. I no longer had to fight to get a ten line review for him or his CDs although few of the obits mentioned the amazing work he'd done with New Age Radio and Mandala Malta (or the fact that, in the late Sixties and early Seventies, he'd toured with Ben E. King, The Drifters, Nicky Thomas, Michael Jackson and The Jackson Five plus a host of others – or the fact he helped introduce solar-powered PAs to Glastonbury's Greenfield Stage, or the fact that his last few recordings were some of the best of his career).

Dave's was an incredibly full life and even now I can quite clearly recall those late afternoons in his Gipsy Hill studio. The work would cease and the coffee, or wine, would flow and time would stand still (not that 'work' there was ever painful for a spectator such as myself; talented artists such as Nick Austin's Profumo, Richard Veal's English Song, the Space Goats, Tony Hadley, Pauline Black, and Cathie H would pass through, each one cutting some wonderful tracks on their way. Beat and Sham 69 bassist Mat Sargent even did most of his much-talked about Sex 'n' Drugs 'n' HIV project at Dave's – look out for the albums and DVDs in the future, they really do exist). You never knew who'd drop by for a chat – Marianne Faithful one day, Glen Matlock the next, Afrika Bambaata the day after.

Of greater interest to me as a writer though was Dave's track record – he had seen, or 'live mixed', most of the bands I loved – from the Pistols, to the Clash, to the Who, Hendrix and the Small Faces – and he had a wealth of stories about them and the culture they sprang from. There was also his marvellous sense of humour and his knowledge of woodlands, of ancient history, of English by-laws, of religions and cults … a dinner, or a drink, with Dave and Kathy really was something to be treasured.

All of the above mean that this book, crammed though I believe it is with incident and anecdote, is merely the opening shot of a trilogy – in atypically typical Goodman fashion he started in the middle. There is a prequel – about Dave's pre-Pistols days – as well as a sequel being edited as I write. The latter covers the period from 1981 to 2005, when he schmoozed his way across America, Germany and Thailand before touring Japan with the likes of Hiroki Okano and his dazzling Tenkoo Orchestra. It was during this time with Hiroki that Dave also first made his presence felt at both Glastonbury's Green Field and in the heart of the eco-warrior movement.

This sequel – which will probably come first, of course – currently has the working title Glastonbury-Tokyo-Malta ...

For me personally though, Dave's departure from this world meant I'd lost direct contact with my oldest friend – since we'd been drinking, usually over-drinking, together since 1978. My oldest Japanese friend, the brilliant herbal doctor Kiekazu Higashikawa, had died the month before and Dave's demise seemed like the last straw. It didn't all fully hit me until Dave's wake at the 100 Club – I drank and drank but couldn't get drunk, stumbling out of that legendary basement close to tears before the live music tributes had even begun.

But one thing to come out of that great, awful, evening was the determination to finish editing both this book and the Dave Goodman documentary I'd half-heartedly started months before (title; Chaos! Ex Pistols' Secret History: Dave Goodman Story Part One). This has now been done, more or less, and that part of my life seems to be now over, in some ways. But I think the inspiration that Dave kindled in me, in so many of us, will live on – like the wild, subtle, positive music he created.

NB This edition could not have been completed without the work of Dave's wife Kathy Manuell, a talented musician and producer in her own right. She – like Richard Veal – has had an enormous, positive input into this project.

Phil Strongman
September 2006

*Ideally, one day I'd like to buy a bit of
land back in old England and build my 'eco-pod'.*

DAVE GOODMAN'S
SEX PISTOLS DIARY

MARCH 1976

Tue 23 MARCH 1976 Nashville Rooms, West London – after THE STRANGLERS pulled out, The Albion agency offered the gig to JOE STRUMMER's pub rock band THE 101ERS. It was the first time that DAVE GOODMAN had worked with STRUMMER and THE 101ERS – and their unknown support band the SEX PISTOLS...

Thu 25 MARCH 1976 Hertfordshire College of Art & Design.

Tue 30 MARCH 1976 100 Club, Oxford St., London – supporting PLUMMET AIRLINES in their 100 Club debut. ROTTEN tries to pick a fight with MATLOCK while onstage, before storming off intending to get a 73 bus home to Finsbury Park. McLAREN demands he go back onstage – he complies only after seeing that an angry JONES has ripped off his guitar strings.

APRIL 1976

Sat 3 APRIL 1976 Nashville Rooms, West London

Sun 4 APRIL 1976 El Paradiso Strip Club, Soho, London – attended by THE ARROWS pop group (including Ben Brierly aka Tommy Trouble) and SOUNDS magazine's JOHN INGHAM.

Thu 8 APRIL 1976 MELODY MAKER review of 3/4/76 Nashville gig says the PISTOLS "do as much for music as World War II did for... peace... I hope we'll hear no more of them".

Sun 18 APRIL 1976 El Paradiso Strip Club, Soho, London – CANCELLED.

Thu 22 APRIL 1976 SOUNDS runs JOHN INGHAM's two page PISTOLS feature and interview. "I wanna change things so there's more bands like us," says ROTTEN. "There's no drugs in this band," says STEVE JONES.

Fri 23 APRIL 1976 Nashville Rooms, West London – VIVIENNE WESTWOOD picks a fight with a long-haired 'straight' who is beaten up by SID VICIOUS, McLAREN and other Sex regulars. ROTTEN joins in as the fight is photographed by JOE STEVENS and witnessed by NEIL TENNANT, a future PET SHOP BOY. The PISTOLS are then BANNED from playing the Nashville. TAPED.

Thu 29 APRIL 1976 Nashville Rooms, West London – supported by TED

CARROLL's Rock On disco, the PISTOLS get around the Nashville ban by hiring the place for a 'private party', Party With The Sex Pistols. The PISTOLS are then BANNED from playing or hiring the Nashville.

NME runs STEVENS' Nashville fight picture under the headline 'Terrorize Your Fans The Sex Pistols Way'. The magazine also runs a letter by future PET SHOP BOY, singer NEIL TENNANT, who writes "the PISTOLS consist of three nice, clean middle class art students and a real live dementoid, Johnny Rotten".

MAY 1976

Wed 5 MAY 1976 The Babalu Disco, Finchley, London – a gig advertised several times on CAPITOL RADIO, describing the PISTOLS as 'the new Who'. Although the PISTOLS rate their own performance only a handful of people turn up. They didn't need my PA for this one but I turned up anyway. Shows what a fan I was becoming.

Thu 6 MAY 1976 North East London Poly. Now this was a happening gig with loads of sweat and encores.

Tue 11 MAY 1976 100 Club, London – supported by synth band KRAKATOA. Attended by PHIL STRONGMAN the diary researcher of this book, SID, SIOUXSIE and TOM ROBINSON.

Wed 12 MAY 1976 PISTOLS record three demos – No Feeling, Pretty Vacant and Problems – with ex-Wombles guitarist CHRIS SPEDDING at Majestic Studios in London.

Mon 17 MAY 1976 Screen on The Green, Islington, London – CANCELLED.

Tue 18 MAY 1976 100 Club, London.

Wed 19 MAY 1976 Northallerton, Yorkshire – PAULINE MURRAY, later of the group PENETRATION is present.

Thu 20 MAY 1976 The Penthouse, Scarborough, East Yorks

Fri 21 MAY 1976 The Crypt, Middlesborough Town Hall – supporting THE DOCTORS OF MADNESS who refuse to let the PISTOLS use their PA.

Tue 25 MAY 1976 100 Club – supported by DOGWATCH.

Sun 30 MAY 1976 Art Department, Reading University.

JUNE 1976

Fri 4 JUNE 1976 Lesser Free Trade Hall, Manchester – seen by IAN CURTIS, BERNARD DICKENS and PETER HOOK – later known as JOY DIVISION – MORRISEY, DEVOTO and SHELLEY. Manchester's first punk event. TAPED.

Tue 15 JUNE 1976 100 Club, London – SID VICIOUS and JAH WOBBLE are involved in a bike chain and knife incident with NICK KENT, a guitarist turned NME journalist who had previously assaulted ex-girlfriend CHRISSIE HYNDE in McLAREN's SEX boutique.

Thu 17 JUNE 1976 Midsummer Music Festival Benefit, Assembly Hall, Walthamstow – supporting KILBURN & THE HIGH ROADS featuring IAN DRURY on drums and THE STRANGLERS, the PISTOLS replacing the now defunct 101ers are seen again by TONY WILSON.

Tue 29 JUNE 1976 100 Club, London – supported by SEVENTH HEAVEN. TAPED

JULY 1976

Sat 3 JULY 1976 Pier Pavilion, Hastings – attended by MARION ELLIOT who's inspired to start group X RAY SPEX with herself fronting the band as POLY STYRENE.

SOUNDS quotes a McLAREN press release – regarding the 100 Club fight involving SID and KENT – in a news piece that incorrectly refers to new groups such as SLAUGHTER and THE DOGS, SUBWAY SEX and SURBURBAN BOLTS who are said to be following in the PISTOLS' wake.

Sun 4 JULY 1976 The Black Swan, Sheffield – supported by the CLASH in their first public gig. ROTTEN baits an unresponsive audience with the words "We were great and you know it! We must have been, we're from London and any band from London is great up here!"

Mon 5 JULY 1976 FAN SID VICIOUS, ROTTEN and at least one other PISTOL are involved in several scuffles and SID (or was it Glen?) throws a bottle at THE RAMONES as they play DINGWALLS, Camden supported by THE FLAMIN' GROOVIES.

Tue 6 JULY 1976 100 Club, London – supported by THE DAMNED in their first public gig after four secret concerts in a West London gay bar.

Thu 9 JULY 1976 The Lyceum, London – supporting the PRETTY THINGS and SUPERCHARGE in an all-nighter. Attending are PAUL WELLER, JOE STRUMMER and MICK JONES.

Sat 10 JULY 1976 The Sundown, Charing Cross Rd, London – the first of two sets ends after 30 minutes and the 2nd set is CANCELLED after the PISTOLS row with both management and bouncers. ROTTEN later waits outside with a 9 inch nail clutched in his hand to defend himself from the latter. PISTOLS are BANNED from Sundown.

Tue 13 JULY 1976 Rock Garden, Covent Garden, London – CANCELLED.

DAVE GOODMAN records the PISTOLS in the band's Denmark Street rehearsal room (which doubles as JONES' home) using his own 4-track deck, over a period of seven days. These he transferred to 8-track to overdub, at Riverside Studios, Chiswick. The seven tracks recorded are Anarchy in the UK, Pretty Vacant, Submission, Seventeen, Satellite, No Feelings and I Wanna Be Me – the best takes of the latter two become the B sides of the PISTOLS' debut single Anarchy In the UK (EMI) and its aborted follow-up God Save the Queen (A&M).

The first issue of MARK PERRY's fanzine SNIFFIN' GLUE appears, although THE HOTRODS and THE DAMNED do get the odd mention SG is mostly dedicated to US acts including THE RAMONES, FLAMIN' GROOVIES, RUNAWAYS, TELEVISION, TODD RUNDGREN and BLUE OYSTER CULT.

Sat 17 JULY 1976 Dingwalls, Camden, London – CANCELLED. The PISTOLS are then BANNED from playing Dingwalls, mainly because of the trouble on the 5th.

Tue 20 JULY 1976 Lesser Free Trade Hall, Manchester – supported by DEVOTO and SHELLEY's new group THE BUZZCOCKS, it's their debut, and SLAUGHTER and DOGS. Attended by future JOY DIVISION members as well as MARK E. SMITH, MORRISSEY, BERNARD SUMNER, MICK HUCKNALL, film student JULIEN TEMPLE and Granada TV's TONY WILSON, host of the channel's new rock show SO IT GOES. 'Anarchy in the UK' is performed for the first time.

Tues 20th July 1976 First Radio Interview – the first PISTOLS radio interview on Manchester's PICCADILLY RADIO. (insert interview)

Sat 24 JULY 1976 National Open Air Music Festival, Burstow Lodge Hill Farm nr Gatwick – CANCELLED.

Fri 30 JULY 1976 GOODMAN mixes the Denmark St. demos at Decibel Studios, North London adding last overdubs and effects – for instance – singing through the spout of a half-filled kettle to create the underwater voice on the intro of Submission.

Sat 31 JULY 76. Under the heading 'Anarchy in the UK', SOUNDS dedicates an entire page to INGHAM's review of the PISTOLS Manchester gig of the 20th.

AUGUST 1976

Sat 7 AUGUST 1976 A two page MELODY MAKER feature on the PISTOLS and the freshly titled PUNK ROCK used the headline 'Punk Rock: Crucial or Phoney?' The story is trailed on the front page and while CAROLINE COON defends the new beat, MM veteran ALAN JONES (later editor of MM and UNCUT) writes that "if the PISTOLS really are the new rock then I am going in the air raid shelter with granny until it all blows over."

Tue 10 AUGUST 1976 100 Club, London – supported by THE VIBRATORS. Attended by EMI A&R MIKE THORNE.

Sat 14 AUGUST 1976 Barbarellas, Birmingham – attended by future members of

DURAN DURAN and POLYDOR A&R CHRIS PARRY, seeing the band for the first time. TAPED.

Thu 19 AUGUST 1976 West Runton Village Inn, Norfolk

Sat 21 AUGUST 1976 The Boat Club, Nottingham.

The Euro Punk Rock Festival in Mont de Morsan, France is played by THE DAMNED, THE HOTRODS, THE GORILLAS, ROOGALATOR, THE TYLER GANG, NICK LOWE and the PINK FAIRIES. The PISTOLS' invitation was withdrawn after the organisers claimed their demands went "too far. Who do they think they are, the Rolling Stones?"

Sun 29 AUGUST 1976 Screen on The Green, London – supported by THe CLASH and THE BUZZCOCKS in an illegal all-nighter special that also featured Kenneth Anger movies and SIOUXSIE and TRACEY O' KEEFE dancing onstage.

Attended by THORNE and his EMI A andR boss NICK MOBBS. TAPED.

Tue 31 AUGUST 1976 100 Club, London – supported by THE CLASH. TAPED.

SEPTEMBER 1976

Wed 1 SEPTEMBER 1976 Granada TV Studios, Manchester – watched by an amused PETER COOK and an outraged stand-up CLIVE JAMES, who'd earlier been upstaged by a fast-talking ROTTEN. The other two bands on the 'new group' bill, GENTLEMAN and BOWLES BROTHERS also get into arguments with the PISTOLS. The PISTOLS play Anarchy in the UK, Problems and Pretty Vacant for the SO IT GOES show – only after onstage dancer JORDAN is asked to cover her swastika armband. She introduces the band with the immortal words "The Sex Pistols are, if possible, even better than the lovely Joni Mitchell" (an ad-lib given her by KIM THRAVES, a partner in GOODMAN's Soundforce PA firm). The three PISTOLS numbers end with total silence from the stunned audience.

Fri 3 SEPTEMBER 1976 Club de Chalet du Lac, Paris – the PISTOLS almost cause a riot, as do the clothes of SIMON BARKER, BILLY IDOL, JORDAN, WESTWOOD, NILS, McLAREN and SIOUXSIE. The latter is threatened with knives and then assaulted, as is COON – there with INGHAM – during the free gig which opens a new nightclub. The crowd queues are so large that the PISTOLS need a police escort to get in. ROTTEN premieres the new McLAREN-WESTWOOD black bondage collection

Sat 4 SEPTEMBER 1976 Club de Chalet du Lac, Paris – the PISTOLS play an afternoon set for Under-17's as well as a 2nd evening show for adults.

The last of the '76 series of TV show SO IT GOES is broadcast in the Granada and London areas – it features the SEX PISTOLS performance of Anarchy in the UK.

Sat 11 SEPTEMBER 1976 Royal Ballroom, Whitby.

After a three month silence following the attack on KENT, NME reviews the PISTOLS Screen on the Green special of 29th Aug.

Sun 12 SEPTEMBER 1976 Fordgreen Ballroom, Leeds.

Mon 13 SEPTEMBER 1976 Quaintways, Chester.

Wed 15 SEPTEMBER 1976 Lodestar, Blackburn, Lancs.

Fri 17 SEPTEMBER 1976 Chelmsford Maximum Security Prison – the day COOK quits his job as an electricians' mate at the Watneys Brewery. INGHAM is present but not allowed out of the dressing room – he does a review. The gig is TAPED through the desk onto GOODMAN's 4-track.

Mon 20 SEPTEMBER 1976 100 Club, London – PUNK FESTIVAL sees the PISTOLS, who earn £440 on the night, supported by CLASH, SUBWAY SECT and 'SUZIE' & THE BANSHEES then featuring SID on drums. France's STINKY TOYS only have time to play a few numbers. The event is filmed by New Zealand Television's GRUNT TV show team. Attended by TV SMITH, GAYE ADVERT, HYNDE, DEBBIE WILSON, SIOUXSIE, SEVERIN etc … GOODMAN allows PARRY behind the mixing desk (as long as he keeps his hands off), he is 'transported'. TAPED.

TWO DAY '100 CLUB' PUNK FESTIVAL

Wed 22 SEPTEMBER 1976 Swansea.

Thu 23 SEPTEMBER 1976 Stowaway Club, Newport, Shropshire – CANCELLED.

Fri 24 SEPTEMBER 1976 76 Club, Burton-on-Trent – TAPED on GOODMAN's 4-track at the request of ROTTEN who supplies two stolen reels of _ inch master-tape. This is the INDECENT EXPOSURE bootleg on 'Rotten Records' in 1977. The bootleg was then itself copied and cleaned-up before being reissued in 1985 by GOODMAN. ROTTEN's management later accepted payment in the name of JOHN LYDON for royalties accrued on this and other releases.

Pinnacle distribution's LAURIE PRYOR apparently gave a sizeable amount of cash to JOCK MacDONALD during this time, as royalties for his PISTOLS bootlegs, most of which were bad copies of the GOODMAN tapes. Unbeknownst to PRYOR, seemingly, MacDONALD was not passing on any of these monies to either the producer or to most members of the band if any.

Mon 27 SEPTEMBER 1976 Outlook Club, Doncaster – EMI A&R NICK MOBBS flies back from Europe to see the PISTOLS for the first time on a night when they earn just over £130.

Tue 28 SEPTEMBER 1976 The Place, Guildford.

Wed 29 SEPTEMBER 1976 Strikes Club, Stoke.

Thu 30 SEPTEMBER 1976 Cleopatras, Derby

OCTOBER 1976

Fri 1 OCTOBER 1976 Didsbury College, Manchester. Sharing the bill with psychedelic folk/rock band Griffin who complimented them with the words "You sound like a modern folk group singing songs about NOW"!

Sat 2 OCTOBER 1976 Priory Ballroom, Scunthorpe – CANCELLED.

Tue 5 OCTOBER 1976 400 Club, Torquay – CANCELLED.

Wed 6 OCTOBER 1976. Wood Centre, Plymouth – CANCELLED.

Thu 7 OCTOBER 1976 Winter Gardens, Penzance – CANCELLED.

Fri 8 OCTOBER 1976 Club Lafayette, Wolverhampton – CANCELLED.

PISTOLS sign with EMI for £40,000, half of it payable in advance – the contract is drawn up and signed in one day, EMI's fastest-ever recording deal. McLAREN puts the PISTOLS on wages of £25 a week each.

POLYDOR's PARRY had forced the label to offer the PISTOLS £20,000, an offer which McLAREN had apparently accepted. So when told about the EMI deal, by GOODMAN on the steps of De Lane Lea studios, an upset PARRY burst into tears.

GOODMAN signs EMI contract to produce the first PISTOLS single. DATE TO BE CHECKED ... (picture of EMI contract)

Sat 9 OCTOBER 1976. The Cricket Ground, Northampton – CANCELLED.

Sat 9 OCTOBER 1976 GOODMAN takes PISTOLS into Lansdowne Studios, West London to record Anarchy in the UK for release on EMI. McLAREN offers the group COCAINE and sprays 'Anarchy' on the control room window before further graffiti from ROTTEN forces complaints from the engineer.

Mon 11 OCTOBER 1976. PISTOLS leave Lansdowne Studios as the latter bill EMI for graffiti damage.

Mon 11 OCTOBER 1976 RGIT, Aberdeen – CANCELLED.

Tue 12 OCTOBER 1976 Dundee Technical College.

PISTOLS sign a £10,000 publishing deal with the connected, but separate, EMI Music company.

Wed 13 OCTOBER 1976 Club Lafayette, Wolverhampton.

Thu 14 OCTOBER 1976 Mr. Digbys, Birkenhead.

Fri 15 OCTOBER 1976 Eric's, Liverpool – supported by THE YACHTS, venue posted as 'Erica's'.

Sun 17 OCTOBER 1976 GOODMAN takes PISTOLS into Wessex Studios, North London to continue recording Anarchy in the UK. Other tracks cut include the seven minute take of No Fun which later becomes, (minus the last 30 seconds), the B side of the 3rd PISTOLS single Pretty Vacant (VIRGIN).

Mon 18 OCTOBER 1976 The GENESIS P. ORRIDGE show PROSTITUTION opens at the ICA with THROBBING GRISTLE supported by CLASH and LSD, the CHELSEA POP GROUP under a pseudonym. An Evening News journalist glasses ORRIDGE and attacks Acme Attractions co-owner STEPH RAYNER before the latter kicks him out. CLASH manager BERNIE RHODES and ROTTEN attend but it is SIOUXSIE, boyfriend STEVE SEVERIN and DEBBIE 'Juvenile' WILSON whose picture is used later in the week by the DAILY MAIL under the heading 'These People Are The Wreckers of Civilization', a quote from a Tory MP. SHANE MacGOWAN has part of his ear lobe bitten off by a girlfriend.

THE DAMNED plays at the Manor Hill School in Finchley, North London, a gig that's attended by members of EATER.

Fri 20 OCTOBER 1976 Bogarts, Birmingham.

Thu 21 OCTOBER 1976 Queensway Hall, Dunstable – supported by THE JAM. Barely 70 fans attend – meaning the PISTOLS earn less than £65 – and PAUL WELLER says to MATLOCK, "I thought you guys were supposed to be big and famous, what's gone wrong?"

Fri 22 OCTOBER 1976 THE DAMNED's New Rose (Stiff) single becomes the first UK punk rock release.

NOVEMBER 1976

Thu 11 NOVEMBER 1976 The PISTOLS perform Anarchy in the UK for BBC TV before ROTTEN and McLAREN take part in a discussion with SOUNDS journalist GIOVANNI DADAMO.

Fri 12 NOVEMBER 1976 Nashville Rooms, London – a secret gig is CANCELLED.

BBC TV's early evening NATIONWIDE show screens the PISTOLS' Anarchy in the UK as performed before SID, SUE CATWOMAN, SM call girl LINDA ASHBY, SIOUXSIE etc… In his intro to the YOUNG NATION slot, host JOHN BLAKE describes the PISTOLS as being "the most nasty aggressive band ever".

Mon 15 NOVEMBER 1976 Notre Dame Hall, Leicester Place, Soho, London – a gig set-up for JANET STREET-PORTER's LONDON WEEKEND SHOW. MATLOCK trashes his bass amp as WESTWOOD dances onstage. Amongst those attending are GLITTERBEST staffer's BOOGIE, BARKER, SOPHIE RICHMOND and art director JAMIE REID as well as Acme Attractions' DON LETTS, JEANETTE LEE, JON SAVAGE, the CLASH's JOE STRUMMER, ANDY BLADE of EATER, TONY PARSONS, POLY STYRENE, LEVINE, MacGOWAN and SID. TAPED.

Fri 19 NOVEMBER 1976 Hendon Polytechnic – the SUBWAY SECT's VIC GODARD is amongst those attending as the PISTOLS perform No Future for the first time, ROTTEN reading some of the lyrics off a sheet of paper. Afterwards COOK is chased by a bottle-throwing heckler – both he and JONES ambush the yob who leaves beaten and bloodied.

Anarchy in the UK was due to be released this day but EMI had insisted that the 'too wild' GOODMAN version be re-recorded by CHRIS THOMAS – who'd worked for THE BEATLES, PINK FLOYD and ROXY MUSIC – which led to a seven day delay.

Sat 20 NOVEMBER 1976 Palace Theatre, Manchester – CANCELLED.

NME report that the PISTOLS forthcoming ANARCHY IN THE UK TOUR will not feature THE RAMONES who have pulled out. The bill now stands as PISTOLS supported by THE CLASH, THE DAMNED, THE HEARTBREAKERS and SIOUXSIE and THE BANSHEES.

Sun 21 NOVEMBER 1976 Talk of The Town, Leicester Square, London – CANCELLED.

Sat 27 NOVEMBER 1976 EMI finally release Anarchy in the UK c/w I Wanna Be Me (EMI 2566). The first 5,000 copies have a mistaken B side credit, falsely naming THOMAS as producer. Since these first few thousand contain the crucial copies that go out to the press, and other industry insiders, GOODMAN consults a lawyer who advises serving an injunction. A high court injunction is prepared but not served.

NME reveals that THE VIBRATORS have pulled out of the ANARCHY TOUR. An under-rehearsed SIOUXSIE and THE BANSHEES have already done the same.

Sun 28 NOVEMBER 1976 LWT screen LONDON WEEKEND SHOW: A Punk Rock Special at 1.15 am, a 38 minute documentary featuring PISTOLS onstage at Notre Dame Hall (15/11/76) – performing No Fun, Submission, Pretty Vacant and Anarchy in the UK – as well as an interview with ROTTEN ("I don't have any 'eroes, they're all useless!"), THE CLASH, SIOUXSIE and posh-sounding SID.

Mon 29 NOVEMBER 1976 Lancaster Polytechnic, Coventry – supported by THE CLASH whose 'White Riot' is heard by the local NUS committee who deem it racist. The PISTOLS' 'No Future' song, and its fascist regime line, also come under scrutiny before the committee holds an emergency meeting and decides not to pay "these fascists". The dispute is eventually resolved and the PISTOLS get paid.

Anarchy in the UK (EMI) sold 1765 copies on this day.

Tue 30 NOVEMBER 1976 McLAREN asks for, and gets, a meeting with EMI's LESLIE HILL who reassures him of the label's commitment to the band.

Anarchy in the UK (EMI) sold 1,635 copies on this day.

DECEMBER 1976

Wed 1 DECEMBER 1976 After hurriedly replacing QUEEN on the early evening THAMES TV TODAY show, the PISTOLS show their MIKE MANSFIELD-directed pop video of Anarchy before swearing at their drunken host BILL GRUNDY, after he chats up SIOUXSIE who's there with SEVERIN, BARKER, SIMONE (SID is absent, appearing in court and being cleared of GBH at the Punk Festival). The resulting fuss jams the THAMES switchboard as the police are called to the studio.

Anarchy in the UK (EMI) sold 2,435 copies this day.

Thu 2 DECEMBER 1976 'THE FILTH and THE FURY!' is the DAILY MIRROR front page lead as the outrage over the GRUNDY swear-in grows.

Anarchy in the UK sold 1,535 copies this day.

Fri 3 DECEMBER 1976 Norwich University – was to have started the ANARCHY TOUR. CANCELLED.

Anarchy in the UK sold 1,780 copies that Friday.

THE SUN front page headline is 'WERE THE PISTOLS LOADED?' – later inspiring the lads' magazine of the same name – as media controversy over the PISTOLS refuses to die down.

Workers at EMI's pressing plant in Hayes, Middlesex refuse to pack copies of Anarchy... although the dispute is resolved by shop stewards by the end of the day.

Sat 4 DECEMBER 1976 Kings Hall, Derby – Derby Council demand to see the PISTOLS play before them, but at the suggestion of GOODMAN the band do not appear. The other groups on the bill are told they can play without the PISTOLS but only THE DAMNED consider it. CANCELLED.

A NEWS OF THE WORLD advert is broadcast on Saturday 4th Dec coast to coast on ITV. "The Sex Pistols Disgusted And Enraged Viewers With Their Foul Behaviour – Punk Rock? We Say Punk Junk! – You'll Be Shocked By This Report On Pop's New Heroes, only in the News of the World this Sunday!"

Sun 5 DECEMBER 1976 Newcastle City Hall – CANCELLED.

The PISTOLS apparently trash the plant display at the Dragonara Hotel, Leeds after being crowded by press photographers who ask the members of the troupe if they'd wreck the display for £20.

Mon 6 DECEMBER 1976 Leeds Polytechnic – the second time on the ANARCHY TOUR when the PISTOLS, HEARTBREAKERS, CLASH and DAMNED actually do play. It is the latter's first and last gig on the tour as they are fired for their attempted 'treachery' at Derby. ROTTEN makes a four-letter dedication to the Queen, Bill Grundy and the Leeds Councillor who objected to the gig. The PISTOLS make £700. TAPED.

Tue 7 DECEMBER 1976 Village Bowl, Bournemouth – CANCELLED.

The PISTOLS and their antics are a last minute item on the agenda of EMI's Annual General Meeting.

Thu 9 DECEMBER 1976 Electric Circus, Manchester – supported by CLASH, HEARTBREAKERS and local heroes THE BUZZCOCKS. TAPED.

Fri 10 DECEMBER 1976 Lancaster University – CANCELLED.

CHARLIE DRAKE releases cash-in 45 'Super Punk' as do the WATER PISTOLS with their 'Gimme That Punk Junk' single.

Sat 11 DECEMBER 1976 Liverpool Stadium – CANCELLED.

Mon 13 DECEMBER 1976 Colston Hall, Bristol – CANCELLED.

A gig at London's Rainbow venue is pencilled in for later in the month.

Tue 14 DECEMBER 1976 Top Rank, Cardiff – CANCELLED.

Tue 14 DECEMBER 1976 Castle Cinema, Caerphilly – last minute replacement for Cardiff Top Rank, supported by CLASH and HEARTBREAKERS as a demo against the gig takes place outside and is filmed by TV crews.

Wed 15 DECEMBER 1976 Apollo, Glasgow – the PISTOLS are BANNED from entering the town of Glasgow. CANCELLED.

Thu 16 DECEMBER 1976 Caird Hall, Dundee – CANCELLED.

Fri 17 DECEMBER 1976 Civic Hall, Sheffield – CANCELLED.

Sat 18 DECEMBER 1976 Kursaal, Southend – CANCELLED.

Sun 19 DECEMBER 1976 Civic Hall, Guildford – CANCELLED.

Mon 20 DECEMBER 1976 Birmingham Town Hall – CANCELLED.

Mon 20 DECEMBER 1976 Winter Gardens, Cleethorpes – CANCELLED.

Tue 21 DECEMBER 1976 Rainbow, Finsbury Park, London – CANCELLED.

Tue 21 DECEMBER 1976 Woods Centre Plymouth – supported by CLASH and HEARTBREAKERS.

Wed 22 DECEMBER 1976 400 Club, Torquay – CANCELLED.

Woods Centre – supported by WIRE, CLASH and HEARTBREAKERS, the last ANARCHY TOUR gig and MATLOCK's last UK gig with the PISTOLS.

Thu 23 DECEMBER 1976 Manor Ballroom, Ipswich – CANCELLED.

Fri 24 DECEMBER 1976 ANARCHY TOUR losses are estimated at £10,000.

Sat 25 DECEMBER 1976 McLAREN's GLITTERBEST office is burgled and some items of 'little value' are removed.

Sun 26 DECEMBER 1976 Roxy Theatre, Harlseden, London – CANCELLED.

Mon 27 DECEMBER 1976 PISTOLS enter Wessex recording studios with THOMAS, recording backing tracks.

Fri 31 DECEMBER 1976 The PISTOLS are present as the CLASH open Covent Garden's new ROXY CLUB.

EMI A&Rs inform MATLOCK that, as the PISTOLS's principle tunesmith, they'd be interested in any solo – or new group – material he might like to offer.

JANUARY 1977

Tue 4 JANUARY 1977 The PISTOLS fly out of Heathrow amid much swearing and drinking – dutifully picked up by the London EVENING NEWS and STANDARD papers (who claimed that band members were vomiting publicly) – to appear on Dutch TV's ROCK CIRCUS show along with GOLDEN EARRING and THE THREE DEGREES.

Wed 5 JANUARY 1977 Paradiso Club, Amsterdam – supported by HEARTBREAKERS. TAPED.

Thu 6 JANUARY 1977 Rotterdam Art Centre – supported by HEARTBREAKERS. McLAREN gets GOODMAN to ask JONES to "stop posing like Johnny Thunders!"

EMI announce end of PISTOLS contract with them by 'mutual' agreement, a phrase disputed by McLAREN.

Fri 7 JANUARY 1977 Paradiso Club, Amsterdam – supported by HEARTBREAKERS. The last PISTOLS gig anywhere with MATLOCK – or, at least, the last gig with MATLOCK for another 20 odd years...

Wed 12 JANUARY 1977 ROTTEN is arrested in London and charged with possession of amphetamine sulphate.

Sat 15 JANUARY 1977 Anarchy in the UK (EMI) has, it is revealed, sold 55,000 copies before being withdrawn – after receiving just five radio plays across the entire UK.

Mon 17 JANUARY 1977 GOODMAN takes PISTOLS into Gooseberry Studios, Gerrard Street, Chinatown where, over a period of four days, they record No Future, Problems, Pretty Vacant, New York, Liar and a new song called EMI.

Wed 19 JANUARY 1977 McLAREN meets A&M Records' UK boss DEREK GREEN.

Thu 20 JANUARY 1977 America's NBC TV film the PISTOLS back at Gooseberry, miming to EMI, New York and No Future.

Fri 21 JANUARY 1977 EMI make official their termination of the PISTOLS contract, giving GLITTERBEST £30,000 with EMI Music adding another £10,000 to end the PISTOLS' publishing deal.

Mon 24 JANUARY 1977 PISTOLS record with GOODMAN in Gooseberry Studios.

Wed 26 JANUARY 1977 PISTOLS record with GOODMAN in Gooseberry Studios again.

Thu 27 JANUARY 1977 McLAREN and the PISTOLS meet Warner Brothers, US. McLAREN and ROTTEN later attack MATLOCK's attitude at the meeting.

Fri 28 JANUARY 1977 GOODMAN mixes, at Eden Studios in Chiswick, the six tracks that were recorded earlier in the month at Gooseberry. With HELEN WELLINGTON-LLOYD as joint roller general.

Mon 31 JANUARY 1977 ROTTEN was born JOHN LYDON on this day in 1956.

FEBRUARY 1977

Tue 1 FEBRUARY 1977 MATLOCK buys a secondhand Sunbeam Alpine sports car in 'Glenn Blue'.

Fri 4 FEBRUARY 1977 Replacing MATLOCK with SID is discussed by McLAREN, ROTTEN, JONES and COOK.

Mon 7 FEBRUARY 1977 McLAREN calls PETER COOK about writing a PISTOLS screenplay as A&M and CBS express some interest in signing the PISTOLS.

Fri 11 FEBRUARY 1977 SID auditions for the PISTOLS in their Denmark Street rehearsal room.

Sun 13 FEBRUARY 1977 McLAREN flies to LA to meet A&M's JERRY MOSS.

Tue 15 FEBRUARY 1977 McLAREN gets in a fist fight with JOEY RAMONE in LA's Whisky A Go-Go club.

Fri 18 FEBRUARY 1977 SID starts rehearsals with the PISTOLS.

Sat 19 FEBRUARY 1977 McLAREN agrees to the PISTOLS doing a tour of Finland as organised by MILES COPELAND, son of the CIA boss of the same name.

Tue 24 FEBRUARY 1977 MATLOCK to leave the PISTOLS saying "onstage John's great, but he'd carry all that into rehearsals and I couldn't handle it ... especially as I'd always felt he was putting it on. He'd put up this front".

Wed 25 FEBRUARY 1977 McLAREN decides that the PISTOLS' Finnish Tour must be CANCELLED.

MARCH 1977

Thur 3 MARCH 1977 PISTOLS recording in Wessex Studios with THOMAS. (for who?)

Sat 5 MARCH 1977 Notre Dame Hall, London – CANCELLED.

Acme Attractions – the shop employing the diary-researcher as a designer – becomes punk shop BOY at 153, Kings Rd.

Wed 9 MARCH 1977 PISTOLS sign with A&M for a prospective £150,000 in the offices of Rondor Music. The money is to be 50% in advance with the rest paid over two years. The first single is to be 'God Save the Queen' aka 'No Future'. The PISTOLS' wages go up to £40 per week.

Thu 10 MARCH 1977 The public signing of the A&M deal takes place outside Buckingham Palace with the new SID PISTOL being filmed by various TV

crews including America's NBC. After a drunken press conference the PISTOLS 'over-celebrate' at the A&M New Kings Road offices, SID apparently smashing windows and a toilet bowl before passing out, as JONES enters the Ladies toilet and gropes various secretaries. McLAREN and GREEN listen to most of the GOODMAN and THOMAS tapes, trying to find the GSTQ B side. "It has to be this version of No Feeling," says GREEN after hearing the £70 take of it that GOODMAN recorded in the Denmark Street rehearsal room.

Fri 11 MARCH 1977 In court ROTTEN is fined £40 for possession of amphetamine sulphate, 'speed', as A&M start to press up 25,000 copies of GSTQ / No Feeling (A&M-AMS 7284).

Sat 12 MARCH 1977 SID, WOBBLE and other friends of ROTTEN are involved in a fracas in London's Speakeasy club – one of the gang threatens to kill the TV host of the OLD GREY WHISTLE TEST, Whispering BOB HARRIS.

Mon 14 MARCH 1977 PHILIP ROBERGE, lawyer for HARRIS – and partner of the manager of A&M's biggest seller, PETER FRAMPTON – delivers letters to A&M, threatening to sue over the death threats against HARRIS. Two further telexes of complaint are received – one, mostly in jest, is from RICK WAKEMAN, the other is said to be from US shareholder JACKIE ONASSIS, the former First Lady of America.

Wed 16 MARCH 1977 Sickened by the threats against HARRIS – and by the damage done to the A&M offices – GREEN fires the 'satanic' PISTOLS from A&M, after first offering his resignation to US boss MOSS. The band – or rather GLITTERBEST – are to receive a total of £75,000 to instantly end the contract. A phone-call from an editor that evening finds McLAREN alone and near to tears in his Dryden Chambers offices.

Thu 17 MARCH 1977 A&M pulp the 25,000 GSTQ / No Feeling singles and destroy the metal masters. BOOGIE and REID put on boiler suits and attempt to rescue copies from the vinyl recycling centre – they break down in giggles, however, and are ejected (apart from two A&M GSTQ 45s sold by Phil Strongman (diary-researcher for this book) to McLAREN, only half a dozen others have ever been seen – and these were allegedly given to the longest-serving staffers after A&M closed down its UK operation in 1998. Consequently a GSTQ / No Feeling A&M single is now worth over £3,000).

'Sacked Again – But the PISTOLS get £75,000' is the half page story in the STANDARD complete with a RICHARD YOUNG photo of the band with McLAREN holding the cheque.

Fri 18 MARCH 1977 CBS say that they're only prepared to issue PISTOLS product without cash advances and label boss MAURICE OBERSTEIN insists that the group and McLAREN cannot visit the company's offices – all meetings are to be held elsewhere. "I know, Obie, your office is in Soho, mine's in Oxford Street, how about meeting on the third bench on the left in Soho Square?" McLAREN sarcastically asks OBERSTEIN – talks continue however.

Mon 21 MARCH 1977 Notre Dame Hall, London – the PISTOLS make their live debut with SID before NBC's cameras and a 100 or so hardcore fans, who manage to squeeze in before the venue's janitor panics and locks the main doors. Attending is NANCY SPUNGEN, a New York junkie – and HEARTBREAKERS' groupie – who happens to be SID's new girlfriend. Another 50 people are locked out – including Phil Strongman and hot-dog twin SIMON – and upon leaving, SID is greeted with cries of 'Where's Glen?' and 'You've sold out!'

Tue 22 MARCH 1977 MATLOCK officially leaves the PISTOLS with a cheque for under £3,000 in lieu of performing royalties.

Wed 23 MARCH 1977 The PISTOLS fly to the island of Jersey for a week's holiday.

Thu 24 MARCH 1977 After being followed by local police for 24 hours the PISTOLS are ordered to leave Jersey.

Sat 26 MARCH 1977 God Save the Queen / No Feeling (A&M) official release date – WITHDRAWN.

Sun 27 MARCH 1977 McLAREN and his friend 'TERRY' pay a surprise evening visit to OBERSTEIN's home address – the door is answered by a leather-clad youth. The McLAREN party barge in and make themselves at home. After an hour of abusing OBERSTEIN's collection of Phillips 2000 videos – all of CBS pop acts – their horrified host loses patience, his bass voice soars into a squeak, and he hysterically orders McLAREN and co. out.

Thu 31 MARCH 1977 CBS finally admit they've dropped out of negotiations to sign the PISTOLS.

APRIL 1977

Sun 3 APRIL 1977 Screen on the Green, London – PISTOLS play a free gig, partly for those turned away from Notre Dame Hall on 21/3/77, after a screening of Sex Pistols No. 1, a 20 minute 16mm documentary edited together from the band's TV footage including excerpts from the Thames TV TODAY show, BBC's YOUNG NATION and STREET-PORTER's LONDON WEEKEND SHOW. Filmed by LETTS for his PUNK ROCK MOVIE. TAPED.

Mon 4 APRIL 1977 McLAREN calls five record companies with a view to getting a new deal for the PISTOLS – all reject his overtures. He's already tried DECCA, PYE and even EMI again with no success although long-time suitors POLYDOR say they may consider an offer.

SID is hospitalized with hepatitis after buying heroin with LEVINE.

Wed 20 APRIL 1977 CBS' OBERSTEIN phones GLITTERBEST to say that American CBS are interested in talking to McLAREN about the PISTOLS.

Fri 22 APRIL 1977 POLYDOR finally say 'no', they are no longer interested in signing the PISTOLS.

Mon 25 APRIL 1977 PISTOLS enter Wessex Studios with THOMAS but without SID who's still being kept, secretly, in hospital.

MAY 1977

Mon 2 MAY 1977 McLAREN and his lawyer STEPHEN FISHER meet VIRGIN Records' solicitor – they discover it's ROBERT LEE, who also represented A&M.

Fri 6 MAY 1977 French label BARCLAY Records sign the PISTOLS to a two year deal – for France, Switzerland, Algeria and Zanzibar – for £26,000.

Mon 9 MAY 1977 ROTTEN gets a tax demand, under his real name JOHN LYDON, for a staggering £18,000.

Tue 10 MAY 77 SIMON JOHN RITCHIE aka JOHN BEVERLY aka SID VICIOUS born this day in 1957.

Thu 12 MAY 1977 CHRYSALIS offer the PISTOLS a deal valid everywhere except the UK, USA and France. As they had nowhere else to turn – Richard Branson eventually got the band.

The PISTOLS – well, JONES, COOK and ROTTEN – sign to VIRGIN Records for £15,000. GSTQ is to be the first 45, out in time for the Queen's June Jubilee, with WALLY NIGHTINGALE's Did You No Wrong on the flip side.

Fri 13 MAY 1977 SID comes out of hospital.

Mon 16 MAY 1977 SID signs the VIRGIN contract.

Tue 17 MAY 1977 At the CBS Aylesbury pressing plant, workers refuse to press up GSTQ. OBERSTEIN doesn't return McLAREN calls and VIRGIN boss RICHARD BRANSON considers using double strength flexi-discs before the pressing plant problem is resolved.

Wed 18 MAY 1977 Printing platemakers refuse to make plates for the controversial REID cover of GSTQ – the image depicts HM The Queen with the words SEX PISTOLS banded across her mouth almost like a gag.

Thu 19 MAY 1977 McLAREN calls CHRYSALIS.

Mon 23 MAY 1977 The PISTOLS sign with the COWBELL gig agency and shoot a pop video for GSTQ at the Marquee.

Tue 24 MAY 1977 The PISTOLS are stopped and searched by police during a photo shoot near VIRGIN's Portobello Rd HQ.

Thu 26 MAY 1977 McLAREN, RICHMOND and REID fly to Paris to show the Sex Pistols No 1 short movie – a large mob of French anarchists and art students wreck the venue, tearing down the screen, ripping up seats and curtains and trying to overturn the projector.

Printers censor a PISTOLS GSTQ advert on the back page of SOUNDS. The ad cleverly stresses, after EMI's withdrawal of Anarchy… and A&M's withdrawal of GSTQ – the potential rarity/collectability of the new single, 'It won't be on the new album and it may not be out at all for very long. So get it while you can'.

Sat 27 MAY 1977 God Save the Queen / Did You No Wrong (VIRGIN VS 181) is issued after 50,000 copies are pressed. Woolworths, WH Smiths and Boots all refuse to stock, or list the 45 and the IBA, Luxembourg 208 and the BBC all ban it from the airwaves. In other record shops punks, straight teenagers and even besuited adults are seen buying two or three copies each.

Despite an absence of obscenity, THAMES TV refuse to show a ten second ad for GSTQ – the latter consisting of ROTTEN (to camera) "You thought you'd gotten rid of us, didn't you old bean? But you were wrong, 'cos we're back – with a vengeance!" JONES (leaning into shot to toast the audience with a GSTQ mug) "God save the Queen, my son!"

A 30 second radio ad for GSTQ is rejected by the four biggest commercial stations.

EATER release Dave Goodman-produced 'Thinkin' of The USA' single on THE LABEL label

JUNE 1977

Fri 3 JUNE 1977 In just five days the GSTQ (VIRGIN) single is reported to have sold in excess of 150,000 copies.

Sun 5 JUNE 77 Eater play The Hope & Anchor.

Tue 7 JUNE 1977 Queen Elizabeth Riverboat Party, Thames – the PISTOLS' Jubilee gig party – complete with TONY PARSONS, O'KEEFE, JORDAN, McLAREN, WESTWOOD, BOOGIE, REID, WOBBLE, DEBBIE WILSON, SAVAGE, BRANSON, ROGER ARMSTRONG of Screen on the Green, TED CAROL, RON WATTS, HELEN, THE SLITS, CARUZO and GOODMAN – ends early after ARMSTRONG is involved in a scuffle and a French cameraman is attacked by WOBBLE. Two police launches force the boat to dock but most guests refuse to leave. In the end they are manhandled down the gangplank and those who retaliate are arrested before – in the cases of REID, WILSON, O'KEEFE, McLAREN and WESTWOOD – being physically assaulted.

Wed 8 JUNE 1977 Only the DAILY MIRROR mentions the police bust of the PISTOLS' QE Riverboat Party as McLAREN appears at Bow Street Magistrates and pleads Not Guilty to insulting behaviour.

The PISTOLS sign with VIRGIN for Europe for £75,000.

Thurs 9 JUNE 1977 Melody Maker run an article on new independent labels including Stiff, Step Forward, Chiswick and Dave Goodman's "The Label".

Sat 11 JUNE 77. The PISTOLS dominate the front cover of RECORD MIRROR, a picture supported by a two page interview inside.

Sun 12 JUNE 1977 'What's Burning Up The Kids?" screams the SUNDAY MIRROR front page in yet another punk rock expose. The article reveals that, with over 200,000 copies sold, GSTQ could turn out to be the 'fastest-selling record' of all time.

Mon 13 JUNE 1977 REID is attacked and has his nose and leg broken by a gang of anti-punk youths.

Fri 17 JUNE 1977 GSTQ does not make No. 1 in the BBC-BMRB Chart, grinding to a halt at No. 2 – although it tops the NME and SOUNDS charts – after VIRGIN and other label-linked shops are taken off the chart returns list during Jubilee week. BPI and WEA head JOHN FRUIN, who was then overseeing the charts, was later sacked after chart-listing irregularities occurred involving artists on the WEA label. The WH Smith shop charts have a gap at No. 2, refusing to name either the PISTOLS or GSTQ.

Sat 18 JUNE 1977 ROTTEN is attacked, along with THOMAS, by a multi-racial gang of a dozen knife-wielding thugs after leaving the Pegasus Pub in Green Lanes, Highbury, North London. ROTTEN and THOMAS had been recording at the nearby Wessex Studios.

Sun 19 JUNE 1977 COOK is attacked and has his scalp cut by a gang of teddy boys in Shepherd's Bush. He needs 15 stitches afterwards.

Mon 20 JUNE 1977 Malcolm calls Dave Goodman to see if he's been the victim of the violence aimed at the Sex Pistols camp. He hasn't but has a long chat with Malcolm, who indicates that he thinks there is something or someone more sinister behind the attacks and advises him to watch his back.

Tue 21 JUNE 1977 'Slashed! Punk Rock Rotten Razored!' is the MIRROR headline in the morning while the EVENING NEWS afternoon lead is 'Another Sex Pistol is Knifed!' a story reporting the attack on COOK.

Thu 23 JUNE 1977 Full page adverts are placed by VIRGIN, celebrating the PISTOLS No. 1 position – in the NME charts. The ad quotes Labour MP Marcus Lipton, "If pop music is going to be used to destroy our established institutions then it ought to be destroyed first", as well as listing all the bans that local and national radio stations, TV stations and venue-owners have imposed on the PISTOLS. The Associated Press agency state that they will refuse to circulate any news stories concerning the PISTOLS.

ROTTEN is attacked in Dingwalls.

SPUNGEN is arrested on offensive weapons charges. Police then discover she has over-stayed her visa.

JULY 1977

Sat 2 JULY 1977 Pretty Vacant / No Fun (VIRGIN VS 184) is released, the flip being the GOODMAN take from the Wessex Studios, October '76.

Sun 3 JULY 77 McLAREN flies to LA to meet cult porno movie-maker RUSS MEYER, a possible director for the PISTOLS feature film.

Tue 5 JULY 1977 A pop video is shot for the PISTOLS' Pretty Vacant.

Thu 7 JULY 1977 In court SPUNGEN receives a token fine for her offensive weapon and visa offences.

Mon 11 JULY 1977 ROTTEN is interviewed by Capital Radio's TOMMY VANCE – the PISTOLS singer also gets to spin his favourite discs, from BEEFHEART to DR. ALIMANTADO.

Wed 13 JULY 1977 Daddy's Dance Hall, Copenhagen, Denmark – BOOGIE mixes sound with help from CLASH roadie RODENT. TAPED.

McLAREN rings BRANSON to insist that the Pretty Vacant video is taken back from TOP OF THE POPS before it can be broadcast – BRANSON claims it is too late.

Thu 14 JULY 77. Daddy's Dance Hall, Copenhagen – TAPED.

'Top of The Punks!' is the MIRROR front page as the Pretty Vacant video is screened on TOP OF THE POPS – carefully sandwiched between the RAMONES and Australia's SAINTS – as the single reaches No.7 in the BMRB Charts.

Fri. 15 JULY 1977 Beach Disco, Halmstad, Sweden – TAPED.

Sat 16 JULY 1977 Mogambo Disco, Helsingborg – TAPED.

The VANCE show, a ROTTEN special, is broadcast late night on Capital Radio, London.

Sun 17 JULY 1977 Disco 42, Jonkoping

Tue 19 JULY 1977 Club Zebra, Kristinehamn

Wed 20 JULY 1977 Pingvinen Restaurant, Oslo, Norway – TAPED.

PAUL COOK was born on this day in 1956.

Thu 21 JULY 1977 Studentsamsfundent Club, Trondheim, Norway.

Sat 23 JULY 1977 Barbarellas, Vaxjo, Sweden – a 'teenagers only' gig as Pretty Vacant hits the Swedish Top Ten.

Sun 24 JULY 1977 Barbarellas, Vaxjo.

Mon 25 JULY 1977 At Wells Street Magistrates Court, London, SId is charged with various offences committed on the 2nd night of the Punk Festival 21/9/76 when a girl had an eye damaged by flying glass. Testimony from CLASH members MICK JONES and STRUMMER as well as COON and INGHAM – then managing GENERATION X – indicate that SID was on the other side of the 100 Club when the glass throwing occurred. A besuited SID is fined just £125 for possession of a flick knife.

Wed 27 JULY 1977 Student Karen Happy House, Stockholm.

Thu 28 JULY 1977 Student Karen Happy House – broadcast on Swedish national radio. TAPED.

Fri 29 JULY 1977 Linkoping, Sweden.

Sat 30 JULY 1977 Dave Goodman/Caruzo Fuller's LABEL label moves into shop premises in Fulham's Dawes Rd. The shop has 2 floors of accommodation above and basement rooms below.

AUGUST 1977

Fri 5 AUGUST 1977 Start of the 2nd two day European Punk Festival – featuring THE DAMNED, THE BOYS, MATLOCK's new group RICH KIDS, POLICE, WAYNe COUNTY and THE ELECTRIC CHAIRS, ASPHALT JUNGLE, THE HOTRODS, DR. FEELGOOD, TYLA GANG, LITTLE BOB STORY and THE JAM.

Sun 7 AUGUST 1977 LWT TV repeat their London Weekend PISTOLS special of the previous Autumn.

Mon 8 AUGUST 1977 MEYER flies in to London for further film negotiations with McLAREN and the PISTOLS.

Thu 11 AUGUST 1977 McLAREN introduces PISTOLS to MEYER.

Fri 12 AUGUST 1977 McLAREN again speaks to WARNERS US about an American deal for the PISTOLS – he also calls UNITED ARTISTS.

Fri 19 AUGUST 1977 Club Lafayette, Wolverhampton – the PISTOLS start their 'Sex Pistols Will Play' secret tour under the name Spots (Sex Pistols On Tour). Attending are THE PREFECTS and RICHMOND.

Sat 20 AUGUST 1977 MM reviews a live PISTOLS bootleg – The Good Time Music of The Sex Pistols – which had been recorded at the Lesser Free Trade Hall in Manchester 4/6/76. MM also mention a 'forthcoming' bootleg, Indecent Exposure, recorded at Burton-on-Trent 24/9/76.

EATER, supported by THE DEAD, play the ROXY.

Sat 21 AUGUST 1977 The Other Cinema, Central London screens the Sex Pistols No.1 and No.2 documentaries, supported by THE SLITS. Attending are ROTTEN, his friend JOHN GREY, WOBBLE, BOOGIE, REID and RICHMOND.

Wed 24 AUGUST 1977 Outlook Club, Doncaster – under the name Tax Exiles, as used by a band at the Roxy auditions the night before. TAPED.

Thu 25 AUGUST 1977 Bury St Edmunds – CANCELLED

Thu 25 AUGUST 1977 Scarborough – under the name Special Guests.

Fri 26 AUGUST 1977 Rock Garden, Middlesborough – under the name Acne Rabble.

GLEN MATLOCK born this day in 1956.

Sun 28 AUGUST 1977 Electric Circus, Manchester – CANCELLED.

Mon 29 AUGUST 1977 The Granary, Bristol – CANCELLED.

Tue 30 AUGUST 1977 McLAREN finally agrees with VIRGIN that all three singles should, despite promises to the contrary, be on the PISTOLS' debut album. SID, JONES, COOK and then ROTTEN are eventually persuaded before entering Wessex Studios with THOMAS.

Wed 31 AUGUST 1977 Woods Centre, Plymouth – under the name The Hamsters. Attending is WOBBLE.

SEPTEMBER 1977

Thu 1 SEPTEMBER 1977 Winter Gardens, Penzance – under the name Mystery Band of International Reputation, last night of the Spots Tour.

Sat 3 SEPTEMBER 1977 STEVE JONES born this day in 1955.

A PISTOLS interview is broadcast by BBC Radio Cleveland.

Tue 13 SEPTEMBER 1977 In court SOPHIE RICHMOND is fined £10 for obstructing a police officer during the Riverboat Party of 7/6/77. DEBBIE WILSON, just 16, is cleared.

OCTOBER 1977

Sat 1 OCTOBER 1977 The forthcoming Holidays In The Sun / Satellite (VIRGIN VS 191) is supported by ads in SOUNDS, MM, NME and RM.

Fri 7 OCTOBER 1977 The budget for the forthcoming PISTOLS feature film is agreed at £750,000 – including £50,000 from GLITTERBEST, £165,000 from VIRGIN, £150,000 from Fox and, its hoped, £200,000 from WARNERS US.

Sun 9 OCTOBER 77. COOK is arrested for criminal damage to a bus.

Mon 10 OCTOBER 1977 WARNERS US take on the PISTOLS' NMTB album – for £50,000 – and agree to invest a further £200,000 in the PISTOLS feature film.

Tue 11 OCTOBER 1977 Filming of the PISTOLS movie, now entitled WHO KILLED BAMBI, begins with MEYER directing a scene which ends with a deer being killed in a Welsh national park.

Wed 12 OCTOBER 1977 Having received insufficient money guarantees – and having rowed with SID and ROTTEN from the start – MEYER walks off the set, never to return.

Sat 15 OCTOBER 1977 Holidays In The Sun is released – and played on Radio One by Alan Freeman despite being BANNED by Capital for its 'offensive' alleged reference to modern holiday camps being the 'new Belsen'.

Thu 20 OCTOBER 1977 The Belgian Travel Service issue a copyright-infringement summons over REID's unauthorized use of their graphics on the Holidays In The Sun colour sleeve – over 50,000 sleeves are taken from VIRGIN and shredded as the old artwork is WITHDRAWN.

Sat 22 OCTOBER 1977 SOUNDS' CHAS DE WALLEY gives a rave review to the GOODMAN-produced SPUNK album, which has appeared as a bootleg – (nothing to do with Dave) "good hard raunchy rock'n'roll ... stunningly inventive ... real definitive rock madness ... Dave Goodman claims that 'I made some great rock'n'roll with the Sex Pistols'. And, of course, he's right."

Sat 29 OCTOBER 1977 The long-awaited official PISTOLS album debut, Never Mind The Bollocks (VIRGIN V 2086) – the title being JONES' suggestion, a repetition of SIMON's catch-phrase – is released with advance orders already topping 125,000, instantly making it a Gold Disc album. The first 5,000 are 11 tracks strong and come with a one-track single of Submission. The rest have 12 songs including, to the disappointment of fans, all four singles – Anarchy in the UK, GSTQ, Pretty Vacant and Holidays in the Sun.

NOVEMBER 1977

Fri 4 NOVEMBER 1977 Never Mind the Bollocks jumps into the album charts at No.1, the first time it has happened since the heyday of THE BEATLES in the Sixties.

Sat 5 NOVEMBER 1977 A Nottingham WPC takes offence at a record shop window display of the NMTB album and informs the shop manager that he may be liable for prosecution as full page ads appear in NME, SOUNDS, RM and MM – the latter two ads have the word 'bollocks' removed.

Thu 17 NOVEMBER 1977 As controversy grows about the NMTB title, and its prominence in certain shop displays, the PISTOLS visit the VIRGIN shop in Nottingham before being interviewed on BBC RADIO NOTTINGHAM, RADIO TRENT and RADIO HALLAM.

Fri 18 NOVEMBER 1977 The PISTOLS visit the VIRGIN shop in Manchester, followed by PICCADILLY RADIO and BBC RADIO MANCHESTER.

Sat 19 NOVEMBER 1977 The PISTOLS blitz VIRGIN shops in Glasgow, Edinburgh and Newcastle with corresponding visits to RADIO CLYDE, RADIO FORTH and METRO RADIO.

DECEMBER 1977

Thu 1 DECEMBER 1977 'Sex Pistol and Girl in Drugs Probe!' is THE SUN frontpage after SID and SPUNGEN are stopped, searched and arrested on drugs charges. They are later released without charge.

Fri 2 DECEMBER 1977 Eater, with Dave Goodman, go on tour of Holland organised by their Dutch distributors.

Mon 5 DECEMBER 1977 Eksit Club, Rotterdam, Holland – the infamous Belsen Was A Gas included in the set.

Tue 6 DECEMBER 1977 Maastright, Holland.

Wed 7 DECEMBER 1977 Pozjet Club, Tilburg, Holland.

Thu 8 DECEMBER 1977 Stokuishal, Arnhem, Holland.

Fri 9 DECEMBER 1977 De Effenaar, Eindhoven, Holland.

Sat 10 DECEMBER 1977 Huize Maas, Groningen, Holland – TAPED.

Sun 11 DECEMBER 1977 Maf Centrum, Venlo, Holland – TAPED.

Tue 13 DECEMBER 1977 De Klinker, Winschoten, Holland.

Thu 15 DECEMBER 1977 St. Andrews Hall, Norwich – CANCELLED.

Fri 16 DECEMBER 1977 Brunel University, Uxbridge – a PISTOLS UK mini-tour starts with ROTTEN wearing a Never Mind The Rich Kids, We're The Sex Pistols t-shirt. TAPED.

Sat 17 DECEMBER 1977 Mr. George's, Coventry – TAPED.

NME dedicates three pages to a SID interview.

Sun 18 DECEMBER 1977 Club Lafayette, Wolverhampton – CANCELLED.

Mon 19 DECEMBER 1977 Nikkers Club, Keighley – TAPED.

Tue 20 DECEMBER 1977 Hamilton Club, Birkenhead – after police discussions with owners CANCELLED.

Wed 21 DECEMBER 1977 Bamboo Club, Bristol – after a mysterious fire CANCELLED.

Wed 21 DECEMBER 1977 Club Lafayette, Wolverhampton.

Thu 22 DECEMBER 1977 Champness Hall, Rochdale – after council pressure CANCELLED.

Fri 23 DECEMBER 1977 Stowaway Club, Newport – TAPED.

Sat 24 DECEMBER 1977 Links Pavillion, Cromer – TAPED.

Sun 25 DECEMBER 1977 Ivanhoe's, Huddersfield – the Xmas evening gig is preceded by an afternoon concert and party – paid for by the PISTOLS – in aid of the children of… A) local firemen – then on strike, B) laid-off workers at the Brown Parks Works factory and C) one-parent families. Filmed by TEMPLE – TAPED.

Mon 26 DECEMBER 1977 The Lyceum – CANCELLED.

Mon 26 DECEMBER 1977 The Greyhound, Croydon – CANCELLED.

Mon 26 DECEMBER 1977 The Other Cinema – CANCELLED.

Thu 29 DECEMBER 1977 There are continuing problems over the PISTOLS' visas for their forthcoming US tour. "Sid Vicious hasn't really got a criminal record," McLAREN tells newsmen, "he's only been done for minor things like knocking a policeman's teeth out."

Sat 31 DECEMBER 1977 New Year's Eve 1977 ends with SID fighting with the singer of French band THE LOUS who'd been supporting THE RAMONES, GENERATION X and THE REZILLOS at the Rainbow, London.

JANUARY 1978

Sun 1 JANUARY 1978 LWT TV screen The Year of Punk, a 45 minute documentary fronted by STREET-PORTER and featuring ROTTEN, SIOUSXSIE and THE BANSHEES and EATER's 15 year old drummer DEE GENERATE who swears, drinks and chain-smokes throughout.

Tue 3 JANUARY 1978 The PISTOLS fly off to start their US TOUR after threatening to 'do' several UK photographers at Heathrow.

Thu 5 JANUARY 1978 The Great South-East Music Ballroom, Atlanta, Georgia – the PISTOLS kick off their US TOUR before 500 curious locals and the world's press. TAPED.

Fri 6 JANUARY 1978 Taliesyn Ballroom, Memphis – TAPED.

Sun 8 JANUARY 1978 Randy's Rodeo, San Antonio, Texas – over 2,000 attend as armed police rush onstage when SID hits a violent heckler with his bass. After being bloodied by a hail of beer cans SID tells the crowd, "You cowboys are all faggots." TAPED.

Mon 9 JANUARY 1978 Kingfish Club, Baton Rouge – ROTTEN collects $30 from the coins thrown onstage as SID is seen afterwards having sex with a groupie in the Gents toilet – TAPED.

Tue 10 JANUARY 1978 Longhorn Ballroom, Dallas – after appearing on the coast-to-coast US TV show VARIETY '77 the PISTOLS play the Longhorn Ballroom, a gig that's broadcast on local radio. At the gig SID – who's onstage shirtless with 'Gimme A Fix' scratched on his chest – is head-butted by LA punk girl Helen Killer. He lets the blood flow. TAPED.

Thu 12 JANUARY 1978 Cairns Ballroom, Tulsa – religious activists picket the gig in this alcohol-free city.

Fri 13 JANUARY 1978 COOK and JONES take part in a phone-in for RADIO K-SAN, San Francisco, JONES asking every female caller, "Have you got big tits … ?"

The PISTOLS are BANNED from using American Airlines and any hotels in the Holiday Inn chain.

Sat 14 JANUARY 1978 Winterland Ballroom, San Francisco – supported by THE NUNS and THE AVENGERS, the PISTOLS' last ever gig with SID VICIOUS is played before 5,000 – occasionally violent – fans as ROTTEN asks the crowd, "Ever get the feeling you've been cheated?" TAPED.

Mon 16 JANUARY 1978 SID VICIOUS overdoses on heroin and has to be taken to hospital.

Tue 17 JANUARY 1978 COOK and then JONES announce that they want to leave the PISTOLS. ROTTEN quits instead, after failing to persuade them to take his side against McLAREN and the Rio trip. SEX PISTOLS now no longer exist except as a legal entity.

Wed 18 JANUARY 1978 ROTTEN arrives in New York and is the first to announce the group's break-up in an interview with the New York Post.

Thur 19 JANUARY 1978 THE SUN announces the band's break-up on front page.

SID flies to New York with Boogie and passes out on the plane, on landing he's rushed to Jamaica Hospital where he is kept under observation.

Fri 20 JANUARY 1978 Studentkaren Happy House, Stockholm – CANCELLED. Photographer ROBERTA BAYLEY rings an isolated SID in hospital, he tells her he'll probably be dead within six months.

FEBRUARY 1978

Fri 3 FEBRUARY 1978 RICHARD BRANSON pays for JOHNNY ROTTEN, now using his own name JOHN LYDON, to fly to Jamaica as a reggae talent scout for Virgin.

Early FEBRUARY 1978 BOOGIE is sent to Jamaica in an attempt to film ROTTEN and ask him the question "Who Killed Bambi"? He gets thrown in the pool for his efforts.

Second week in FEBRARY 1978 McLAREN joins COOK & JONES in Rio where they record "A Punk Prayer" – later known as "Cosh the Driver" and released as "No One is Innocent" – and a reworking of "Belsen was a Gas" with vocals by ex-Great Train Robber RONNIE BIGGS.

Third week in FEB. 1978 McLAREN flies to LA where Warners have attempted to arrange a reconciliatory meeting between him and LYDON – the latter refuses to play ball and the meeting ends in hostility.

Fri 24 FEBRUARY 1978 ROCK AGAINST RACISM hold a relatively peaceful concert at Central London Poly featuring SHAM 69 and Southall Rastas MISTY.

MARCH 1978

Beginning of MARCH 1978 McLAREN still writing to Warners that his "first priority is to keep the four Sex Pistols together as a performing group".

Sometime in MARCH 1978 SID, BOOGIE, JULIEN TEMPLE & MALCOLM fly off to Paris to shoot SID performing My Way etc.

29 MARCH 1978 DAVE GOODMAN born on this day in 1951. COOK & JONES return from Rio and LYDON's lawyer BRIAN CARR sends a letter to Glitterbest asking for his accounts as contracted.

APRIL 1978

30 APRIL 1978 ROCK AGAINST RACISM organise march from Trafalgar Square to Victoria Park, Hackney where 100,000 people gather and dance to X-RAY SPEX, TOM ROBINSON, STEEL PULSE and the CLASH to name just a few.

MAY to JULY 1978

27 MAY 1978 NME announces on it's front page, the birth of JOHN LYDON'S new band PUBLIC IMAGE

End of MAY 1978 DEBBIE WILSON gets a phone call from LYDON informing her that her best friend TRACEY O`KEEFE has died from leukaemia. She was eighteen.

MAY, JUNE, JULY 1978 McLAREN & TEMPLE work on script for movie. JONES, COOK & GOODMAN rework July 76 Wessex sessions "No Lip", "Stepping Stone", "Substitute" etc.

End of JUNE 1978 SEX PISTOLS release their first single since the split. A double A with "Punk Prayer" one side and "My Way" on the other. It was a big hit, selling more copies than "Holidays" or "Queen".

AUGUST 1978

9 AUGUST 1978 Complete draft of film script prepared.

Middle AUGUST 1978 Shooting began on movie, latest title "The Great Rock'n'Roll Swindle". SID & NANCY kept outside JOHN LYDON's Gunter Grove flat by his axe-wielding mates.

SEPTEMBER – DECEMBER 1978

7 SEPTEMBER 1978 SID plays Max's, New York with MICK JONES, JERRY NOLAN and KILLER KANE in his backing band.

During OCTOBER 1978 McLAREN and STEPHEN FISHER are involved in confidential negotiations with Virgin solicitor JAMES WARE for a Virgin buy-out of Glitterbest.

Wed 12 OCTOBER 1978 SID is arrested inside the Chelsea Hotel, New York and charged with second degree murder of his girlfriend NANCY SPUNGEON. McLAREN is alerted in England by a New York Times reporter, calls SID's mum then flies over straight away.

Thur 13 OCTOBER 1978 SID appears in court and is granted bail for $50,000 – McLAREN allegedly gets a promise from Virgin to send the monies over on Monday 17th.

Sun 16 OCTOBER 1978 MRS VICIOUS, Anne Beverly, arrives in New York and visits her son in Rikers Island prison. NANCY SPUNGEN is buried in Philadelphia.

Mon 17 OCTOBER 1978 SID is released on bail and is rushed away from the prying eyes of the media. PUBLIC IMAGE release their first single "Public

Image" on Virgin.

Sat 22 OCTOBER 1978 SID attempts suicide and ends up in the psychiatric ward of Bellvue Hospital.

31 OCTOBER 1978 STEPHEN FISHER writes to JAMES WARE at Virgin asking for a minimum £500,000 for the buy-out of GLITTERBEST.

Early NOVEMBER 1978 CLASH release their second album 'Give 'Em Enough Rope', dubbed 'Give 'Em Enough Dope' by a highly cricital GARRY BUSHELL in the pages of SOUNDS.

10 NOVEMBER 1978 JOHN LYDON starts High Court proceedings to wind up the SEX PISTOLS partnership. The case is adjourned until a hearing date can be fixed.

21 NOVEMBER 1978 SID's next court hearing, where District Attorney Al Sullivan allows bail to stand at $50,000 providing SID reports to New York homicide and the city's Manhattan methadone clinic.

Early DECEMBER 1978 STEVE JONES flies to America to do some production work with the AVENGERS and ex-RUNAWAY JOAN JETT.

9 DECEMBER 1978 SID gets into a fight with PATTI SMITH's brother TODD. SID bottles TODD who ends up in hospital.

10 DECEMBER 1978 SID is sent back to Rikers Island prison.

12 DECEMBER 1978 SID's next court hearing where Judge Leff decides to keep SID in custody while reports are prepared.

13 DECEMBER 1978 PUBLIC IMAGE release their first album.

19 DECEMBER 1978 CLASH play a London benefit gig for SID.

25 DECEMBER 1978 PUBLIC IMAGE LTD organise their own Christmas Day gig at The Rainbow Theatre, London.

JANUARY – MARCH 1979

1 FEBRUARY 1979 SID is in court and after an impassioned plea from his lawyer, James Merberg, is released by lunchtime (a day ahead of schedule)

2 FEBRUARY 1979 SID overdoses on near pure heroin while with his mother.

3 FEBRUARY 1979 SID's death makes the tabloid front pages.

"SEX `n` DRUGS `n` ROCK`n`ROLL `n` KNIVES `n` DEATH!".

Wed 7 FEBRUARY 1979 Hearing begins in the Chancery Court re: J.Lydon and others V Glitterbest/Matrixbest. SID is cremated in New York.

Tue 13 FEBRUARY 1979 Steve and Paul, furious at the alleged misuse by

McLaren of money owing to them, change sides and lawyers and move to Lydon's/Virgin's camp.

Wed 14 FEBRUARY 1979 Mr Justice Browne Wilkinson delivers his verdict, taking control of the Sex Pistols away from Malcolm and placing it into the hands of court receivers Spicer & Peglar. Malcolm immediately flies to Paris in search of a record contract for an album of standards.

Mon 19 FEBRUARY 1979 SEX PISTOLS release 'Something Else' an Eddie Cochran cover sung by SID that sells 320,000, outdoing "God Save the Queen".

Mon 27 FEBRUARY 1979 Virgin rush release "The Great Rock'n'Roll Swindle" soundtrack album.

15 MARCH 1979 Malcolm now back in London, sends a letter of complaint to the receivers about the new 'Swindle' film edit: "a pathetic scrapbook butchered about by people with no direction. Stop it now!" Within a day, he carries out his threat and walks off the film.